RIVALS

CONFERENCE

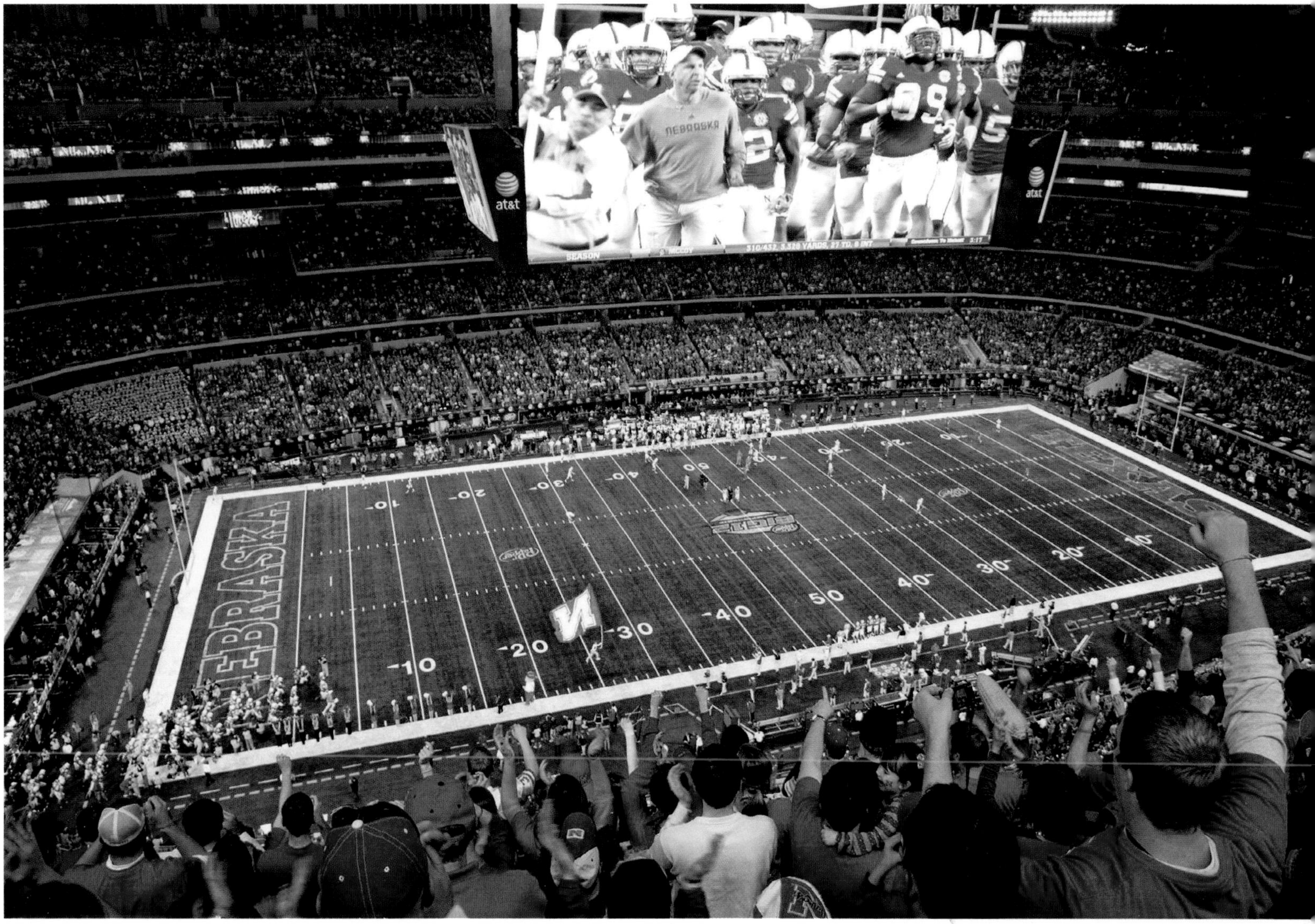

Omaha World-Herald

56

BIG RED RIVALS

FAREWELL TO A CONFERENCE

Editor
Dan Sullivan

Designer
Christine Zueck

Lead writer
Michael Kelly

Executive Editor
Mike Reilly

President and Publisher
Terry Kroeger

Omaha World-Herald Co.
1314 Douglas St.
Omaha, NE 68102

First paperback edition
ISBN: 978-0-615-41175-0
Printed by Walsworth Publishing Co.
Marceline, MO

« Nebraska's Herm Rohrig (25) looks for yards in a 13-7 victory over Oklahoma in 1939. Rohrig later served as the Big Ten's supervisor of officials.

On the cover: Johnny Rodgers' punt return for a touchdown against Oklahoma in 1971.

Title page: Nebraska fans cheer the Huskers at the 2009 Big 12 championship game in Arlington, Texas.

Nebraska takes the field for the 2008 Kansas State game at Bill Snyder Family Stadium in Manhattan.

TABLE OF CONTENTS

7
SOONERS
7
OU

Lee Barfknecht

has 36 years of memories from attending or covering Big Eight and Big 12 football games.

« Husker fan Ron Freiburger (left) and friend Jack Land, an Oklahoma fan, have different perspectives on the 2009 game in Lincoln.

DEAR COLLEGE FOOTBALL FANS,

Barring some odd calamity, Nebraska's move to the Big Ten Conference in 2011 should be as successful as projected when it was announced in June 2010.

The school gains massive benefits academically, nails down long-term security athletically and shields itself forever from dealing with Texas on the Longhorns' terms. Talk about a win, win, win.

Yet there are losses to calculate, too. Not financial or physical, but emotional.

Only the oldest people on the planet would be able to recall Nebraska not being in the Big Eight (or its precursors) or the Big 12 Conference.

NU was one of five original members of what was known as the Missouri Valley Intercollegiate Athletic Association, which formed in 1907. The others were Kansas, Missouri, Iowa and Washington University of St. Louis.

In 1928, at a meeting in Lincoln, six state institutions – Nebraska, Kansas, Kansas State, Missouri, Oklahoma and Iowa State – reorganized into the Big Six. Colorado made it the Big Seven in 1947 and began play a year later. Oklahoma State made it the Big Eight in 1957 and began playing conference football in 1960.

That's a lot of history to let go of – and tons of memories to process in the short time left. Memories, such as:

• Barry Switzer's "We gotcha again" grin after another episode of Sooner Magic that put Oklahoma closer to one of its seven national championships.

• Bill Snyder's "How dare you" stare after a Kansas State mistake, something the coaching veteran wouldn't tolerate while turning the Wildcats from the nation's worst program into a regular bowl participant.

• Ralphie the live buffalo's "I'm more out of control than you want to believe" romp around Colorado's Folsom Field twice a game. Ask Kansas running back L.T. Levine, a victim of a Ralphie pancake block.

• Dan McCarney's "I'm going to bury this mess in enough whipped cream" brand of positive thinking that led Iowa State to five bowl games in six years during the 2000s after the school had gone to only four bowls previously.

• Kansas' "This is what a college campus should look like" view from Campanile Hill above Memorial Stadium. That's something Nebraskans may never see again, after playing KU in football 117 times.

• Missouri's "Hey, let's hire this guy" philosophy, which led to five coaching changes in 21 years after the Tigers compiled more victories in the 1960s than any other Big Eight school.

• Oklahoma State's "Where the heck did they find that guy" roster of little-hyped but highly talented players from Walt Garrison to Leslie O'Neal to Barry Sanders.

As for memories of the four Texas schools that joined in 1996, well, let's just say the primary one is that of a forced marriage that few from the old Big Eight found fulfilling.

Our hope is that the following pages of stories and photos from The World-Herald archives help you recall the past fondly and prepare you for the new world that lies ahead.

Now, pass me a tissue. Better make it the whole box.

Sincerely,

CONFERENCE CHRONICLE

1890s

• Nebraska's earliest affiliation was with the Western Inter-State University Foot Ball Association, along with Iowa, Kansas and Missouri. League play, which took place from 1892 through 1897, was marked by disputes over scoring and objections to Nebraska and Iowa including African-American players on their squads. Above is the 1894 Nebraska team.

1900s

• Nebraska, Iowa, Kansas, Missouri and Washington University of St. Louis formed the Missouri Valley Intercollegiate Athletic Association in 1907. Two months after the initial meeting, Iowa State and Drake were admitted.

• The Cornhuskers began play in the Missouri Valley in 1907 under coach W.C. "King" Cole, defeating Kansas in Lawrence 16-6. Conference games were added against Iowa and Iowa State in 1908 and Kansas State in 1913. Iowa retained its membership in the Western Conference, later called the Big Ten, and competed as a Valley member only through 1910. Later Valley additions were Grinnell in 1919, Oklahoma in 1920 and Oklahoma A&M in 1925.

1910s

• Nebraska fans got their first taste of conference dominance with the arrival of coach **Ewald O. "Jumbo" Stiehm** (pronounced "steam") in 1911. The "Stiehm Rollers" won or shared five Missouri Valley titles, at one time putting together a 34-game unbeaten streak.

• Stiehm's five seasons of success – he left for Indiana in 1915 – boosted Nebraskans' pride in their team and spurred talk of quitting the Valley for the bigger and more prestigious Western Conference.

• The most famous of the Huskers during this period was halfback **Guy Chamberlin,** whose career earned him spots in the college and pro football halls of fame. After Chamberlin led Nebraska to a 35-0 victory over Kansas to claim a Valley title in 1914, a reporter wrote, "If you can imagine a piano-mover doing the hundred in 10 seconds, you might have some idea of how this man Chamberlin looked."

• Missouri Valley play was suspended in 1918 because of World War I, and Nebraska competed as an independent during the 1919 and 1920 seasons.

1920s

• The Cornhuskers rejoined the Valley in 1921, winning three straight titles under coach Fred Dawson, with the third coming in their new home, Memorial Stadium. While conference titles were nice, fans seemed more interested in big-time nonconference opponents like Illinois, with Red Grange, and Knute Rockne's Notre Dame, featuring the Four Horsemen. Both powerhouses lost to NU teams featuring All-American **Ed Weir.**

• A student publication marked Jumbo Stiehm's death in 1923 with this: "For Stiehm, it was not enough that Nebraska have a good team; he early established the ideal for which Nebraskans would strive – never to suffer defeat. He jerked the blindfold of timidity from Cornhusker eyes." It is the standard by which Nebraskans still judge their football team.

• The pull of big-time football in the 1920s eventually led Nebraska, Missouri, Oklahoma, Kansas, Kansas State and Iowa State to form the Big Six in 1928, leaving behind Valley rivals Drake, Grinnell, Oklahoma A&M (later Oklahoma State) and Washington University of St. Louis.

• In 1928, Nebraska claimed the first Big Six title with a 5-0 record under Ernest Bearg, capping the season with an 8-0 Thanksgiving Day win over Kansas State.

1930s

• Nebraska won six conference titles in the 1930s, with Kansas, Kansas State, Oklahoma and Missouri picking up one each. By the end of the decade, the Cornhuskers had won or shared first place 20 times during the combined 30 seasons of Big Six and Missouri Valley play.

1940s

• Conference play continued through World War II, although controversy arose over whether schools should allow the use of military recruits from nearby bases. "The (Nebraska) athletic board is considering laying down some ground rules regarding participation with teams loaded with naval trainees. Oklahoma, Kansas, Iowa State and possibly Minnesota would be affected by such a ruling," The World-Herald reported.

• The conference was shaken in 1946 by news that the University of Chicago had announced its withdrawal from the Big Ten and that Nebraska and Iowa State – along with independents Notre Dame, Michigan State, Pittsburgh and Marquette – were mentioned in news reports as possible replacements.

• Nebraska officials hedged their bets on the possibility of joining the prestigious Big Ten. "The University of Nebraska would feel complimented for an opportunity to join so fine a conference as the Big Ten," said acting Athletic Director A.J. Lewandowski. "Such an invitation would have careful consideration by the university's athletic board." He added, "But we are very happy in the Big Six." John Bentley, NU's longtime sports information director, wrote in a World-Herald column, "There has been both thought and talk about Nebraska's changes whenever this perennial question pops up. Committees have been formed, but none was ever able to report progress."

• An invitation didn't arrive for Nebraska. The Big Ten instead added Michigan State, closing its membership until the addition of Penn State in 1990.

• Big Seven football was born in 1948 with the entry of the University of Colorado. Nebraska had played the Buffs six times earlier, the series beginning with a road trip to Boulder in 1898.

CONFERENCE CHRONICLE

1950s-60s

• The Big Seven was first forced to deal with television issues in 1951 when the Nebraska Legislature adopted a proposal asking the university to seek a review of the conference's stand on television. According to a World-Herald report, "Sen. Robert McNutt of Lincoln reminded that minor sports at the university are financed by football profits and said he fears the school will have to ask tax dollars to support athletics if television cuts football attendance. He said he understands the university got about seven hundred dollars from television rights during the 1950 season – enough to pay for about 47 season football tickets."

• Oklahoma State joined in 1957 to make the league the Big Eight and began conference football in 1960.

• The arrival of **Bob Devaney** in 1962 revived Nebraska football, allowing the Big Eight to boast of another national power along with Oklahoma.

1970s-80s

• Talk of Nebraska moving to the Big Ten arose again in 1977, when university regents reported that they had received calls asking if the Huskers would be interested in a change if Northwestern were to drop out. "This whole thing is news to me," Athletic Director Bob Devaney said. Northwestern's president, Robert H. Strotz, responded to the report: "There's been absolutely no discussion of Northwestern leaving the Big Ten. It's not even being considered." One of the Nebraska regents who reportedly had been contacted was a critic of the Big Eight's 50-50 split of gate receipts, saying that Nebraska was subsidizing the conference.

• Nebraska and Oklahoma were either champion or co-champion for 27 consecutive conference seasons through 1988, a streak that began after Colorado's title of 1961 and ended with the Buffs' 1989 crown. When Barry Switzer left as OU's coach in 1989 amid NCAA sanctions, it ended the NU-OU domination of the conference, and Nebraska and Oklahoma never again played in November for a Big Eight title.

1990-2000s

• As it turned out, the 36 seasons of Big Eight football represented the longest and most stable period of Nebraska's conference affiliations. The landscape of college football began to change dramatically in the 1990s. The move of Arkansas from the Southwest Conference to the SEC led the way to future realignment and season-ending conference championship games.

• 1996 was the inaugural season of the Big 12, made up of the members of the Big Eight and four schools from the Southwest Conference – Texas, Texas A&M, Texas Tech and Baylor. The split of the schools into North and South Divisions meant that Nebraska's string of annual games with Oklahoma and Oklahoma State would come to an end.

• Nebraska's national championship in 1997 boosted the Big 12's prestige.

• Big 12 teams played for the football national championship seven times from 2000 to 2009, with titles to Oklahoma and Texas. Conference teams played in 17 BCS games overall during the span, including Nebraska's loss to Miami in the 2002 Rose Bowl.

2010 **2011** **2012**

• In May 2010, Nebraska Athletic Director **Tom Osborne,** Big Ten Commissioner **Jim Delany** and Chancellor **Harvey Perlman** met secretly at an undisclosed location to discuss Nebraska and possible conference realignment.

• In June, Perlman received an ultimatum from the Big 12: You have one week to let us know whether Nebraska is committed to the conference. Perlman was concerned about the future stability of the Big 12 – Texas and five other Big 12 schools were in serious discussions with the Pac-10 Conference – and he was greatly intrigued by the athletic and academic benefits of the Big Ten.

• After Perlman made an urgent call to Delany, the Big Ten presidents and chancellors vetted Nebraska academically and athletically. Delany called Perlman with their verdict: "The presidents would be receptive to an application from Nebraska."

• On June 11, Delany announced the Big Ten's approval of Nebraska as the conference's 12th member, and Colorado accepted an invitation to join the Pacific 10 Conference. The remaining Big 12 members will continue conference play in 2011.

• The Cornhuskers in 2010 mark the end of Big 12 football play after 15 seasons and the disruption of series stretching as far back as 1892.

IN 2011, THE BIG TEN WILL BE SPLIT INTO TWO DIVISIONS:

Nebraska	Illinois
Iowa	Indiana
Michigan	Ohio State
Michigan State	Penn State
Minnesota	Purdue
Northwestern	Wisconsin

NEBRASKA'S BIG TEN SCHEDULES

2011	2012
Oct. 1 at Wisconsin	Sept. 29 Wisconsin
Oct. 8 Ohio State	Oct. 6 at Ohio State
Oct. 22 at Minnesota	Oct. 20 at Northwestern
Oct. 29 Michigan State	Oct. 27 Michigan
Nov. 5 Northwestern	Nov. 3 at Michigan State
Nov. 12 at Penn State	Nov. 10 Penn State
Nov. 19 at Michigan	Nov. 17 Minnesota
Nov. 26 Iowa	Nov. 24 at Iowa

Husker fan Adam Loecker was a Big Red weed in the waving wheat at the 2007 game in Lawrence.

KANSAS

A LONG HISTORY OF ROMP-STOMP CAKEWALKS

BY MICHAEL KELLY | WORLD-HERALD STAFF WRITER

THE LONG-RUNNING KANSAS-NEBRASKA act was unique – the lengthiest uninterrupted series in major-college football, 105 games before NU's move to the Big Ten. Though lots of good athletes played on both teams, fans remember the Nebraskan who got away to Kansas. Gale Sayers, who became a college and pro hall of famer, grew up in Omaha, graduated from Central High and announced in 1961 that he would attend Nebraska. But he changed his mind three months later and headed to Mount Oread, the KU campus. "Think of the fame that may be awaiting him," wrote The World-Herald's Wally Provost. "Think of the University of Nebraska fans who are trying hard not to think of the fame that may be awaiting him."

Nebraska and Kansas first met in football in 1892. After an 1898 NU victory, students celebrated with a bonfire on the field in which "everything that was moveable was thrown on the fire." The only break in the NU-KU series came in 1904 and '05, when Kansas refused to play, alleging that Nebraska's Johnny Bender had violated his amateur status by accepting money to play baseball over the summer. The series resumed, but an argument ensued in 1913 because of NU lineman Clint Ross, who was black. KU served notice that Ross should not show up at Lawrence, but NU coach Jumbo Stiehm countered by saying Ross would play or Nebraska wouldn't show up. NU won 9-0, Ross had a good game and news accounts reported that the African-American population of Lawrence treated him to dinner before the Husker train pulled out for Lincoln. Nebraska and Kansas played for the Missouri Valley Conference title in 1914, NU winning behind Guy Chamberlin's four touchdowns. A writer said folks in Lawrence had known Jesse James, but that Guy was "the worst bandit who ever galloped through this town." Though Nebraska's first game in Memorial Stadium was a win over Oklahoma in 1923, the stadium-dedication game was the next week against Kansas, which stopped the Huskers four times inside the 10-yard line. The game was inconclusive – a 0-0 tie. But Nebraska has dominated the series conclusively, including a 9-0 win in 1953 that was NU's first of the season in the Big Seven Conference. The card section at KU featured a large K and J and a Jayhawk head, with the word "Husker" superimposed on an ear of corn. Kansas won five in a row over Nebraska, 1957 to 1961, and was led the last three of those years by future pro quarterback John Hadl. Bill Jennings, fired as NU coach after the '61 season, became an assistant coach at KU. Before leaving Nebraska, Jennings said: "We can't feed the ego of the state of Nebraska with the football team."

In spite of a loss in Lawrence in 1967, the Huskers lodged no complaints about anyone listening in on their sideline strategy.

In 1969, Nebraska had the help of a controversial call in a 21-17 victory over the Jayhawks. The win marked the start of a 32-game Nebraska unbeaten string that included two national championships. It also started a streak of 36 consecutive NU wins over Kansas. The Huskers' drive for their winning touchdown was kept

ROAD TRIP TO

LAWRENCE

University of Kansas

Founded: 1866

Enrollment: 30,000

Colors: Crimson and blue

Conference history: Founding member of Big Six in 1928

Stadium: Kivisto Field at Memorial Stadium, capacity 50,071

History of "Jayhawks": Early Kansas settlers first took the name, a combination of two birds – the quarrelsome bluejay and the stealthy sparrow hawk. The message of the name, according to KU: Don't turn your back on this bird.

Distance from Memorial Stadium in Lincoln: 197 miles

Worth remembering:
"Rock, chalk, Jayhawk, KU" is puzzling to outsiders, even though it's accepted as one of college sports' best-known cheers. A chemistry professor in the 1880s came up with the cheer "rah, rah, Jayhawk, KU" for his science club. The sound apparently offended the ear of an English professor, who suggested the change "Rock Chalk" because it rhymed with Jayhawk and would symbolize the chalky limestone of Mount Oread in Lawrence. Unforgettable as well is the sight of fans "waving the wheat" by swaying their arms over their heads when they celebrate.

Quote:
"You who saw the boys carried bodily from the train when they came home from that victory at Kansas know what enthusiasm is. Well, that is the kind of support pennant winners need."

– "The Hesperian," the University of Nebraska student publication (1895)

The end of Nebraska's 36-game winning streak over KU was a reason for Jayhawk fans to celebrate in Lawrence in 2005.

alive when an official flagged KU for interference on Nebraska end Jim McFarland on a fourth-down pass, then added 15 yards for unsportsmanlike conduct when a Jayhawk player argued. A sportswriter who opened Kansas coach Pepper Rodgers' post-game press conference with a "tough game to lose" remark was answered by an obscenity from Rodgers. "Let's see you print that!" he shouted. An assistant coach picked that moment to hand a sack lunch to his irate boss. After a few more angry remarks, Rodgers rolled his lunch sack into a ball and threw it against the locker room wall. "How about that?" he shouted. "There's your story. Rodgers throws sandwich against wall with vengeance – and by the way, it was beef!" The legend of the locker-room sandwich toss grew over the next few years, variously told as beef, bologna and ham. While Rodgers never set that matter straight, he did offer a further explanation of the episode when he returned to Lincoln in 1973 as coach of the UCLA Bruins. "It was the mayonnaise," he said. "I like mustard on my sandwiches. I got mad when I found mayonnaise on it." So to keep Pepper from blowing red hot, the lesson was to hold the mayo.

During the 36-game streak from 1969 through 2004, the Huskers often won in routs, though it took a fourth-quarter field goal to win by a point in 1973. People filled Memorial Stadium, some going to lengths to get in. Before the 1979 game, a member of the Board of Regents said he had spotted short adults wearing Boy Scout uniforms, pretending to be ushers to get in free. The 1983 game marked the final Lincoln appearance of "The Triplets," Irving Fryar, Turner Gill and Mike Rozier, who won 67-13 with Rozier running for four touchdowns and 285 yards in a Heisman Trophy-winning season. In 1985, behind Omaha Central grad Keith Jones, NU won 56-6, scoring 35 points in an 11-minute stretch of the first half. Nebraska fell behind by 17 points in 1991, but another Omaha Central grad, Calvin Jones, came off the bench to run for a then school record 294 yards. In 1993, the Huskers won 21-20 when KU went for a two-point conversion in the final minute but a pass failed. Asked when he decided to go for two with the game on the line, KU coach Glen Mason replied: "When I first took this job and saw what a lopsided series this was." In 1999, a week after Gale Sayers inspired KU with a speech before the Jayhawks beat Missouri, coach Terry Allen said: "Unfortunately, we will not have Gale Sayers around this week. If we did, we'd suit him up." KU played the Huskers tough before losing 24-17.

Then came 2005 and the end of the streak – a 40-15 Kansas win. "It feels unbelievable," a KU linebacker said. "It means no more talk about that stupid streak." The goal posts in Lawrence were torn down, and coach Mark Mangino and his KU players returned from their locker room to the field to pose for pictures in front of the scoreboard. The next year it took overtime for NU to beat Kansas. And in Lawrence in 2007, Nebraska fortunes hit bottom. The eighth-ranked Jayhawks scored 48 in the first half and won 76-39, the most points ever against Nebraska. NU coach Bill Callahan was fired after that season, replaced by Bo Pelini. Just as Devaney had inherited good players from Bill Jennings 45 years earlier, Pelini arrived and met the likes of defensive lineman Ndamukong Suh, who was named the Associated Press national player of the year. With a few exceptions, the long series with the "Rock Chalk Jayhawks" included a lot of Nebraska romp-stomp cakewalks.

A MEMORY OF LAWRENCE

"One year I went to KU with Bev Melton and our kids, so that meant five kids in the van. We found a parking space not far from the stadium. After the game, Tom and John (Melton) decided to drive back with us. But we couldn't find the van. Then we saw a no-parking sign down the block that we hadn't seen. All the cars on that block had been towed. So we all walked to the police station. There were fans from both sides there in the holding cell who had been arrested. The Kansas Jayhawk (mascot) was there because he had gotten into a fight with a Nebraska fan. And all these fans recognized Tom when he came in. It was quite a scene."

– Nancy Osborne, related in 1997

YESTERYEARS

1908: Kansas defeated Nebraska 20-5 in the first Missouri Valley Intercollegiate Athletic Association game played in Lincoln. The Cornhuskers had played Iowa State in a league game earlier that year in Omaha.

1954: Nebraska coach Bill Glassford, shown with co-captains Bob Wagner (65) and Bob Smith (41), clinched second place in the Big Seven with a 41-20 victory over Kansas. Why was that a reason to celebrate? Conference rules did not allow champion Oklahoma to go to the Orange Bowl in consecutive years, so the Huskers made the trip to Miami, losing 34-7 to Duke.

1935: The Cornhuskers captured a 19-13 homecoming win on their way to the first of three straight Big Six titles. Nebraska did not lose to the Jayhawks from 1917 until a 20-0 defeat in 1944. However, KU battled NU to a painful 0-0 tie in 1923 at the official dedication for Memorial Stadium in Lincoln.

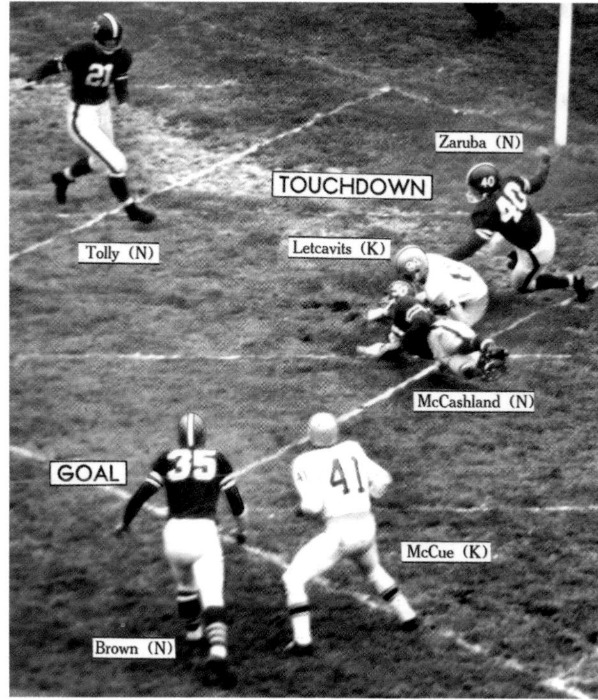

1957: Kansas won 14-12 in Lincoln, its first of five in a row over the Huskers, as it scored the winning points on a controversial touchdown reception. "It was trapped on the ground," NU center Dick McCashland said. Not so, insisted Jim Letcavits, who made the winning catch. "I had just enough room between me and the ground to get my hand under the ball." The World-Herald reported that the home crowd left quickly when the game ended, with most passing up a request to stand for "There Is No Place Like Nebraska." Said one alumnus, "I stood, but I didn't sing. I cussed."

« **1960:** The 31-0 beating by the Jayhawks at the time was the worst Nebraska defeat in the series. "Ineptness of the Nebraska backs may have been due to the fact that on defense they worked overtime backing up a weak line," The World-Herald's Gregg McBride wrote.

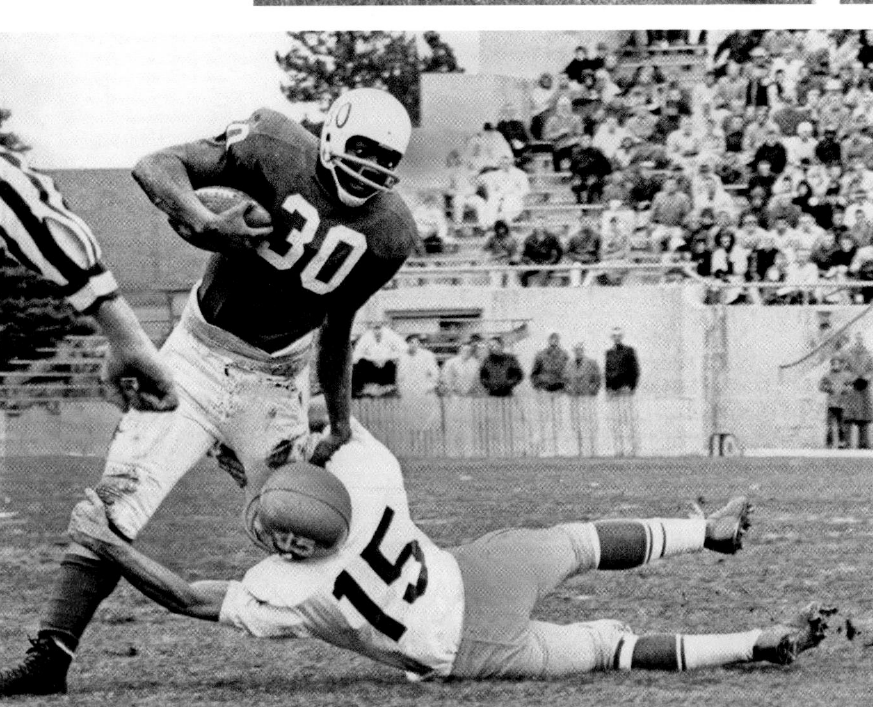

« **1961:** Husker fullback Thunder Thornton (30) was held to 46 yards in a 28-6 loss in Lincoln. KU quarterback John Hadl, a future San Diego Charger star, ran for a touchdown and threw for another in the Jayhawks' fifth straight win in the series. "I know Nebraska is a young club, but they hit real hard," Hadl said. Thornton, who also played defense, returned the compliment. "I've never played against anybody that moves as fast as that Hadl. We've got a young team, but this losing carries over. We've got to get the winning spirit, get rolling and over this hump."

⌃ **1962:** Nebraska routed Kansas 40-16 in the Huskers' first game against Omaha prep star Gale Sayers and Bill Jennings, who was in his first season as a KU assistant after getting fired at Nebraska. The Huskers scored the first four times they had the ball, and The World-Herald reported that Sayers "sat downcast on the bench during most of the nightmare of the first quarter. Kansas didn't have the ball enough for him to get his shirt dirty." While Husker players said they enjoyed beating their former coach, Bob Devaney was more generous in victory. "I have a lot of respect for Bill Jennings, and we certainly cannot complain about the material he left us," he said. That "material" would include halfback Willie Ross (21), who had three touchdowns. Leonard Barwick, who had played quarterback for the 1904 Cornhuskers, watched from the sideline. "I want to score again," the 79-year-old said when the score had reached 40-0. "I want to make it really lopsided."

"THAT LAD WE ALL KNOW SO WELL"

BY DAN SULLIVAN | WORLD-HERALD STAFF WRITER

After graduating from Omaha Central in 1961, Gale Sayers first announced that he would attend Nebraska, then switched to Kansas, explaining that he felt he could "get a better break" at KU. "I believe that they do more for the Negro athlete," he added.

Nebraskans' regrets over losing the high school star grew even stronger after he broke the Big Eight single-game rushing record in his first season, running for 283 yards against Oklahoma State. Even though Sayers had left for KU before Bob Devaney arrived in Lincoln in 1962, the Nebraska coach still got an earful about the Huskers losing out on the star running back.

At a luncheon talk in Lincoln before the 1963 game, a fan asked the coach about Sayers, referring to him as "that lad we all know so well." Devaney shot back, "If you all know Sayers so well, I wonder why you never enrolled him here at Nebraska"

Devaney couldn't resist jabbing again after the "Kansas Comet" had dashed 99 yards for a touchdown against the Huskers. "We would have held Kansas to 167 yards rushing and passing if it hadn't been for the 99-yard run by that lad 'you all know so well.'" Devaney never lost to Kansas while Sayers was in Lawrence.

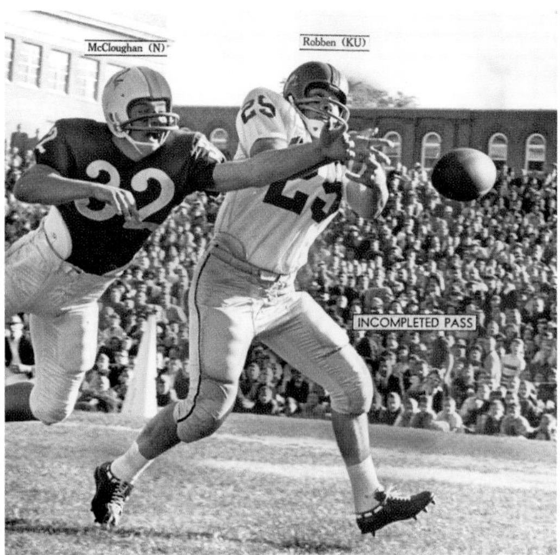

« **1963:** Husker defensive back Kent McCloughan (32) tipped away a potential KU touchdown pass in a 23-9 win in Lincoln. McCloughan, a four-time Nebraska high school sprint champion, later starred for the Oakland Raiders. Much of the talk after the game was about a 99-yard touchdown run by Gale Sayers. "We worked against it all week and were not asleep," NU coach Bob Devaney said. "Kansas simply executed the play well."

⌃ **1964:** While the game was held in Lawrence, it had an all-Nebraska coin flip: The Jayhawks were represented by Sayers (48) of Omaha, Ron Marsh (67) of Omaha and Sid Micek (10) of Scottsbluff; and standing up for the Huskers were Lyle Sittler (52) of Crete and Bob Hohn (18) of Beatrice. Nebraska and Kansas came into the game leading the Big Eight with 4-0 records, with the Jayhawks already having beaten Oklahoma. But Bob Churchich's 92-yard touchdown pass to Freeman White, a school record at the time, helped boost the Huskers to a 14-7 victory and an 8-0 overall record. "We are the worst pass defense team in the country, without a doubt," lamented KU coach Jack Mitchell.

≈ **1965:** NU halfback Ron Kirkland (20) ran for 147 yards and a touchdown in a 42-6 rout. "I had no idea that any team in the nation could take that ball and whip us like that," Kansas coach Jack Mitchell said. "Our scout says Nebraska is the finest squad he has seen in the conference, and he'd seen the good ones at Oklahoma."

» **1966:** Nebraska spoiled the Jayhawks' homecoming theme of "Huskers' Last Stand" with a 24-13 win in Lawrence. NU quarterback Bob Churchich threw for 101 yards and ran for 27 to erase Dennis Claridge's school career record for total yardage.

« » **1967:** Junior quarterback Bobby Douglass led winless Kansas to a 10-0 upset of an unbeaten Cornhusker team favored by 13 points. "I thought we could stop their quarterback rollout," NU coach Bob Devaney said. "We worked on it all week. Then (Douglass) ran it for a touchdown." Douglass came into the game as the Big Eight's leading passer. "You've got to respect him doubly as a passer or runner," Devaney said. "He fakes very well." Even a fiery sideline talk from Husker assistant Mike Corgan (right) couldn't help the NU offense avoid the shutout.

» **1968:** The Jayhawks won again, this time 23-13 in Lincoln, with Don Shanklin's touchdown providing an early lead. The Huskers were forced to counter his speed to the outside, leaving the inside open for runs by quarterback Bobby Douglass and halfback Junior Riggins. "With a guy like Shanklin in there, you can't afford to concentrate too much on the middle," Bob Devaney said.

« **1969:** Paul Rogers (30) received congratulations from coach Bob Devaney after a 55-yard field goal in a 21-17 win in Lincoln. He had missed two field goal attempts and an extra point the year before against the Jayhawks. The Huskers also had the help of a controversial call: Their drive for the winning touchdown was kept alive when an official flagged KU for interference on Nebraska end Jim McFarland on a fourth-down pass. The Jayhawks were penalized 15 more yards for unsportsmanlike conduct when a player argued the call.

≚ **1970:** Nebraska fell behind 20-10 but quarterback Van Brownson (12) ran for two touchdowns and threw for two in leading the Huskers to a 41-20 win.

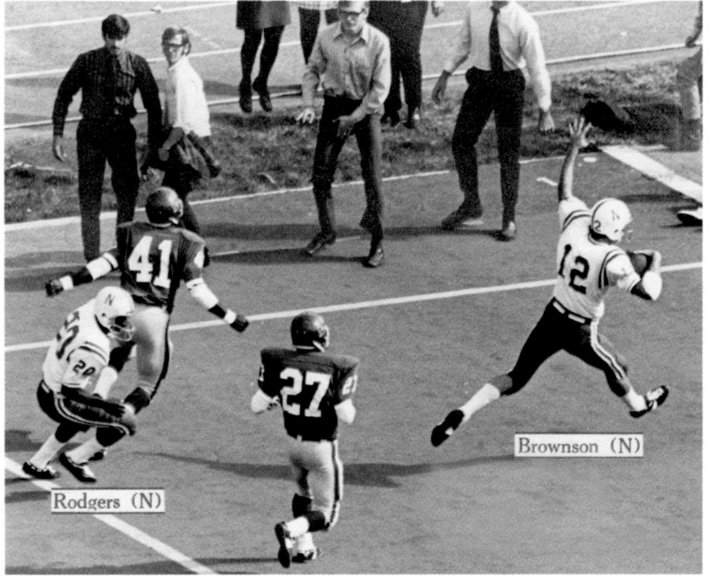

» **1971:** NU drilled Kansas 55-0 in what was the first of six blowouts in the 1970s. Rich Glover (79) and the Blackshirts compiled 100 yards in tackles for losses, recovered five fumbles and intercepted three passes. It was Nebraska's most lopsided victory since a 59-0 romp over Kansas State in 1911.

≈ **1972:** How easy was the fifth-ranked Huskers' 56-0 win in Lawrence? Several Husker players gathered around an NU regent on the sideline who had a radio tuned in to Missouri's game against eighth-ranked Notre Dame. A roar of delight went up from the bench when it was announced the Big Eight's Tigers had upset the Fighting Irish. Kansas quarterback David Jaynes (12), nursing an injured shoulder, called it quits when the game got out of hand, rather than face the rush of Willie Harper (81) and John Dutton (90).

» **1973:** Husker fans weren't ready for a tough 10-9 victory in Lincoln. Scattered boos were heard when first-year coach Tom Osborne decided to run out the clock at the end of the first half with a 7-3 lead. "When you come off the field and the fans are booing, that's ridiculous," said Nebraska defensive captain John Dutton (90). "The fans have to accept the fact this conference is tough. Everybody is almost equal." A letter in The World-Herald's Voice From the Grandstand letters column a few days later provided some perspective for the boobirds: "Most of those wet-noses were in grade school when I watched six years of third-down punts and only passing on second-and-one on the opponent's 20-yard line. In those years, a 4-6 season was a good one. I never missed a game then and won't now, as long as I can get a ticket."

» 1974: FAMBROUGH DEFENDS OSBORNE

Kansas coach Don Fambrough didn't have much to celebrate on his 52nd birthday, enduring a 56-0 bush-whacking by Nebraska in Lawrence. Nebraska went into the game with a disappointing 4-2 record, and Husker coach Tom Osborne was taking heat at home. KU was 4-1 and feeling its oats.

NU quarterback David Humm completed 23 of 27 passes for 230 yards, helped by the sticky fingers of Ritch Bahe (24). The defense held Kansas to four first downs.

Afterward, Fambrough said, "I wish some people would get off Osborne's back. This guy's a hell of a football coach. If the fans want to know how good he is, they shouldn't ask the guy next to them in the stands; they should ask our players. They know!

"And I don't have to say that. I don't have to save my job. I'm not in a bad position security-wise."

Fambrough, much revered as a Jayhawk player, longtime loyal assistant and four-year head coach, was fired at the end of the season. So much for security. He was rehired as head coach in 1979 and fired again in 1982.

In 2007, the university dedicated a $17,000 concrete bench overlooking Memorial Stadium in Lawrence. The plaque on the bench reads: "Coach Fambrough has shown a love and commitment to the University of Kansas and KU football unequaled by anyone in the history of the university."

– Tom Ash

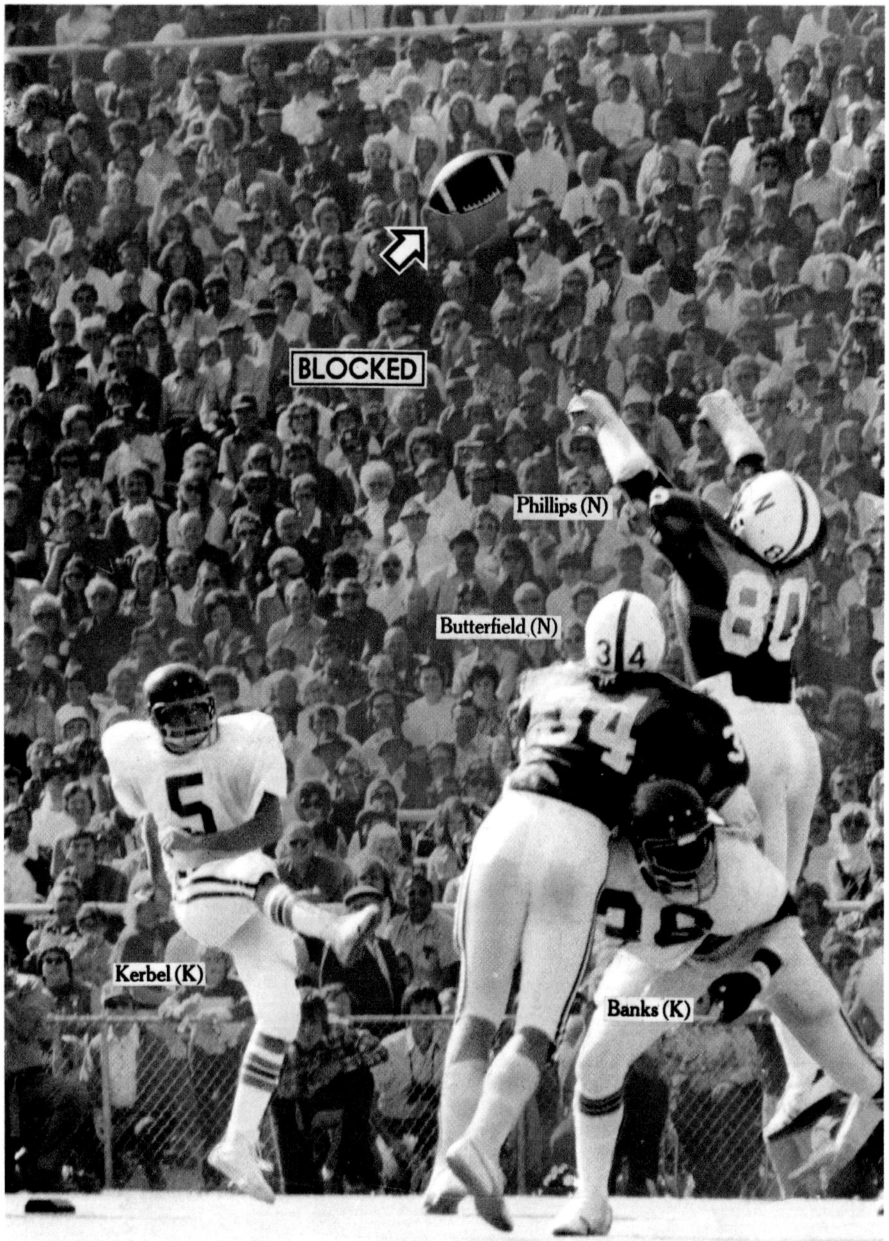

« **1975:** Nebraska's Ray Phillips (80) blocked a field goal attempt just before halftime, the last Kansas scoring threat in a 16-0 Husker win in Lincoln. The Blackshirts held KU wishbone quarterback Nolan Cromwell to 62 yards rushing and two pass completions after defensive coordinator Monte Kiffin had warned his troops that Cromwell had already broken Gale Sayers' single-game rushing record at Kansas.

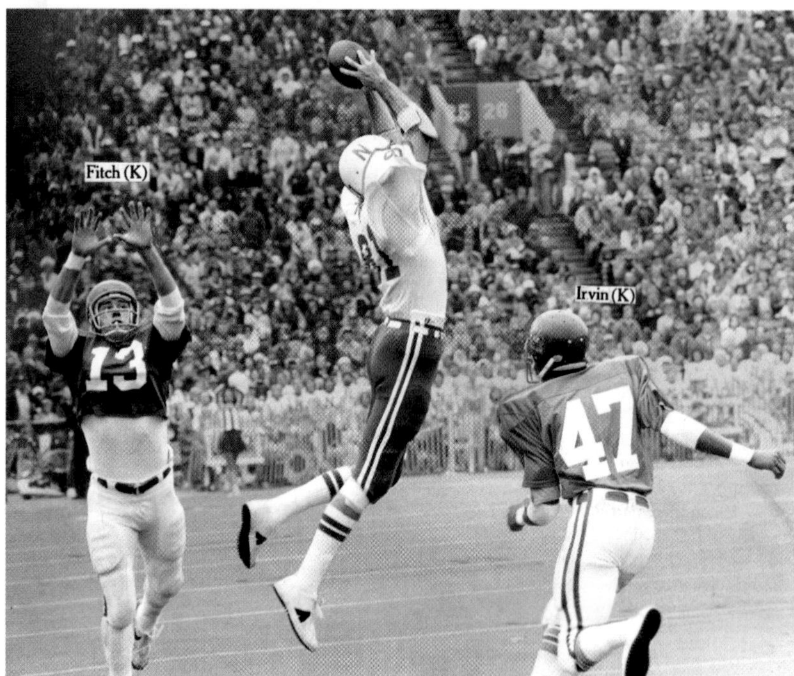

⌃ **1976:** NU coach Tom Osborne was worried about how his team would respond after a tough loss to Missouri the previous week. But quarterback Vince Ferragamo led the Huskers to 483 yards in total offense in a 31-3 victory. Ferragamo ran for one touchdown and threw for two, including one to Dave Shamblin (81). "If we had lost again, we'd close the locker room," Osborne joked afterward, referring to Oklahoma coach Barry Switzer and Colorado's Bill Mallory announcing bans on postgame interviews of players.

» 1977: GIVE HIM THE BALL

Quarterback Ed Burns (17), an Omaha Rummel product, never rose above the third team and never threw a touchdown pass during his career at Nebraska. But Burns stuck with the New Orleans Saints as a free agent and spent two seasons (1978 and 1979) backing up Archie Manning.

Burns touched off an emotional tribute by his teammates when he scored on a 3-yard option around right end and was awarded a rare game ball following his final Memorial Stadium appearance – a 52-7 conquest of Kansas.

In the locker room, the Huskers went wild after co-captains Greg Jorgensen and Jeff Carpenter presented Burns with the game ball.

"Eddie! Eddie! Eddie!" they chanted. Burns wept at the tribute paid him. His cheeks were still soggy moments later when the press was allowed into the room.

"Yes, those are tears," he said. "I'm embarrassed to cry before you guys, but . . . " His voice trailed off. He blinked a couple of times, then broke into a smile.

Burns said coach Tom Osborne called the option play that led to the only touchdown of his Husker career.

"I think I made my mind up early that I wasn't going to pitch it," he said. "After I scored, the whole team came over and congratulated me. I thought I would start crying then."

– Larry Porter

≈ 1978: KU SPOTTED HIS TALENT

Rick Berns (35) opened scoring in a 63-21 rout before leaving with a thigh bruise. With injuries also slowing I.M. Hipp and Tim Wurth, Nebraska turned to fourth-team I-back Craig Johnson.

Kansas had tried hard to recruit Johnson out of Omaha Westside. His decision to stay in Nebraska didn't work out well for the Jayhawks. Johnson, a sophomore, scored on plays covering 64, 78 and 60 yards, finishing with 192 yards on 10 carries. "That's pretty good," said Mike Corgan, NU running backs coach in his best deadpan. Johnson's 78-yard score came on a screen pass. His contributions helped the Huskers to a school and Big Eight record of 799 total yards.

– Steve Sinclair

≈ 1979: STARTING WASN'T EVERYTHING

While Craig Johnson rarely took center stage during his career as a backup I-back at Nebraska, his performance against Kansas again demanded attention in a 42-0 NU win.

Johnson unleashed a 94-yard touchdown run – at the time the longest scoring run in NU history – as a junior against the Jayhawks. Roger Craig matched Johnson's 94-yard blast against Florida State in 1981. Quarterback Eric Crouch broke the record in 2001 with a 95-yard scoring run against Missouri.

But Johnson owned the record the day he torched Kansas. And he did it as a third-string I-back behind Jarvis Redwine and I.M. Hipp.

"It's a thrill for me," Johnson said after erasing the record of 84 yards set by John Edwards in 1954 against Oregon State. "There have been so many great running backs here, and there are so many great ones here now that I wonder: Why me? Why do I have it now?"

Johnson could have started at many other major colleges, but he accepted his backup status as a Husker. "A lot of people say that I could start at other places," Johnson said. "But here's Jarvis at Oregon State. He really wasn't a starter there. Then he comes here to a school like Nebraska that should have more competition than Oregon State. He's super. He's a great running back. He's an all-class guy.

"When people say maybe I could play someplace else, well, going someplace else doesn't always solve your problem. Jarvis wasn't a starter there. Maybe I wouldn't be a starter at another place, either.

"I'm satisfied with my role here in the respect that when you have Isaiah and Jarvis, it's hard for anyone to play in front of them. It's hard for me to sit on the bench for two quarters and watch, but that's hard for any competitive football player.

"The biggest thing of all," Johnson concluded, "is that I feel I've contributed. If you can contribute and play with a team like this, it's an honor."

– Larry Porter

≈ **1980:** Sophomore I-back Roger Craig (21) had three touchdowns in a 54-0 rout. Ahead 33-0 after scoring in the last minute of the first half, Nebraska coach Tom Osborne chose to go for a two-point conversion, leading some Jayhawks to skip handshakes after the game. Osborne defended the move afterward, but he backpedaled the next day after talking to his wife. "That whole thing had to do with perspective on the game," he explained. "Nancy was in the stands, and she said their fans felt after we got ahead a touchdown or two it was over. They thought we were rubbing it in. I wasn't sure we had it put away."

≈ **1981:** Kansas led late in the third quarter before falling 31-15 in Lincoln, as the Huskers tied a school record from 1910 with their fifth straight game without allowing a touchdown. Still, the Blackshirts gave up five field goals. "That's kind of a lousy way to get it," Nebraska linebacker Brent Evans (48) said. "It would have been nice to have shut them down and held them under 100 yards and do it in fashion, instead of the way we did it."

« **1982:** Tony Felici (46) and the Blackshirts held Kansas to 69 total yards in a 52-0 shutout. Nebraska defenders attributed their performance to a TV interview with KU quarterback Mike Bohn the night before the game. "He said on television that we have a poor defense," safety Bret Clark said. "That really fired me up." The Blackshirts gave up just 6 yards rushing, 63 yards passing and seven first downs. "John Elway or any other great quarterback would have a tough time throwing against Nebraska today, the way their defense really came at us," Bohn said after the game.

RECRUITING WAR

Nebraska and Kansas went head to head in recruiting prized running backs Jeff Smith (28) and Kerwin Bell (4) in 1980. Smith, a Wichita native, ended up picking Nebraska after Husker coach Tom Osborne said he'd back off on recruiting Bell. Kansas fans might have forgiven Smith for leaving the state, since they ended up with Bell, if not for the fact that Smith later provided evidence in an NCAA investigation of Kansas.

A newspaper story quoted Smith as saying that KU assistant John Hadl had promised him $30,000 to sign a letter of intent. Hadl, who had since left to coach in the NFL, called Smith a liar. Another former Kansas assistant said that if Smith had been offered money, "he should have taken it, because he ain't worth a quarter."

While Bell rushed for over 1,000 yards in his freshman year, injuries and eligibility issues kept him off the field for much of the rest of his career. Kansas ended up on probation, partly because of alleged illegal payments the former Jayhawk staff offered to Smith when it tried to recruit him.

Smith never lost to his home-state school in four games. "It's great we've played so well against Kansas in the years I've been at Nebraska," he said after a 41-7 win as a senior in 1984. "It's a good feeling to know that Nebraska has been a great choice for me."

« 1983: SAY GOODBYE TO MIKE

Mike Rozier (30) made his final home game one to remember.

The Nebraska I-back rushed for a school-record 285 yards and four touchdowns as the Huskers blasted Kansas 67-13.

"I always wanted the record," Rozier said. "This week they let me get it."

Rozier had 230 yards and all of his touchdowns in the first half as the Huskers surged to a 41-0 halftime lead. Coach Tom Osborne kept Rozier in the game until after he surpassed Rick Berns' single-game school record of 255 yards.

"I wanted to break it here, in my last home game," Rozier said. "I'm not out for individual records, but I'm glad coach Osborne let me stay in."

Rozier's touchdowns boosted his season total to 28 to break the NCAA record of 26 by Penn State's Lydell Mitchell in 1971.

"I'll be able to tell people I blocked for that guy," NU center Mark Traynowicz said. "His name won't be forgotten around here for a long time."

– Steve Sinclair

« **1984:** Nebraska coach Tom Osborne once again had to answer questions about a decision before halftime, this time in a 41-7 victory. Kansas fans booed when the Cornhuskers tried to score late in the second quarter with a 28-0 lead. "All I can say," Osborne said on his television show the next day, "is take a look at the Miami game yesterday." No. 6 Miami led Maryland 31-0 at halftime but lost 42-40. "You better score all you can score in the first half and the third quarter to make sure that doesn't happen to you," Osborne said. Nebraska clinched a share of its fourth consecutive Big Eight championship with the victory.

» 1985: BLACKSHIRTS' STREAK

Nebraska's defense in 1985 put together a string of 15 straight quarters without allowing a touchdown.

The Blackshirts' streak started in the final three quarters of a 17-7 win over Colorado and continued through a 41-3 win over Kansas State, a 49-0 win over Iowa State and a 56-6 win over Kansas.

But the defense suffered a blow in the Kansas game when junior linebacker Marc Munford suffered a serious knee injury that required surgery the next day. Munford had five unassisted tackles in the first 20 minutes before he was injured. He was named the Huskers' defensive player of the game for the third time in the season.

"It's a big loss for us," NU defensive coordinator Charlie McBride said. "Marc and Mike Knox, along with those kids up front, have been the heart of our defense all year long. Having a guy with Munford's ability out of the (Oklahoma) game sure isn't going to help."

Munford was lost for the season. He suffered kidney problems after his knee operation and was briefly on dialysis but returned for the next season.

The week after Munford's injury, the Huskers lost to OU 27-7. Sooner tight end Keith Jackson ended NU's streak of not allowing a touchdown when he went 88 yards on a reverse to score 3:19 into the game.

– Steve Sinclair

≈ 1986: A GOOD START

The first career start for quarterback Clete Blakeman (12) went about as smoothly as possible.

Nebraska scored two touchdowns before Kansas took a center snap in the 70-0 victory in 1986. The loss was the worst in Jayhawk history, and NU's margin of victory was its biggest shutout win since World War I.

"I was just happy to get in there, get the start, and move the team like we did," said Blakeman, a junior from Norfolk filling in for the injured Steve Taylor.

"I've been waiting a long time for this chance. It showed that Coach Osborne has the faith in me to play me like that."

Blakeman threw three touchdown passes and ran for another.

In 1987, Blakeman started against Kansas for the second straight year, again with Taylor out because of an injury. This time, Blakeman completed 10 of 12 passes for 100 yards and a touchdown and ran for 26 yards in a 54-2 Husker win.

So the Huskers outscored the Jayhawks 124-2 in Blakeman's two starts.

– Steve Sinclair

« **1987:** Neil Smith (99) and the Nebraska defense allowed just 74 yards rushing and 64 passing in a 54-2 shellacking. The Jayhawks, under instructions from coach Bob Valesente, headed straight for the locker room after the game, skipping the customary midfield handshakes between opposing players. Valesente said there were no hard feelings, just that his team "didn't deserve to mingle around the field after the game."

≈ **1988:** Tyreese Knox (34) ran for 120 yards and a touchdown in a 63-10 romp in Lawrence. Coach Glen Mason, in his first year at Kansas, praised his young team for not quitting when Nebraska built a big first-half lead. "If you think it's not tough playing against Nebraska, you're crazy," said Mason. "I didn't see any volunteers come out of the stands and put their helmets on, wanting to go out there."

« **1989:** Kansas scored on its second possession, giving the Jayhawks their first lead over the Huskers since the first quarter of the 1985 game. But Jeff Mills (42) and the Blackshirts shut down the Jayhawks, as Nebraska scored the next 44 points to end up a 51-14 winner. KU's Glen Mason said he was looking for a way to make his escape after the Jayhawks went ahead 7-0. "I was taking the rule book out and figuring if there was any way I could call the game off right there," he said. "I wish I was a little bit smarter. Maybe I should have said, 'Let's head to the buses.'"

» **1990:** Much of the talk after Nebraska's 41-9 victory was about KU's onside kick after taking a 3-0 lead early in the game. The ball went out of bounds at the KU 41, and the Huskers took the lead for good four plays later on a 35-yard touchdown pass from Mickey Joseph (2) to Johnny Mitchell. "We weren't expecting an onside kick that early," coach Tom Osborne said. "I guess they felt if they scored that they would try to put one on us early. It just didn't work."

» **1992:** Seventh-ranked Nebraska made No. 13 Kansas look more like a pretender than a contender in hammering the Jayhawks 49-7. The Huskers benefited from three touchdown passes from quarterback Tommie Frazier, including a 46-yarder to Corey Dixon (2).

« **1991:** Redshirt freshman Calvin Jones (44) broke Nebraska's single-game rushing record with 294 yards and scored six touchdowns in NU's 59-23 victory at Lawrence. "We gave him a couple of extra carries," said Tom Osborne afterward, noting that Jones was still playing late in the runaway game. "We don't normally make concessions to records, but we thought in that case we wanted to make sure he got it."

« 1993: THE GREAT ESCAPE

Nebraska linebacker Trev Alberts said he hated to use the word "lucky" in describing how the Huskers escaped with a 21-20 victory, but perhaps no other word applied. Nebraska's defense was looking to stop the run on the Jayhawks' try for two points after a 3-yard run by June Henley (20) pulled KU within one point in the final minute. The Jayhawks passed. As fate would have it, the ball fell incomplete, preserving the Huskers' perfect record. "This is our season on that one play," Alberts said. "We were probably lucky today. I don't like to use the word 'lucky' so much. We came through." KU's Glen Mason was questioned about his decision after the game. "Sometimes you think with your heart and not your head," he said. Tom Osborne applauded Mason for going for the victory. "That's what I would have done," he said, "and I respect him for that decision. Only about 30 to 40 percent of two-point plays are effective. When you do that, you know it's the chance you take."

¥ **1995:** Quarterback Tommie Frazier (15) broke Nebraska's career total offense record in a 41-3 rout, finishing with 99 yards rushing and 86 yards passing. He also broke Dave Humm's record for career touchdown passes in the win over the Jayhawks, who ended the season with a 10-2 record after a win over UCLA in the Aloha Bowl.

≈ **1994:** NU quarterback Brook Berringer (18) completed 13 of 18 passes for 267 yards, with two touchdowns and no interceptions in a 45-17 victory. With tongue in cheek, he thanked Colorado coach Bill McCartney for the game plan. "He said we had to throw to our wide receivers," Berringer said. "So that's what we did." The remark was in reference to comments the CU coach made after losing to Nebraska 24-7 the previous week. When asked if Berringer had "replaced" the injured Tommie Frazier at quarterback, McCartney said NU's new starter needed to keep proving himself each week and had to learn to throw to his wide receivers. "I don't care what Bill McCartney thinks," Berringer said. "And I don't care what anybody else says, either."

« **1996:** Jayhawk coach Glen Mason said he wasn't shocked by Nebraska's Scott Frost (7) throwing for 254 yards in a 63-7 rout. It was Frost's best passing yardage day since he played for Stanford two years earlier. "(Coach) Bill Walsh recruited him to Stanford as a passer, and he's in the Hall of Fame and I'm riding the bus home eating a bologna sandwich," Mason said. Frost said he didn't know whether the game would silence critics during his first year as Nebraska's starting quarterback. "I don't hear the critics anymore," he said. "I learned my lesson after the first two weeks. After the first week, everyone was telling me how great I was. After the second week, they were ready to tar and feather me and put me out of the state."

» **1997:** Two days removed from a liquid-only diet and a fairly severe case of tonsillitis, Nebraska defensive tackle Jason Peter (55) survived 40-degree temperatures, 30 mph winds and a cold, steady rain for three hours in the Huskers' 35-0 win. Peter showed little effect of his illness, notching five tackles, including two behind the line of scrimmage, one sack and a pair of pass breakups. "I felt a little sluggish out there," Peter said. "When it comes time to playing a game, you're not really thinking about how sick you are and how banged up you are." Peter, Tony Ortiz (37) and the Blackshirts held Kansas to 48 total yards in the game.

« **1999:** Nebraska spent the first half of the game swimming upstream against Kansas, but Bobby Newcombe (12) threw the Huskers a life preserver in the second half of a 24-17 victory. Newcombe broke an 86-yard punt return to wipe out a 9-3 Kansas lead with 2:14 to play in the third quarter, then caught a 49-yard touchdown pass from Eric Crouch with 3:24 left in the game for the deciding score over 32-point underdog KU.

« **1998:** Correll Buckhalter (36) scored three touchdowns, as the Huskers piled up 545 total yards in a 41-0 victory. "I would venture to say they had 350 to 400 yards between the tackles," first-year Kansas coach Terry Allen said. "They just rammed it down our throats." The shutout was Nebraska's second straight against the Jayhawks and the 10th in its 30-game winning streak against Kansas.

» **2000:** Dan Alexander (38), Eric Crouch and Correll Buckhalter all had 100-yard games, as the Huskers totaled 557 total yards in a 56-17 victory. The Nebraska running game was so dominant that ABC chose center Dominic Raiola for its offensive player-of-the-game award.

« **2001:** Nebraska made itself feel right at home in Lawrence, winning 51-7 in front of a red-clad horde of Husker fans that made up more than half of the sellout crowd of 50,750. "Before the game, we were joking around whether this was a home game or not," said NU I-back Dahrran Diedrick (30). "We had more people than they did. When we're on offense, we can hear everything. That twists the whole home-field advantage to us. Our crowd was cheering so loud it disrupted their offense."

» **2002:** "I'm not really an excited guy. I just want to win," NU quarterback Jammal Lord (10) said after leading the Huskers to a 45-7 victory. In the game, he became the 18th quarterback in NCAA Division I history to rush and pass for 1,000 yards in a season. Lord ended the season with more total yardage than Eric Crouch had the year before in his Heisman Trophy-winning season. His biggest play of the day came in the third quarter, when he sprinted for a 42-yard run. KU safety Johnny McCoy stopped him by grabbing his face mask and twisting his helmet off. "That's just football," Lord said.

» **2003:** Safety Josh Bullocks (20) got his nation-leading and school record ninth interception of the season in a 24-3 win, but his attention was more on twin brother Daniel, who got his first. "I was real proud of him," said Josh, the younger of the brothers by one minute. "We're competitive, and he was getting behind. I tell him, 'If you get one, I'm going to get one. No, if you get one, I'll get two.'"

» **2004:** Four turnovers, two missed field goals and a last-second Hail Mary pass in the end zone couldn't stop Nebraska from pulling out a 14-8 win, its 36th straight in the series. Adam Barmann heaved a prayer into the end zone as the clock expired, and the ball bounced off Daniel Bullocks (14) and Fabian Washington (3) and dropped to the ground. It was the third straight game for the 3-1 and 1-0 Huskers that was decided by a knocked-around pass in the end zone in the final seconds. "It would be nice to win by a few touchdowns and relax a little," said NU linebacker Barrett Ruud.

2005: THE STREAK ENDS

BY RICH KAIPUST | WORLD-HERALD STAFF WRITER

There was some symbolism in the 41-yard interception return by Kevin Kane (45) that finished off Kansas' 40-15 win over Nebraska, unless you were a disgusted Husker fan who already had looked away after the linebacker swiped a late pass by Zac Taylor (13). As Kane sprinted toward the end zone, one Jayhawk blocker absolutely creamed I-back Cory Ross and another shoved aside a helpless Taylor. Appropriate to the way things had gone all afternoon in Lawrence, Kan.

Kansas gained 428 total yards despite coming into the game averaging 251.2 against Big 12 foes. Nebraska managed just 138.

Happens, right? Well, not in this series, where KU had never reached 40 points in any of the previous 111 meetings. Before that Saturday, Nebraska had won 36 straight games vs. Kansas, at the time the second-longest active streak by one NCAA Division I-A opponent over another.

For all the streaks that would come to an end during Bill Callahan's four years as head coach, he seemed to understand the significance of this one more than most. He was then 10-10 in his second year as NU head coach, sitting through a tense postgame press conference in a cramped interview room that was not able to handle all those who wanted to get in. "It's not good," Callahan said. "It's God-awful, in my opinion. It's disturbing to me. It bothers me."

Two years later, it actually found a way to be worse. The Huskers were drilled 76-39 in Lawrence – the most points ever given up by a Husker team – and Callahan would coach only two more games at NU.

« **2006:** A 75-yard touchdown catch by Frantz Hardy (7) was the break Nebraska needed in its 39-32 overtime victory. The big play came on third-and-18 with four minutes left in regulation and the Huskers down by a point. "I just threw it up, and Frantz made a play on it," quarterback Zac Taylor said. "You know what, we'll take what we can get," said NU fullback Dane Todd. "We're not going to complain about how we got it done."

≽ **2007:** KU scored more points against Nebraska in its 76-39 victory than it did in a 10-year stretch from 1995 to 2004 (69) and a 14-year stretch from 1971 to 1984 (75). Quarterback Todd Reesing (5) led eighth-ranked Kansas to its highest point total ever against NU. During one stretch, the Jayhawks scored touchdowns on 10 of 11 drives and on the one time they didn't score in that stretch, they ran out the clock before halftime after taking over with five seconds left.

2008: Nebraska coach Bo Pelini awarded Blackshirts to his defensive unit after a 45-35 win over Kansas. While the defenders allowed 422 total yards, Pelini said the unit played with a physical nature and great effort, and made plays sideline to sideline. "It's a dream come true," said NU sophomore cornerback Anthony West. "When I walked down and saw it in my locker, I almost didn't believe it. I thought somebody was joking at first. I didn't see any numbers on it. It was kind of tucked away. I just saw the black. I walked up to it and held it out. Man, it means a lot, just knowing the history and the past Blackshirts and the tradition. It means a lot."

2009: Kansas took a 17-16 lead with 7½ minutes remaining in Lawrence, but Roy Helu scored two fourth-quarter touchdowns as NU pulled away for a 31-17 win. Niles Paul (24) had 244 all-purpose yards, but coaches also raved about his blocking. "We knew he had a chance to make some big plays," receivers coach Ted Gilmore said, noting that confidence was never an issue for Paul. "Niles likes Niles Paul. I don't ever have to worry about that part of it."

STILL HAVING NIGHTMARES ABOUT . . .

BOBBY DOUGLASS

Quarterback

Think fast: What former Kansas backfield star beat Nebraska twice in the 1960s and later set rushing records that still stand for the Chicago Bears?

It's not who you think. Omaha Central grad Gale Sayers never beat Bob Devaney's Huskers. But three years after Sayers left KU, Bobby Douglass quarterbacked the Jayhawks under coach Pepper Rodgers to victories over downtrodden NU teams in 1967 and '68.

Douglass, a bruising runner from El Dorado, Kan., scored the only touchdown in the '67 game, a 10-0 Kansas win. A year later in Lincoln, he rushed for two TDs in the final five minutes to finish a 23-13 comeback, KU's last win in Lincoln.

"I would put those wins right at the top of any that Kansas would have liked to have when I played there," Douglass said. "That was the team we wanted to beat – Missouri and Nebraska and, of course, Oklahoma. If Kansas can beat Nebraska, that makes it a pretty good season."

The Jayhawks had to savor those Douglass-directed wins for nearly four decades, going until 2005 without another victory over the Huskers.

"I remember him as a big, very strong guy, tough to bring down," said Tom Osborne, on the staff under Bob Devaney for those Kansas wins. "He had some running ability and had a very strong arm. They had pretty good players around him, and we probably weren't quite as talented as we had been."

Nebraska's 6-4 marks in '67 and '68 led Devaney to ask Osborne to retool the offense, which in turn led to his ascension to head coach four years later.

So Douglass, in a roundabout way, helped set into motion the events that led to the greatest era in NU football history, starting with national championships in 1970 and '71.

Douglass played 10 years in the NFL, including the first seven with the Bears. He set NFL records for quarterback rushing yardage in a season and per game that stood for more than 30 years until topped by Michael Vick.

– Mitch Sherman

JOHN HADL

Running back/ Quarterback

Directed the Jayhawks to three straight wins over Nebraska from 1959 through '61 before a standout NFL career as QB.

JOHN ZOOK

Defensive end

Earned All-America honors for the 1968 Orange Bowl team that notched KU's last win over Nebraska until KU finally did it again in 2005.

JUNE HENLEY

Running back

Gouged NU for 148 rushing yards in 1993 but inexplicably stayed on the sideline for a failed last-second two-point conversion in a one-point Husker win.

TODD REESING

Quarterback

Accounted for 12 touchdowns in three games against NU, including six through the air and 354 passing yards in a 76-39 KU win in 2007.

Nebraskans have had plenty to celebrate on their road trips to Ames over the years, including a 35-7 victory in 2008.

IOWA STATE

THE WIND HAS BLOWN MOSTLY IN ONE DIRECTION

BY MICHAEL KELLY | WORLD-HERALD STAFF WRITER

THE NEBRASKA FIGHT SONG SAYS, "We'll all stick together in all kinds of weather," and that often was tested in trips to Ames for games at Iowa State – a team whose very nickname is related to the weather. A Chicago newspaperman wrote in 1895 that a defeated Northwestern team might as well have played a cyclone from the plains, and the Cyclone nickname stuck. Under legendary coach Pop Warner, the Cyclones began their annual series with Nebraska the next year. Husker rooters are no mere fair-weather fans, as they have proved by traveling to Ames over the years on some disagreeably cold and rainy weekends.

Lincoln isn't always balmy, either. But what happened at NU in 1907 remains a point not of meteorological but of historical disagreement: Iowa State says it won 13-10; Nebraska claims it won 10-9. Trailing, Iowa State attempted a late field goal (four points at the time), which landed short but bounced over the crossbar and was ruled no good. Cyclone Coach Clyde Williams appealed to Walter Camp, "the father of American football," who said that under the rules then, a ball that bounced over should count. Nebraska never accepted that, and each school to this day lists the game as a victory.

The Huskers have dominated the long series, giving the Cyclones more losses by far than any other opponent. At times, Iowa State seemed jinxed. In 1947, the 'Clones set a school record that still stands by holding NU to two first downs – but lost 14-7 when a bad snap over the punter's head and a blocked kick set up the Huskers for touchdown drives of four yards each. In the '50s, coach Vince DiFrancesca was asked after another low-scoring, close defeat if the breaks might soon turn the other way, as in a craps game. "Not when we play Nebraska," he said. "I'm tired of continually throwing sixes." The problem was not scoring enough sixes. But in a 13-0 ISU win in 1957, The World-Herald reported: "The Cyclones did more than bury a Cornhusker jinx of long standing – they plowed it under."

Husker student manager Pete Smith helped out lineman Tom Alward on a muddy day in Ames in 1974.

ROAD TRIP TO

AMES

Iowa State University

Founded: 1858

Enrollment: About 28,000

Colors: Cardinal and gold

Conference history: Founding member of Big Six in 1928

Stadium: Jack Trice Stadium, capacity 55,000

History of "Cyclones": Originally the Cardinals, the name was changed after an 1895 newspaper account about a victory referred to the team as a cyclone from Iowa that tore across the plains. Cy the cardinal became the official mascot in 1954.

Distance from Memorial Stadium in Lincoln: 221 miles

Worth remembering:
Games in Ames might not have produced a lot of last-second touchdowns and goal-line stands in high-stakes games. But fans won't forget the feel of the light coating of ice on the handrails, the sound of a flagpole rattling in the north wind or the sight of the stands on the opposite side of the field dimmed by a downpour of rain.

Quote:
"Our guys love to play Nebraska. It's the darnedest thing I've ever seen. You wouldn't think that would be a normal reaction. But they couldn't wait to play this game."

– ISU assistant coach Jimmy Burrow (1994)

Iowa State punter Carl Gomez had trouble coming to grips with a cold and snowy day at Jack Trice Stadium in 1998.

In 1961, Cyclone coach Clay Stapleton gave a back-handed compliment and perhaps a prediction of a turnaround, calling the sub-.500 Huskers "the best losing football team I've seen." Bob Devaney arrived as NU coach in 1962, soon calling his first-team defense the Blackshirts because of their black practice jerseys. Iowa State mimicked that in 1965 with red practice jerseys and a "Red Devil" defense. Alas, NU won 44-0. That Nebraska offensive explosion was followed the next year at Ames with a real explosion – on the field, three hours before the game. An Iowa State chemistry student had planted a homemade bomb the night before, saying "there wasn't enough excitement or interest in the game." No one was hurt, and he received a suspended sentence.

In 1972, the year after NU's second straight national title, the teams played to a 23-23 tie on a muddy field at Ames. A disgusted Devaney said the Huskers performed "like a bunch of farmers on a picnic, waiting on somebody to bring their lunch." Iowa State coach Johnny Majors, though, called it "the greatest game ever at Iowa State." The next year the Huskers handed the 'Clones their lunch, 31-7, and in 1974 won the final game between the schools at old Clyde Williams Field – though it was again so muddy and the student body so unruly that coach Tom Osborne called it "a sorry place to play." At the new stadium in Ames in 1976, Iowa State won 37-28, and coach Earle Bruce, similar to Majors four years earlier, called it "the greatest thing that ever happened to Iowa State."

From 1978 on, NU won 13 in a row, including a 35-0 game in 35-degree weather in Ames in 1980, and a 1981 Senior Day game in Lincoln, where wingback Anthony Steels became the first Husker to take the microphone and sing the pregame national anthem. The low-scoring games of old were history as Nebraska rang up wins of 72-29, 49-0 and 51-16. The Huskers, though, trailed at halftime at Ames in 1986, when their normally taciturn coach let them have it. "Coach Osborne basically blew his stack," said defensive coordinator Charlie McBride. "It's a little bit uncharacteristic of him, but he got their attention." NU won by three touchdowns. In 1992, the Husker victory streak ended when an obscure fifth-year quarterback, Marv Seiler, led the 'Clones to a 19-10 win. Coach Jim Walden called it "the height of my coaching career in terms of watching my kids perform. They played a perfect game."

The Huskers returned to lopsided victories in the '90s, including 73-14 in 1995 and 77-14 in 1997, but the final decade of the rivalry included Iowa State victories in 2002 (knocking NU out of the national rankings for the first time since 1981), in 2004 and in 2009 – a 9-7 win at Memorial Stadium in Lincoln, where the Huskers had more turnovers (eight) than points. No cyclone had blown in from the plains, but the Huskers and their fans felt a little under the weather.

CHANCELLOR'S SUPPORT AFTER A LOSS

Nebraska Coach Tom Osborne in 1977 still managed to display a sense of humor when he addressed the Extra Point Club following the 24-21 loss to Iowa State – the Huskers' second straight loss to the Cyclones. Lending support during the weekly luncheon held at the Cornhusker Hotel was Chancellor Roy Young. "I'm pleased Roy Young came down," Osborne said. "But he told me the main reason he came was that he wanted to listen to a man who had more problems than he does."

– Larry Porter

YESTERYEARS

≽ **1935:** Nebraska won its Big Six opener in Ames 20-7 on the way to its first of three straight conference titles under coach Dana X. Bible. He left for Texas after the 1936 season, his 50 victories at NU trailing only Tom Osborne, Bob Devaney and Frank Solich.

» **1944:** Iowa State defeated Nebraska 19-6, its second of three straight wins – the Cyclones' longest streak in the series. Nebraska's squads were depleted during the war years. In fact, the 1943 roster was made up of 11 players classified 4-F for the military draft, seven who were awaiting their draft notices and 15 who were too young to register for the draft. ISU, however, chose to use more physically fit naval trainees. "Without naval athletes, the Cyclone management has declared it could not field a team," The World-Herald reported.

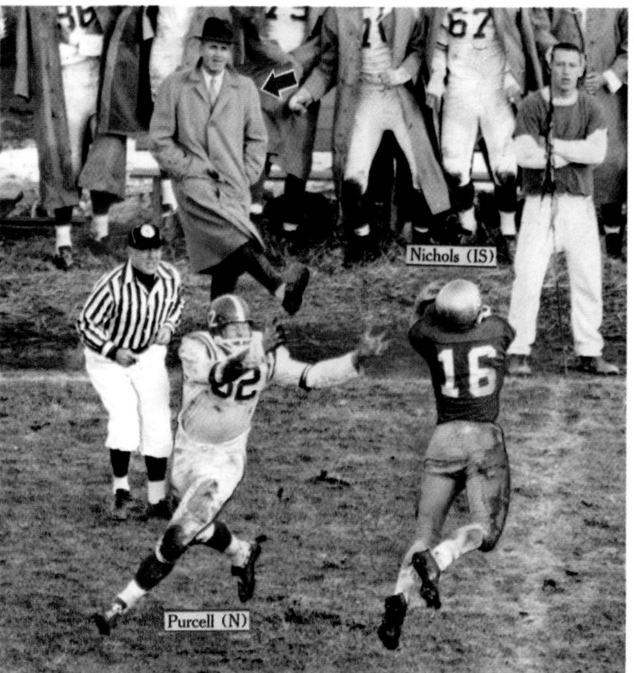

≼ **1959:** Nebraska coach Bill Jennings kicked the turf as Iowa State's Dwight Nichols (16) intercepted a pass intended for NU's Don Purcell (82) in the Cyclones' 18-6 win. The game was the week following the Huskers' dramatic 25-21 upset of Oklahoma to snap the Sooners' 74-game conference winning streak. The ISU victory was no upset, however. Coach Clay Stapleton's "Dirty Thirty," so named because of the small ISU roster, entered the game as a 3½-point favorite.

≼ **1956:** Nebraska running back Jerry Brown provided a 71-yard touchdown run in a 9-7 victory, the Huskers' 11th straight in the series. The winning points came on a field goal with 45 seconds left. The World-Herald's Gregg McBride reported: "As the final gun popped at Memorial Stadium Saturday, an Iowa State old-timer, slamming his hat down onto the cold concrete, snorted: 'Well, I'll be damned, they did it to us again.'"

« **1960:** Cyclone fans celebrated a 10-7 victory, ISU's first in Lincoln since 1944, and had to be held back from bringing down the goalposts in Memorial Stadium. Sophomore Larry Schreiber's field goal provided the difference in the game. "The boys seem to be in a daze," a reporter said to NU coach Bill Jennings. "They can't figure out what happened." Replied Jennings: "They got beat."

1961: NU upset the Cyclones in Ames 16-13 as sophomore quarterback Dennis Claridge (24) upstaged Iowa State star tailback Dave Hoppmann (16), who came into the game leading the nation in total offense. Claridge ran for 33 yards and a touchdown, threw for 83 and averaged 40 yards on five punts in a game marred by fights and ejections. "Someone stuck their finger through my face guard," said Husker fullback Thunder Thornton, who was tossed in the third quarter. "Guess I shouldn't have lost my head."

» **1962:** The Huskers avoided a letdown in the game following a dramatic victory over Michigan in Ann Arbor. First-year coach Bob Devaney was more enthusiastic after the 36-22 win over ISU than he had been after beating the Wolverines. "We made mistakes, sure, but they were mechanical – not of the heart," said Devaney, adding that he thought Iowa State's players were superior to Michigan's.

⌃ **1963:** Husker lineman Lloyd Voss (71) needed a break during Nebraska's 21-7 victory, as the thermometer hit 93 in Lincoln. "Players were allowed an extra salt pill and the squad ambled onto the playing field instead of sprinting," The World-Herald reported. NU was sparked by a tough halftime talk from Bob Devaney. The coach "had some words and he used them well," said All-American lineman Bob Brown, who broke his helmet for the second straight week.

⌃ **1964:** Quarterback Bob Churchich (15), a sophomore from Omaha North, led the way after starter Fred Duda suffered a broken leg in the first quarter. "Sure, I was nervous, but not for long," Churchich said after the 14-7 win in Ames. "The boys all chattered, 'You can do it, Bob. We're for you 100 percent. We'll make it go for you.'"

» **1965:** NU quarterback Fred Duda (10) threw for two touchdowns and ran for another in a 44-0 win. ISU coach Clay Stapleton before the game had compared playing Nebraska to going bear hunting armed with a stick. "I may be a sorry coach today, but I'm sure a darn good prognosticator," he said after the beating. Asked if he had praise for any of his players, he responded, "I'd have to say all the kids played about the same – poorly."

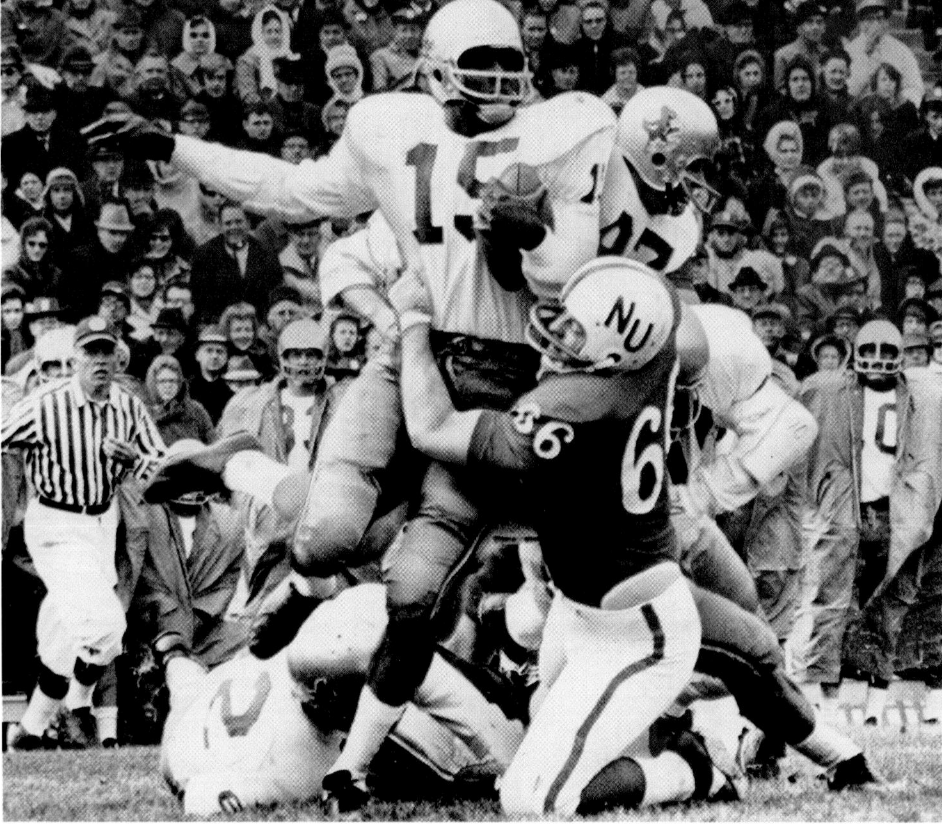

» **1966:** A snag by Tom Penney (85) helped quarterback Bob Churchich (15) to 203 passing yards in a 12-6 Nebraska win. Paul Critchlow, an Omaha Benson graduate who had considered going to ISU, was happy to contribute a fourth-down run that kept NU's winning drive alive in the fourth quarter. Cyclone coach Stapleton "wrote a letter saying in view of my eyesight and after viewing the films, Iowa State was not interested in me," said Critchlow, who wore contact lenses. He said he kept the letter and framed it. Harry Wilson (31) scored the winning points on a 36-yard run with 3:45 left.

« **1967:** Nebraska defensive lineman Wayne Meylan (66) had nine unassisted tackles in a 12-0 shutout on Band Day in Lincoln. "Meylan did bother me a couple of times storming in," said ISU quarterback John Warder. "I've been rushed harder by ends, but I've never been rushed so hard from the middle before."

» **1968:** First-year Cyclone coach Johnny Majors was pleased in spite of a 23-13 loss in Ames, saying "we did so well, but not well enough." Fans talked afterward about a trick play in which quarterback John Warder (15) lined up on one side of the field, then flipped the ball to his teammates on the other side. "That's our cow pasture play," Majors said. "We've had it for some time but just didn't have the guts to use it before. Being behind just two touchdowns, we figured it was as good a time as any."

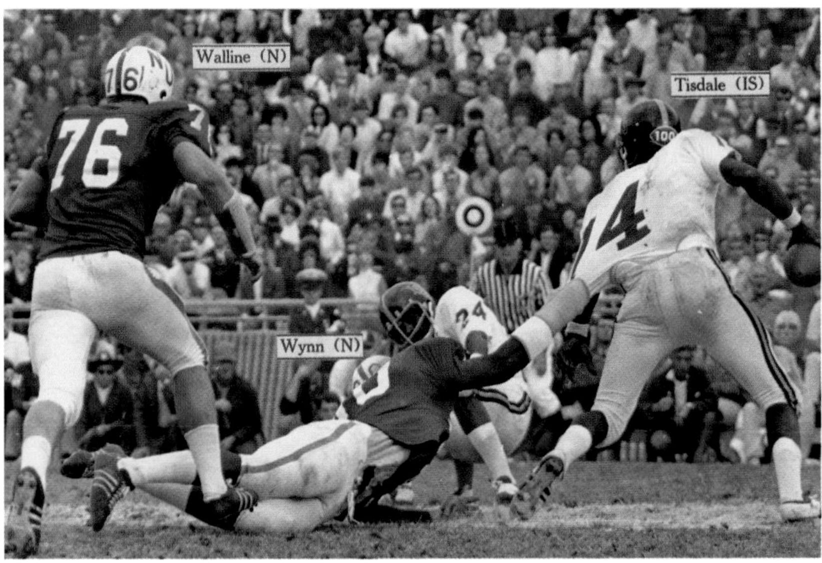

^ **1969:** Bob Devaney claimed his 100th career coaching victory with a tough 17-3 decision in Lincoln. "The first couple of years after I came here, it was pretty much if you beat Missouri and Oklahoma you'd win the Big Eight. It's not that way anymore. Everybody's tough. Iowa State is one of the better defensive clubs we've played."

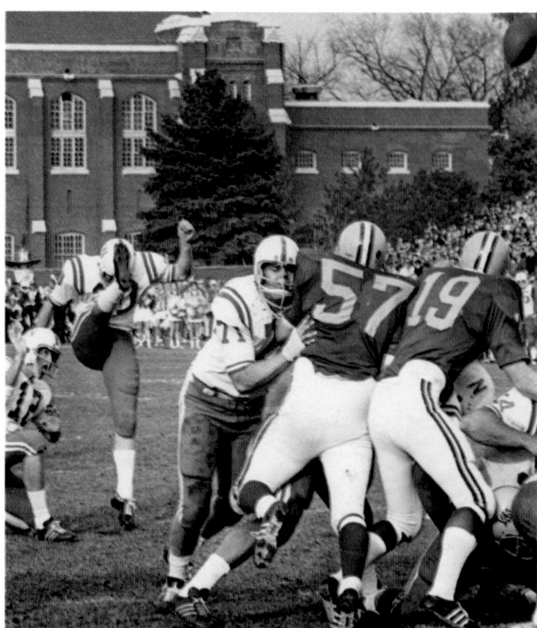

« **1970:** The Huskers' 54-29 rout was full of milestones, as they built the longest unbeaten streak of the Bob Devaney era to 16. Kicker Paul Rogers (30) had six extra points to break the conference career record with 82. And running back Joe Orduna, an Omaha Central grad, had 69 yards to take the lead in career rushing yards since Devaney arrived. Iowa State set a record with 36,000 in attendance at Clyde Williams Field, boosted by a large group of visiting Husker fans.

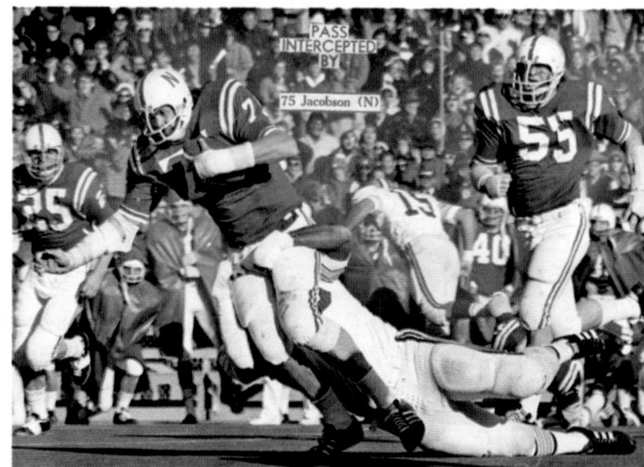

« **1971:** The Blackshirts intercepted three passes, including one by defensive tackle Larry Jacobson (75), in a 37-0 romp at Memorial Stadium. The game also featured a spectacular 62-yard punt return by Johnny Rodgers. "The prolonged roar of the crowd was as great a tribute as any Husker has received in years," The World-Herald's Wally Provost wrote.

» 1972: HUSKERS WERE LUCKY TO GET THE TIE

Bob Devaney, Nebraska's Hall of Fame coach, took his Huskers to Ames for the final time and was fortunate to escape with a 23-23 tie. Nebraska was trying to hold onto a six-point lead with the nation's No. 1 defense, 74 yards to protect and 58 seconds to evaporate.

But George Amundson (12), a composed senior Cyclone quarterback, made it with 28 seconds to spare. Pass completions of 12, 18 and 20 yards preceded a dramatic 24-yard pitch to flanker Willie Jones to tie it. All kicker Tom Goedgen (29) had to do was add the point, which he had done in 29 of his previous 31 attempts. He missed wide left.

Said Devaney: "I have never been so disgusted with a Nebraska team in a long time." His team "played like a bunch of farmers on a picnic, waiting on somebody to bring their lunch." Devaney later apologized to all the farmers who were offended.

– Tom Ash

Goedjen (IS)
Thornton (N)
Pate (N)
Blahak (N)
Pitts (N)
Amundson (IS)
Branch (N)
Manstedt (N)
Dutton (N)

≈ **1973:** Both teams piled up more than 200 yards rushing, but the Huskers were helped in a 31-7 victory by two ISU fumbles that allowed them to score two touchdowns in 51 seconds. "That's a good football team, and you just can't do that against Nebraska," said Cyclone coach Earle Bruce.

» **1974:** Nebraska's 23-13 victory spoiled the Cyclones' final game on Clyde Williams Field. Rain turned the grass field into a muddy mess, keeping both schools' bands in the stands during halftime and providing ample justification for the artificial turf in the new stadium. ISU students provided a lowlight for the game, unleashing smoke bombs before the game and pelting the benches with apples and oranges. "In short, it was a poor performance by the Cyclone students," NU coach Tom Osborne said in a letter to boosters later. He also complained about noise from the students making it hard for Nebraska on offense. Responded ISU's Earle Bruce: "Nobody gets louder than Nebraska fans when you get down close to their goal."

» **1975:** Quarterback Vince Ferragamo (15) threw for two touchdowns and ran for another as Nebraska clinched a share of the Big Eight title with a 52-0 win. Word that Missouri had beaten Oklahoma set off a wild locker room celebration over an outright title, but the Huskers soon found out that the Sooners had rallied to win and the mood changed quickly.

˅ 1976: 'BIGGEST IN THE HISTORY OF THE SCHOOL'

Earle Bruce called the game "the biggest game of the year for us and, maybe, the biggest in the history of the school. We've got a greater opportunity than we've ever had before."

Nebraska was 7-1-1 and ISU 7-2. The Huskers could clinch a share of the Big Eight championship with a win. A sign in the Cyclone locker room read: "Win to become the best team in ISU history." Bruce's secretary answered the phone all week with "Beat Nebraska." It had been 16 years since that happened. Nebraska lost six fumbles and had a pass intercepted en route to the 37-28 loss, but it was hardly a fluke. The Cyclones out-yarded Nebraska 321-77 on the ground. They lost star quarterback Wayne Stanley for the season in the second quarter, but sub Buddy Hardeman rushed for 93 yards and a touchdown.

Bruce said in the pandemonium of the locker room: "Beating Nebraska is the pinnacle of our program. Now, I won't have to feel bad whenever I go to Omaha." Bruce was an Ak-Sar-Ben horse racing aficionado.

– Tom Ash

» 1977: PRACTICE FILM AT 10

Iowa State backed up its 1976 upset of Nebraska in Ames with a 24-21 stunner in Lincoln by taking apart new Husker defensive coordinator Lance Van Zandt's attack defense with 294 rushing yards.

Making the game more memorable was an alleged spying incident during ISU's Friday afternoon warmup drills at the University of Nebraska at Omaha. The Cyclones were reportedly incensed when they saw one of the trick plays they were working on during a Friday night TV sportscast.

In the rehash in following days, reports said Cyclone coach Earle Bruce (at right with quarterback Terry Rubley) spotted a TV reporter and cameraman filming the practice and demanded that they leave. Bob Cullinan, the KETV reporter, said Bruce stopped practice and started yelling at them. He quoted Bruce as saying, "You act like this is amateur night." Bruce was "yelling near the top of his lungs," he said.

But Cullinan and the cameraman didn't leave. "We didn't want him to see us, so we went around to the north side of the field and shot through some bushes. Then we went to the fifth floor of the Chemistry Building overlooking the field and shot some more. At that point, we felt like we were playing cops and robbers."

After the game, Bruce said of the incident, "Oh, some guy wasn't very ethical or morally minded. But that's my opinion."

Then, referring to the next week's game at Oklahoma, "We're going to go to Omaha again and put in a few more wrinkles on the way to Norman." Did ISU use the trick play seen on TV against Nebraska? "No," Bruce said, "but you tell him (Cullinan) that I think he won us the football game. Maybe it will cost him his job."

– Tom Ash

« 1978: BACK ON TRACK

There was a time when Nebraska players weren't certain they could beat Iowa State. The 1976 and 1977 losses were fresh in the minds of the Huskers when they traveled to Ames in 1978.

After taking a 9-0 lead, Coach Tom Osborne challenged the Huskers in a halftime speech to get a shutout. They responded by blanking the Cyclones 23-0.

"It sure feels good to beat these guys," junior defensive tackle Rod Horn said. "It showed they can be beaten. The shutout also showed we hustled all the time. In the Big Eight, getting a shutout means something. Let up once and they'll score on you."

– Larry Porter

^ 1979: SIZING UP THE MISMATCH

After Donnie Duncan moved from Oklahoma, where he was an assistant, to the head coaching job at Iowa State, he said, "Now I have no time of my own. I've had to give up some of my duties at home, like mowing." Duncan took his first team to Lincoln, and it absorbed a 34-3 licking.

In particular, he lamented the mismatch between his 167-pound cornerback Mike Schwartz and Nebraska's 235-pound tight end Junior Miller. "It looked like a pair of pliers competing with a forklift," Duncan said. Shamus McDonough (53) was another Cyclone who had a rugged afternoon.

– Tom Ash

« 1980: ON SECOND THOUGHT . . .

Nebraska was ranked fourth and owned an 8-1 record going into its next-to-last game of the 1980 season.

At midweek, ISU coach Donnie Duncan proclaimed that NU would get his vote as the No. 1 team. But Duncan changed his mind during the Cyclones' 35-0 loss to the Huskers, with Steve Damkroger and the Blackshirts holding ISU star Dwayne Crutchfield (45) to 69 yards.

"No," Duncan said in the Cyclones' locker room when asked if he still considered the Huskers the nation's best team. "They weren't as good as I thought they were going to be."

Perhaps Duncan, a former Oklahoma assistant, realized that the Huskers needed more than the ability to shut out ISU to successfully contend with Sooner Magic. Oklahoma came to Lincoln the following week and once again broke the hearts of the Huskers.

– Larry Porter

1981: A COSTLY VICTORY

Nebraska clinched the 1981 Big Eight championship when it erupted for 24 points in the fourth quarter to defeat Iowa State 31-7. But the game also produced bad news for the Huskers when it was learned that sophomore quarterback Turner Gill (12) suffered mysterious nerve damage in his right leg. The injury kept Gill out of the Oklahoma game and the Orange Bowl loss to Clemson.

Gill couldn't move his right foot because of the nerve damage. Everyone wondered if he would ever play again. He had surgery twice and went three months without movement in his foot. But doctors were optimistic he would recover, and he did. He held the ball for a field goal and extra points in the spring game. By the time practice started in the fall, he was running full speed. Gill performed at a high level in the 1982 season, leading the Huskers to a 12-1 record and a No. 3 ranking in the national polls.

Nebraska's 1981 victory over Iowa State and Missouri's win over Oklahoma the same day clinched the Big Eight title for the Huskers a week before the annual NU-OU game. Nebraska became the first school in the 54-year history of the Big Six-Big Seven-Big Eight to wrap up the league championship when each team had at least one conference game remaining.

– Steve Sinclair

THE ULTIMATE SENIOR DAY

Anthony "Slick" Steels (33) was given some extra work before his final game in Memorial Stadium. And that chore turned on the water works prior to the Nebraska-Iowa State kickoff in 1981. The senior wingback was believed to be the first Nebraska football player to sing the national anthem prior to a game. He took the microphone, told the fans goodbye and said he wanted to dedicate his performance "to the 22 seniors, the entire team and to the fans."

Steels had enough stage presence to turn and face each section of the stadium during his rendition. But he was never able to focus clearly on the crowd. The sea of red was blurred through his tear-filled eyes. The fans roared as Steels released his final note. Then, waving his arms in the air, he ran toward a field gate, disappeared under the South Stadium and rejoined his teammates in the locker room. "I have never felt as much emotion in my life," Steels said of that moment. "The players told me they heard me in the locker room. They said it fired them up. Every time one of them said, 'Good job,' I felt like crying. I had to turn my head. Everybody's eyes were watery."

Steels capped his memorable day by leading the Husker receivers with three catches for 28 yards, including a 3-yard touchdown pass from Turner Gill that provided a 24-7 lead. "This was the biggest day in my life," said Steels, who walked on at Nebraska from Zaragoza, Spain, where his father was stationed in the military. "I did almost everything I ever wanted to do. I sang in front of the fans, I scored and had a good day, we won the game and we wrapped up the Big Eight championship."

– Larry Porter

« **1982:** Fullback Doug Wilkening (34) got the Huskers started with a first-quarter touchdown on the way to a 48-10 win in frigid Ames. The Cyclones entered the game seventh in the nation in total defense but gave up 460 yards. "As I said earlier in the week, Irving Fryar and Turner Gill and Mike Rozier can go all the way on every play," ISU coach Donnie Duncan said.

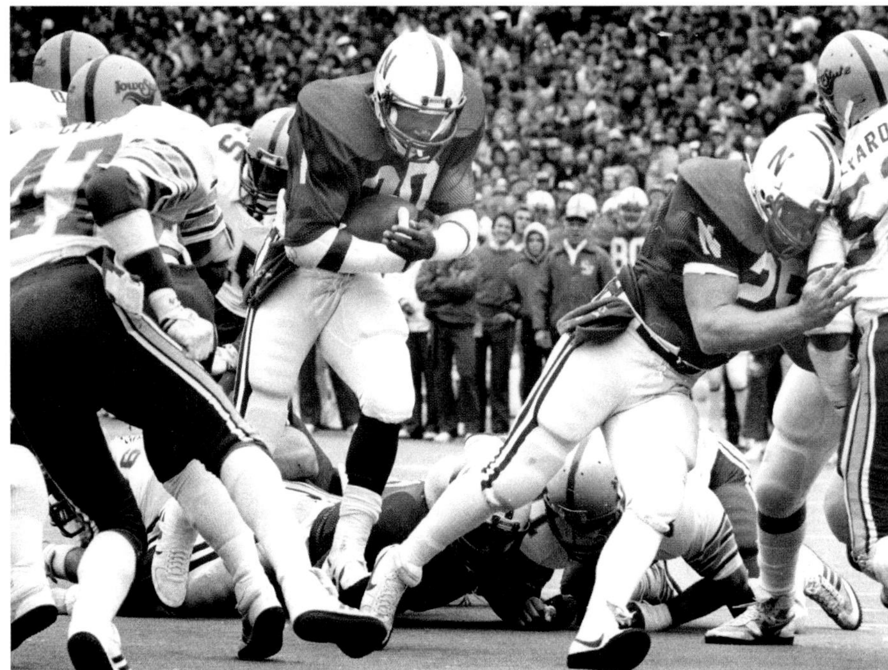

« **1983:** The two teams' offenses combined for 1,170 yards and 101 points, as Nebraska claimed a 72-29 victory. "I wish we could shut people down better," NU's Tom Osborne said. "I guess you win and lose as a team. If we can score more than they can, then I'm happy." I-back Mike Rozier (30) pitched in 212 yards rushing and four touchdowns, breaking Johnny Rodgers' school records for career totals in touchdowns and points. "I'm pretty proud about breaking his records," Rozier said. "He's a legend around here." He also surpassed Bobby Reynolds' record for rushing touchdowns in a season.

« **1984:** Nebraska's 44-0 shutout of Iowa State boiled down to one simple fact. "Nebraska is a much better defensive team than we are an offensive team," said ISU coach Jim Criner. Iowa State's offense mustered just 53 total yards, and the Cyclones never got closer than Nebraska's 37-yard line. Bret Clark (10) led the ball-hawking Blackshirts, who intercepted four passes and recovered two ISU fumbles.

⌃ 1985: ANOTHER SHUTOUT

The Blackshirts again stuffed Iowa State in a 49-0 win, with linebacker Kevin Parsons (35) and company holding the Cyclones to 137 yards of total offense.

Nebraska junior I-back Doug DuBose led the Huskers with 114 yards, passing the 1,000-yard rushing mark for the second straight season.

He became only the third Husker to rush for more than 1,000 yards twice, joining Jarvis Redwine and Mike Rozier. DuBose finished the 1985 season with 1,161 yards and his career with 2,250.

DuBose didn't get a chance at three straight 1,000-yard seasons, because his career ended prematurely with a knee injury in a 1986 preseason scrimmage.

– Steve Sinclair

⌄ 1986: MAY I HAVE YOUR ATTENTION?

Nebraska responded when coach Tom Osborne raised his voice. The Huskers trailed 14-7 at halftime when Osborne gave his players a tongue-lashing.

"I've never seen Coach Osborne like he was," defensive end Broderick Thomas said. "He was highly upset."

Osborne's mood improved in the second half as the Huskers rallied for 28 points in their 35-14 win, and Danny Noonan (95) and the Blackshirts held the Cyclones scoreless. The Huskers' primary offensive weapons were I-back Tyreese Knox and fullback Ken Kaelin, who each gained 126 yards and did ironman duty in the victory.

Knox, a sophomore from Daly City, Calif., was the only NU I-back to touch the ball as he carried 29 times. Osborne said during the week that Knox, making his first start, might shoulder a heavy load because of an injury that sidelined Keith Jones, the Big Eight's leading rusher who underwent thumb surgery the week before the game.

Kaelin, a senior walk-on from Westerville, Neb., carried 25 times.

"I was really proud of the effort both Tyreese and Ken gave," said Frank Solich, Nebraska's running backs coach. "They did an excellent job of taking care of the ball and making yards after contact."

Kaelin said Osborne's halftime speech aroused the Huskers. "People think he's really reserved, but he can raise his voice," Kaelin said. "He doesn't have to say a cuss word or anything. All he's got to do is say 'dadgum it,' and everybody shuts up. And we come out of that locker room ready to kill people."

– Steve Sinclair

« **1987:** The Huskers gained 666 total yards in a 42-3 victory, but four turnovers and three wasted scoring opportunities bothered coach Tom Osborne. "I was really not too pleased with some of the execution," he said. "At times, we played sloppy football. At times, we didn't play very intelligent football." Fortunately, linebacker Steve Forch (38) and the Blackshirts held up their end, forcing four ISU turnovers.

⌃ **1988:** "I thought we were really fairly good to Iowa State," Osborne said the day after the Huskers' 51-16 victory over the Cyclones. "We substituted liberally very early in the game. We gave them a chance to get a couple toward the end that they probably couldn't have gotten against our first-team defense. And I don't think there's any question we could have scored in the 60s or 70s if we'd wanted to." Iowa State fans booed the Huskers as they left the field with a 31-0 halftime lead. Nebraska had called two timeouts and completed two long passes to set up a field goal with no time left. "We were ahead of Oklahoma State 42-0 at one point in the second quarter, and it turned out that wouldn't have been enough," Osborne said, referring to an earlier 63-42 victory. "You have to score all the points you can." Hardy Husker fans had the stadium to themselves at the end in Ames, where the wind screamed out of the northwest at 25 to 40 mph, snow fell sideways and the wind chill dropped to 3 degrees.

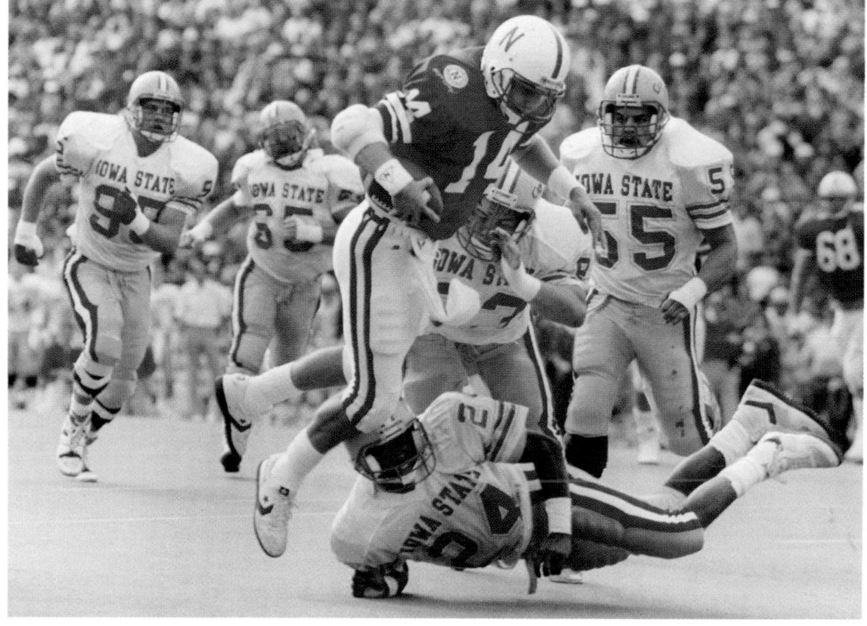

⌃ **1989:** Senior quarterback Gerry Gdowski (14) took advantage of a new wrinkle in the Huskers' option, setting an NU quarterback record with 176 rushing yards and accounting for six touchdowns in a 49-17 win.

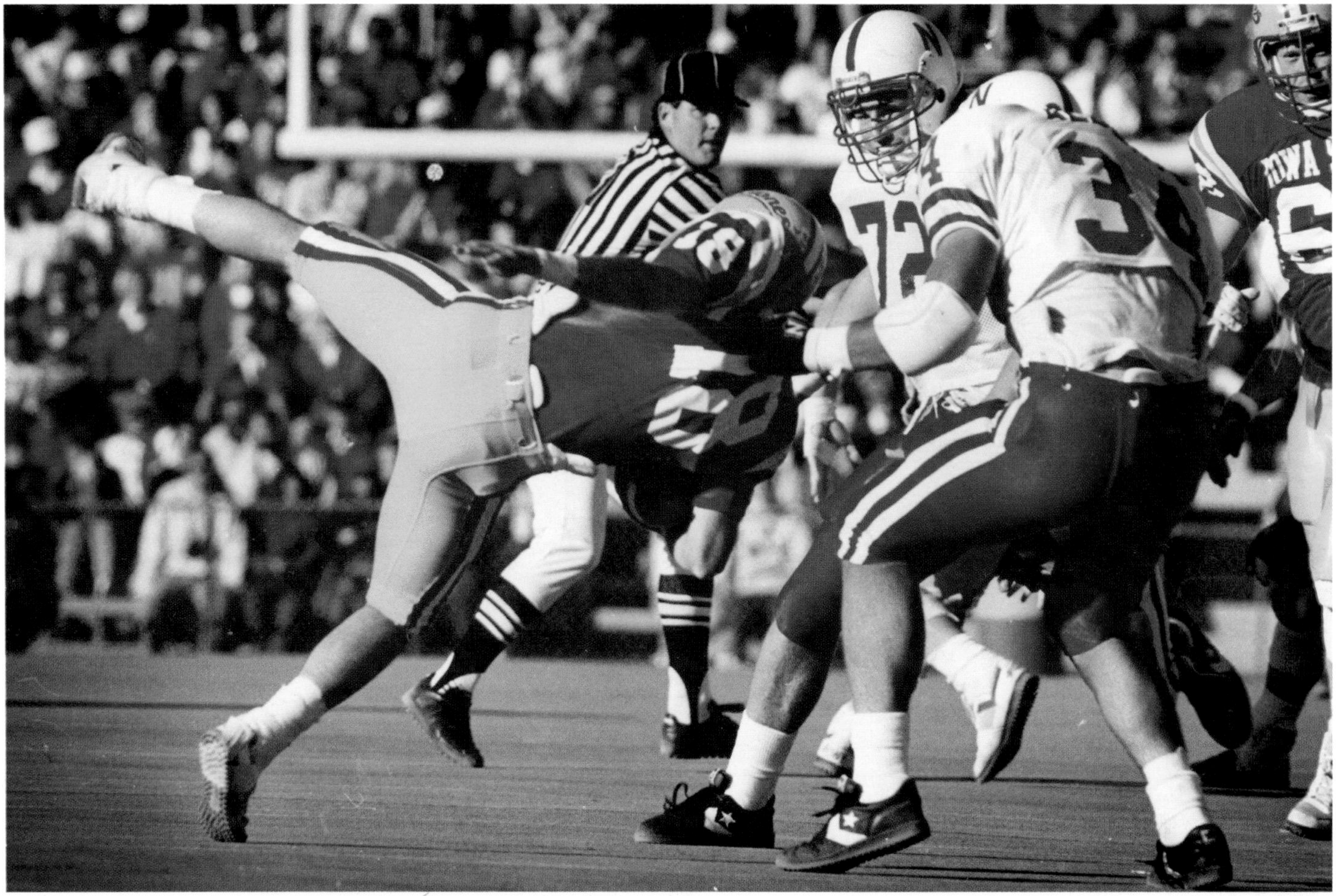

» **1990:** Nebraska rush end Trev Alberts (34) had three sacks in a 45-13 win in Ames. Like coach Jim Walden's first three ISU teams, this one couldn't stop Nebraska's basic running plays, and the Huskers threw just four passes. Mickey Joseph completed all four, including two for touchdowns to freshman tight end Johnny Mitchell. "We'll probably get criticized for not throwing enough," coach Tom Osborne said. "But we did what we felt like we had to do."

» **1991:** NU I-back Derek Brown (21) ran 107 yards and a touchdown in a 38-13 win, as the Huskers gained 525 yards and averaged 9.4 yards per play. ISU coach Jim Walden said he was puzzled by criticism of Nebraska's offense. "I don't know what these people are looking at, because I've never seen a team score so many points from so far out so often," Walden said.

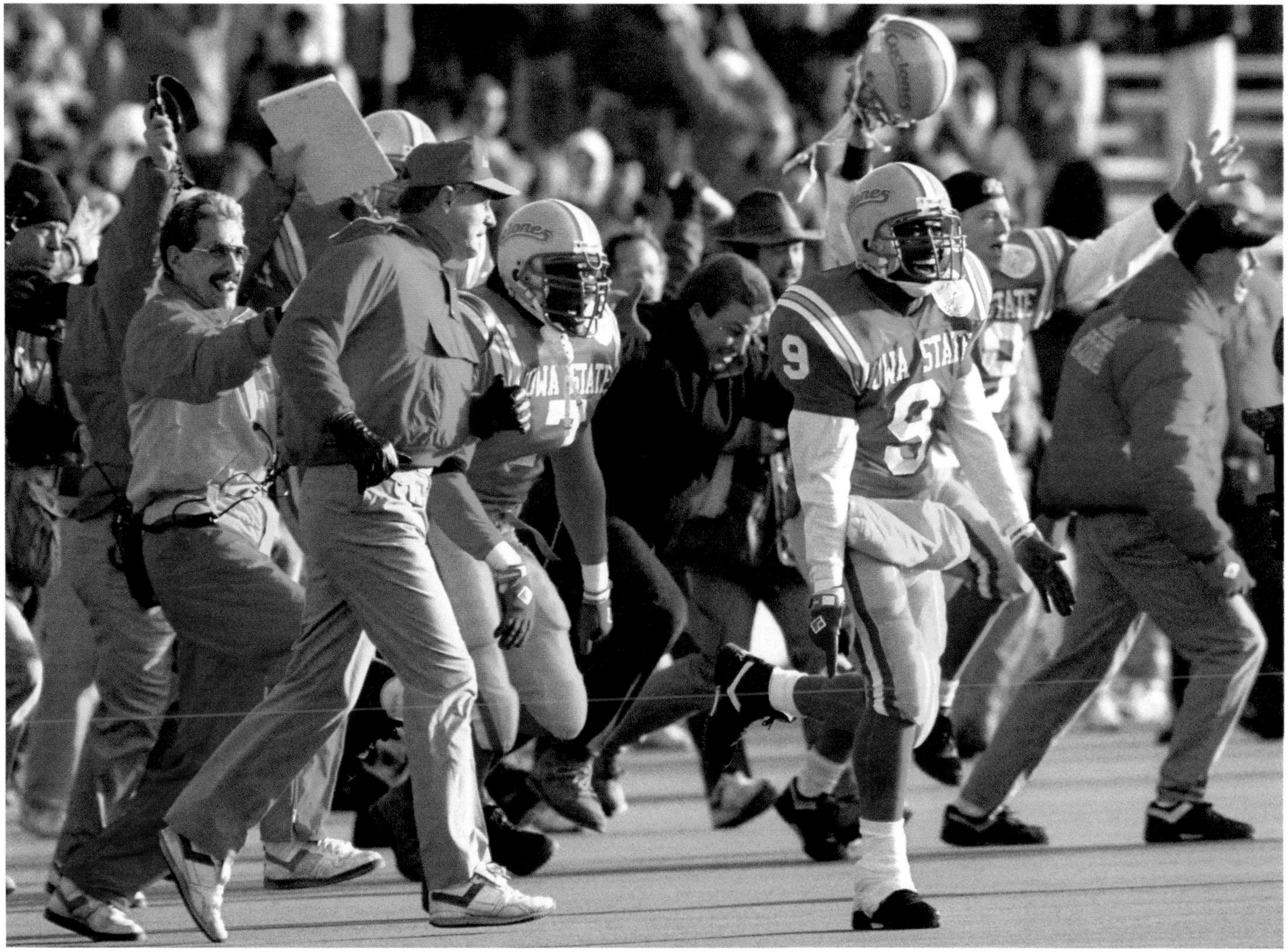

« **1992:** Quarterback Marv Seiler (14), who led Iowa State to a 19-10 upset, began the season as the third-string quarterback and played only because the starter was injured. Coach Jim Walden joked that Seiler probably thought he was being thrown to the wolves, because Nebraska was a huge favorite and had beaten Iowa State 14 straight times. But the fifth-year senior was undaunted and broke a 78-yard run in the fourth quarter to set up the game-clinching touchdown. "Realistically, you had to look at it and say we didn't have a chance," Seiler said. "But if we go out there and play, anything can happen." Nebraska's Tom Osborne managed to keep his sense of humor. "We've heard a lot of complaints that we can't win the big one and all we can do is win the little ones," he said, then mentioned recent victories over ranked Colorado and Kansas. "Well, we won two big ones and lost a little one."

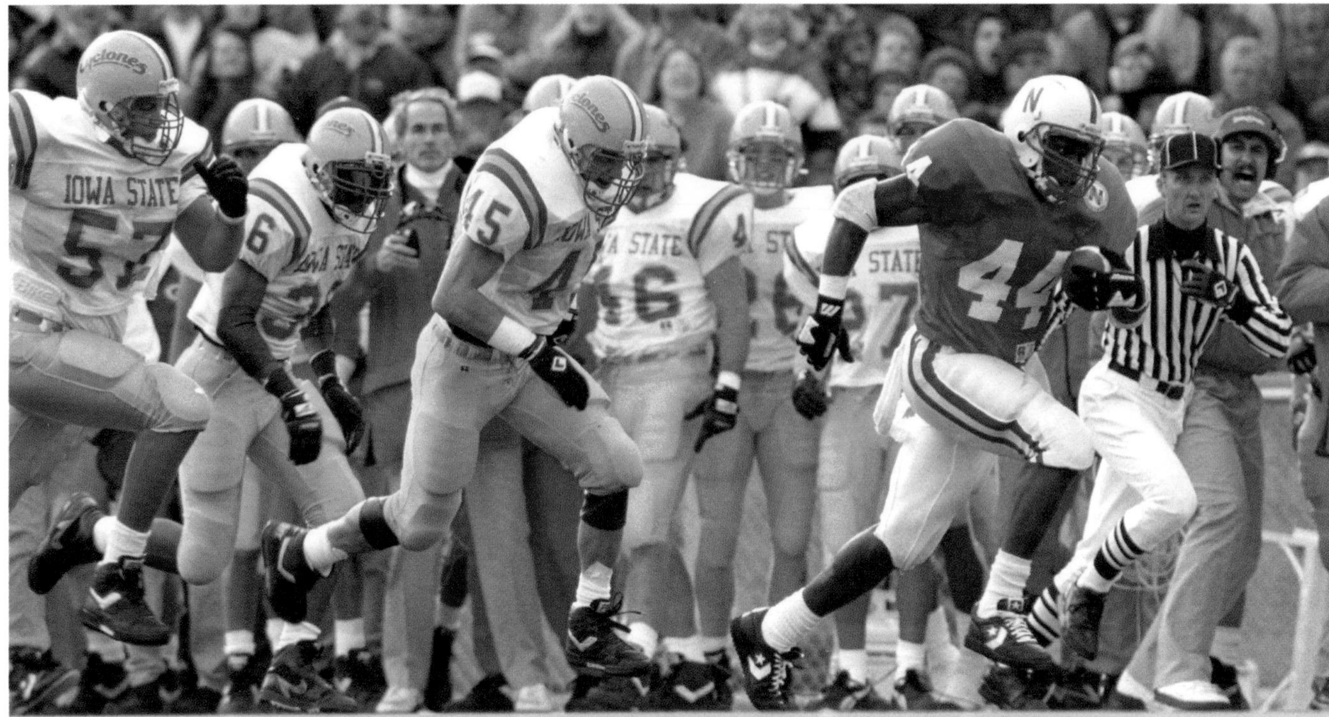

» **1993:** Huskers wrapped up the Big Eight title with a 49-17 win, as I-back Calvin Jones (44) became Nebraska's No. 2 all-time rusher. "I'm glad that's over," Tom Osborne said. "We played pretty well. At times we had trouble stopping them. They are not an inept football team."

» **1994:** One team entered Cyclone Stadium without a win, and the other came in without a loss. But deep into Nebraska's 28-12 victory, it wasn't always clear which team was which. The Cyclones closed to within one point late in the second quarter, were within two points entering the fourth quarter and had a touchdown called back with 9½ minutes left in the game. Eight players from the state of Nebraska started for Iowa State. Linebacker Matt Nitchie of Lincoln Southeast had 18 tackles. Linebacker Michael Cooper of Omaha Westside had 12. Place-kicker Ty Stewart (2) of Westside had field goals of 35 and 37 yards into a 20-mph wind. And quarterback Todd Doxzon of Millard North threw for 151 yards.

« **1995:** Nebraska scored on its first 10 possessions and ran for 624 yards in a 73-14 victory. I-back Ahman Green (30) kept a lot of the spotlight off the return of I-back Lawrence Phillips, who had been suspended after the assault of his ex-girlfriend. Green ran for 176 yards in 12 carries, setting an NU record for rushing yards by a freshman. "Ahman played great," Tom Osborne said. "He's got that extra step that you need."

⌃ **1996:** Blackshirts Mike Minter (10) and Terrell Farley (43) kept Iowa State running back Troy Davis from reaching 2,000 yards for the season in Nebraska's 49-14 victory in Ames. Davis turned down interview requests after the game. Iowa State offensive tackle Tim Kohn said Davis' silence may have reflected his disappointment. "I think it was important for him to break the record at home so he could share it with some of the Cyclone fans," Kohn said. (Davis broke the 2,000-yard mark in ISU's next game.) Tom Osborne also didn't have much to say afterward. "There was nothing real remarkable about the game," he said. "We played about the way I thought we would."

» **1997:** Nebraska's 77-14 rout of ISU capped an emotional senior day in Lincoln. Quarterback Scott Frost's two seasons as a Husker had been a mix of ups and downs, of brilliance and boos. "I don't have any regrets," said Frost (7), who transferred to Nebraska after spending his first two seasons at Stanford. "I've left everything I had on the field, and I played as hard as I could. Looking back, if I have any regrets it's that I had only two years to play in this program. It's a class-act program, and anyone who wants to play college football, this is where they should come." Frost wasn't the only senior to become emotional during his last game at Memorial Stadium. "It was tough trying to choke everything back," Nebraska rush end Grant Wistrom said. "I tried to take everything in one last tunnel walk, one last time hearing the roar of the Memorial Stadium crowd. There are some things that are going to be tough to let go of. No matter where I go and where I end up, this place is always going to be home for me. We've won a lot of football games here, and if I had it all to do over again, I wouldn't wear any other color but the red and white." It was also Tom Osborne's final game as a coach at Memorial Stadium.

« **1998:** Sophomore defensive back Joe Walker (25) scored on a 65-yard interception return in Nebraska's 42-7 win, becoming only the fifth Division I-A player to score touchdowns in the same season on punt, kickoff and interception returns. "It feels great to go down in history," Walker said. "Since I don't get to play offense, I have to take advantage of all the opportunities I do get. Every time I touch the ball, I feel like I can score."

» **1999:** Ralph Brown (22) recovered a blocked kick for a Nebraska touchdown in a 21-point first-quarter blitz. By the end of the 49-14 homecoming victory the Huskers had shut down what had been the country's leading rushing team and had buried what had been the nation's No. 5 defense with an avalanche of 524 yards.

» **2000:** NU's Correll Buckhalter (36) rushed for only 20 yards, but he scored three touchdowns in Nebraska's 49-27 victory in Ames. The Huskers, leading 21-20 after three quarters, rolled up 184 yards on 26 plays in the fourth quarter and scored on all four of their possessions, transforming a raucous Jack Trice Stadium into one with Nebraska fans outnumbering the home fans by game's end. "Until we turn this program around, we need to learn to play fourth quarters," Cyclone junior defensive end Kevin DeRonde said. "It's what separates a good team from a great team."

» **2001:** The Huskers built a six-touchdown lead after one half before settling for a 48-14 victory that extended their streak of home wins over the Cyclones to 12. "It was complete domination by Nebraska in the first half," said Iowa State coach Dan McCarney. "We didn't block. We didn't tackle. We didn't do anything on special teams. We didn't do a good job of coaching. They were all over us." Four touchdowns by NU quarterback Eric Crouch (7) gave him 51 career rushing scores to break the NCAA Division I-A record for quarterbacks. He also surpassed Mike Rozier's team record of 49 rushing touchdowns.

2002: The Nebraska fan exodus began in earnest with 7 minutes left, as the Husker reserves ran out in Iowa State's dominating 36-14 victory at Jack Trice Stadium. Those Nebraska fans who remained in the boisterous crowd of 51,888 witnessed another unusual sight: Iowa State fans celebrating their team's fourth win over Nebraska in 42 years. In a light rain, ISU's Jon Calease (93) gave coach Dan McCarney an icy shower while cardinal and gold fans tried unsuccessfully to topple Iowa State's "indestructible" goal posts.

» **2003:** Blocked punts by Demorrio Williams (7) and Josh Bullocks led to 14 points for Nebraska in a 28-0 win in Lincoln. Bullocks said coach Frank Solich had focused on blocking punts during the week's practice. "We can pretty much win just about any way the coaches want us to," Bullocks said. "It all boils down to the players and how bad they want to get it done."

^ **2004:** Iowa State receiver Todd Blythe (1) caught eight passes for 188 yards and a touchdown in a 34-27 win in Ames. Cyclone offensive coordinator Barney Cotton, who had lost his job at Nebraska the previous season, smiled and hugged Nebraska players as they trudged off the field. "He told me, 'Good job,'" said NU I-back Cory Ross, "and that he misses us."

^ **2005:** Nebraska captain Cory Ross (4) finished with eight catches for 131 yards in a 27-20 double overtime win. The 5-foot-6 senior enjoyed one of the most unusual games of his career. He ran wild as a receiver while gaining just 32 yards rushing on 15 attempts. "I've always thought he was not only a good runner but that he was one of the best receiving backs I've ever coached," running backs coach Randy Jordan said.

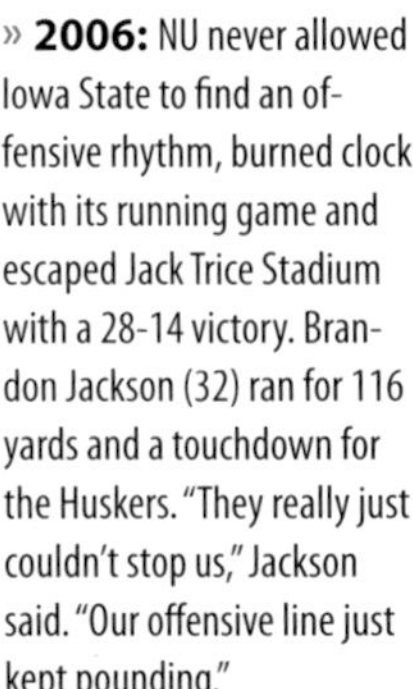

» **2006:** NU never allowed Iowa State to find an offensive rhythm, burned clock with its running game and escaped Jack Trice Stadium with a 28-14 victory. Brandon Jackson (32) ran for 116 yards and a touchdown for the Huskers. "They really just couldn't stop us," Jackson said. "Our offensive line just kept pounding."

⌃ **2008:** Zach Potter (98) helped anchor a defensive front that contributed 15 tackles, including four stops behind the line of scrimmage, in a 35-7 victory. The line also forced two fumbles and knocked down three passes. "They're a very proud bunch, and they're very close-knit," said Nebraska defensive coordinator Carl Pelini. "I think they took some criticism a year ago, and they have been very focused and determined to play at a high level this year."

⌃ **2007:** Iowa State led for nearly 17 minutes of the first half, but Nebraska gradually seized control and went on to the 35-17 victory, its 15th straight home-field win over the Cyclones. Cortney Grixby tipped a third-and-goal Cyclone pass into the air, and Bo Ruud (51) snatched it and raced 93 yards for the backbreaking score. "Guys doing their jobs," said Ruud, who added a game-high 14 tackles. "When the opportunity arises, you've got to take a chance and make a play."

⇑ **2009:** Eight Nebraska turnovers made it hard for anybody to dare try to pinpoint one being more damaging than another. However, one play might have best told the story, as Iowa State stunned the Huskers 9-7 and claimed their first victory at Memorial Stadium since 1977. Receiver Niles Paul (24) took a long pass from Zac Lee, eluded the last ISU defender and headed for a touchdown. But Paul, without contact, lost the football, watched it bounce down the field, scrambled to get it back, retained it for a moment and then lost it into the hands of the Cyclone defenders.

STILL HAVING NIGHTMARES ABOUT . . .

^ **MARV SEILER**

Quarterback

Tom Osborne came into the 1992 game against Iowa State having never lost to a team that would finish the season with a below-.500 record. All that changed when the Huskers met the 29-point underdog Cyclones, who had five losses in their past six games.

Quarterback Marv Seiler, a fifth-year senior making his first career start, led ISU to a 19-10 upset in Ames, rushing for more yards in the game – 144 – than in the rest of his career combined. The big play of the game was Seiler's 78-yard run to set up the Cyclones' only touchdown early in the fourth quarter, using every bit of his 5.1 "speed" to drive a stake through Nebraska's heart.

"Seiler has to be a big hero in my heart – all 5.1 of him," Iowa State coach Jim Walden said. "As he was sprinting down that field, he looked faster than any quarterback I've ever seen."

Osborne called it a sad day for Nebraska, but a great day for Iowa State, which hadn't beaten the Huskers since 1977. "We've had a lot of good days against Iowa State," Osborne said. "I want them to realize what they did, and they need to have credit for it. "My hat's off to Jim Walden and his staff and his players. They did a good job."

DAVE HOPPMANN

Tailback

Ran out of the single-wing in 1960 to lead the Cyclones to their first win in Lincoln since 1944 and created headaches in losing efforts in 1961 and 1962.

GEORGE AMUNDSON

Quarterback

Directed game-tying TD drive in last minute to dash NU title hopes in 1972 and snap an 11-game NU streak in the series.

LUTHER BLUE

Receiver

Returned a kickoff 95 yards to complete a stunning 17-point first quarter for the Cyclones in their 37-28 win over the Huskers in 1976.

DEXTER GREEN

Running back

Led the Cyclones to back-to-back victories in 1976 and 1977. Nicknamed "Money" by his teammates, he gashed Nebraska as a receiver and on several draw plays in 1977 as ISU stunned the Huskers for their first win in Lincoln since 1960.

TY STEWART

Kicker

Turned down a walk-on spot at NU as a senior at Omaha Westside. Booted four field goals – from 37, 32, 45 and 30 yards – in the Cyclones' 1992 upset.

TROY DAVIS

Running back

Rushed for 259 yards in 1994 and 1995, although ISU never came close to beating Nebraska's great teams.

SENECA WALLACE

Quarterback

Had 270 yards and three TDs in 2002 as ISU won 36-14, its most decisive win over NU since 1899.

JEROME TILLER

Quarterback

Refused to make mistakes as a late replacement in 2009, accounting for 167 yards and a 45-yard TD pass in a 9-7 win.

Missouri students in 2007 showed their support for the Tigers and sent a message to visiting Nebraska fans as well.

MISSOURI

HARD HITTING, HARD FEELINGS AND HARD LOSSES

BY MICHAEL KELLY | WORLD-HERALD STAFF WRITER

RIVALS TO THE END, Nebraska and Missouri have met more than 100 times, often contentiously, since first playing in 1892. With all the bickering, feuds and controversies, it's a miracle the teams didn't kill each other. They certainly played a lot of close games. And speaking of miracles: The most memorable Nebraska play in the long series occurred on a Columbia night in 1997. Trailing by a touchdown with a minute left and the ball at their 33, the Huskers drove to the Mizzou 12 with time for one more play – a play for the ages, the "Miracle in Missouri." Scott Frost fired a pass for Shevin Wiggins, who was hit hard. As he fell, he said later, he was "just trying to keep the ball alive." He kicked it (doing so intentionally is supposed to be a 15-yard penalty), and Matt Davison of Tecumseh, Neb., made a diving catch for a touchdown. Neither a designed play nor a trick "flea-flicker" play, it became known as the "Flea-Kicker." NU coach Tom Osborne called it a "one-in-a-thousand play," and MU coach Larry Smith deplored it as "that last stinking play – a fluke play." The Huskers won the game in overtime, and keeping the ball alive also meant keeping their national-championship hopes alive. Nebraska later defeated Tennessee to win the '97 coaches' national title.

Husker fans did their best to make sure Missouri's 2000 game at Memorial Stadium in Lincoln was a red-letter day.

NU played more "big games" against Oklahoma, but have the Cornhuskers enjoyed and endured a fiercer rivalry than the one with the Missouri Tigers? Except for a 24-year NU victory streak starting in 1979, the schools have played each other almost evenly – though not always with even dispositions. NU's Bob Devaney and MU's Dan Devine, former colleagues at Michigan State, became two of the top head coaches in the country, "both in the $20,000 salary bracket," The World-Herald reported in 1965. In 1964, both threw their clipboards to the turf. Devine questioned the honesty of the chain gang in Lincoln and sent an assistant coach to the NU sideline to keep an eye on things. Devaney angrily complained that a Missouri coach so close by could spy on the Huskers, and officials sent him back. The next year, the Big Eight supervisor of officials had to go down to the field to settle a dispute about whether the next play was third down or fourth down. Before the 1966 game in Lincoln, the head of the university's health service announced that henceforth, a heart specialist would be on duty at Memorial Stadium. Over the years, there were plenty of heart-stoppers. But also some bad blood. Three times in four years – 1979, 1980 and 1982 – Osborne complained or implied that Missouri players intentionally tried to injure Huskers. MU coach Warren Powers, a former Husker player and assistant coach, denied that and said he was sick of Osborne's "complaints and gripes." Things eventually cooled, and Osborne said it wasn't worth a civil war – but at times the rivalry could be uncivil.

ROAD TRIP TO

COLUMBIA

University of Missouri

Founded: 1839

Enrollment: 31,000

Colors: Old gold and black

Conference history:
Founding member of Big Six in 1928

Stadium:
Faurot Field/Memorial Stadium, capacity 71,004

History of "Tigers":
Guerrilla activity before the Civil War prompted citizens in Columbia to form an armed guard to protect the town. The reputation of the unit, called "the Missouri Tigers," prompted raiders to bypass the area.

Distance from Memorial Stadium in Lincoln:
325 miles

Worth remembering: The letter M on the hill behind the north end zone is one of the nation's best stadium landmarks. The M, made of whitewashed rocks and measuring 90 feet wide and 95 feet high, was built by the freshman class of 1927. The mascot, Truman the Tiger, was named after the president from Missouri and has won competitions for the nation's best mascot. Those are the sights, now the sound: an ROTC cannon fires when Mizzou scores. Nebraskans also will remember Columbia as one of the least friendly sites for a road game.

Truman the Tiger took an active interest in the work of World-Herald photographer Rudy Smith at a game in Lincoln in 1991.

Sometimes there were just pranks. Before the 1957 game in Columbia, interlopers rearranged the M rock pile above the earthen end of the horseshoe-shaped stadium and made it into an N. It was rebuilt by game time. When Missouri students pelted sign-carrying NU cheerleaders with apple cores and soft-drink cups in 1965, Carl Samuelson, a former Husker from the late 1940s, drew cheers from Nebraska fans and boos from Mizzou by chest-bumping an MU student and sending him sprawling. Nebraska sent the Tigers sprawling that day, too, after Devaney read the Huskers a quote from UCLA coach Tommy Prothro, who said eighth-rated Nebraska should be ranked 49th. The players voted after the game to award Prothro a game ball, but Devaney declined to send one. The most ingenious prank wasn't aimed at Missouri but occurred at the 1972 game in Lincoln. Someone had substituted instructions for the NU card section, so instead of a salute to the Navy when the cards were turned, they read "Devaney for president" and "Johnny R is shifty." The card caper eventually was blamed on six students, who were privately reprimanded.

In 1988, Osborne gingerly addressed another crowd matter, saying there wasn't much excitement at Memorial Stadium anymore unless NU was the underdog, which happened rarely. His team trailed Mizzou at halftime and heard boos, but fans continued their ritual of applauding visitors afterward, win or lose. "We don't need to carry boos into the locker room with us," the coach said after his team won. "That was kind of a paradox when our fans aren't happy with us at the half and then cheer the opponent at the end."

The Missouri-Nebraska rivalry has included great games and great plays. In 1950, NU All-American Bobby Reynolds scored three touchdowns, kicked five extra points and ran for 175 yards. But a most unforgettable play began at the Mizzou 33, where he started to his left, got hemmed in, retreated, got trapped again, reversed his field, picked up a half-dozen blocks and kept running for a touchdown. It went in the books as a 33-yarder, but Reynolds ran a good 100 yards backward, sideways and forward. In 1975, on fourth down at the Missouri 40, NU dropped into punt formation – and ran a trick play known as the Bummeroosky (named for college and pro coach Bum Phillips). The ball was snapped not to the punter but to blocking-back Tony Davis, who sneakily handed the ball forward between the legs of bent-over John O'Leary. As fellow Huskers ran right and Tigers slipped past him in pursuit, O'Leary paused and then ran left for a touchdown. In 1981, sophomore quarterback Turner Gill survived constant blitzes and NU scored a touchdown with 23 seconds left to win 6-0. In 1985, Dale Klein set an NCAA record by kicking seven

5 YARDS FOR STRUTTING

Nebraska barely escaped a referee's call of delay of game in its 1956 game against Missouri in Lincoln after a lengthy halftime that included a homecoming ceremony and the parading of the Victory Bell. "The performance of the Nebraska and Missouri bands and strutting of campus brass set a halftime marathon record," The World-Herald reported.

consecutive field goals in a game without missing. In 1992, Tommie Frazier became the first true freshman to start at quarterback for Nebraska, scoring three touchdowns at the start of a heralded career. "He has an air about him," said Gill, then an NU assistant coach. "He knows how to lead. Some people have it, and some don't." In 2000, Bobby Newcombe scored on a then Nebraska record 94-yard punt return, breaking the mark of 1972 Heisman Trophy winner Johnny Rodgers, who attended the game. And in 2001, on the way to his own Heisman, quarterback Eric Crouch dropped back, retreated to the end zone in Columbia and set sail on a signature 95-yard touchdown run, the longest from scrimmage in NU history.

Missouri also gave its fans plenty to cheer about -- and to sing about in the fight song: "Missou-RAH! Missou- RAH!" The Tigers won six in a row from 1957 to 1962. But the next year, the Huskers won by a whisker – 13-12 – and NU All-America tackle Bob Brown had his goatee shaved by teammate Tony Jeter in the locker room. Mizzou won in 1969, NU's last loss before a 32-game unbeaten string that included two national titles. In 1973, Nebraska lost 13-12 when first-year head coach Osborne – in a harbinger of a fateful play in a national-championship game a decade later – decided to go for a two-point conversion in the final minute instead of kicking an extra point for the tie. Mizzou intercepted, and MU coach Al Onofrio called it "the greatest game we've ever had." After a Missouri win the next year, Onofrio again deemed it "the best game I've ever been involved in." MU burned the Huskers with a 98-yard pass play to win in 1976. But the killer was 1978, when Nebraska upset Oklahoma and needed a victory the next week to play for the national title. Mizzou won 35-31 in Lincoln behind James Wilder's four touchdowns. Missouri also handed NU multiple losses in the first decade of the 21st century.

Omaha native Bob Gibson walked the sideline after a World Series championship for St. Louis, and Cardinal legend Stan "the Man" Musial attended in Lincoln as a guest of the NU president. Beginning in 1927, student honor societies from Nebraska and Missouri handed a 19th-century Victory Bell back and forth to the victor. The series surely wasn't all antagonistic, but it was tough. Said NU assistant coach Jim Walden in 1971: "It's like a backyard fight between brothers. No matter how strong you seem to other people, when you start fighting in the family, nobody is afraid of you." Now the long and sometimes bitter series is over, though the Huskers and Tigers truly were rivals to the end. When the Big Ten Conference signaled that it might expand, Missouri made its interest known. But when the decision was made, the nod went to Nebraska.

Nebraska's Benard Thomas and Missouri's Zack Abron proved in 2003 that there was no shortage of hard feelings in this series.

Quotes:

"I suppose we punished them. I know they sure punished us."

– Missouri coach Dan Devine after a 17-7 victory (1969)

"It's a big rivalry, and there may be a little bit of hatred. It's nothing personal. It's just that good teams bring out the best in each other."

– Missouri lineman Brad Edelman (1981)

TIGERS WERE THE NO. 1 RIVAL IN 1970

The Game of the Century in 1971, followed by Tom Osborne's series of battles with Barry Switzer, may have forever established Oklahoma as Nebraska's primary rival in the Big Eight. But before the season in 1970, Nebraska's players were asked to designate the school's foremost rivalry. "The players did come through with a strong vote favoring Missouri," The World-Herald's Wally Provost reported. "Second place went to Oklahoma, third to Colorado."

YESTERYEARS

« **1947:** Missouri won 47-6, the Tigers' third of five straight victories in the series. In all, they took 19 of 25 games from 1938 to 1962, although Nebraska legend Tom "Train Wreck" Novak (68) wasn't ready to give up the fight in the '47 game in Columbia. In 1949, his senior year, Novak wore 60, which became the first number officially retired by Nebraska.

» **1939:** Missouri won 27-13 in Columbia in an early November game that ended up deciding the Big Six title and handing the Huskers their only loss of the season. The Tigers were led by Paul Christman, who threw three touchdown passes, including one to each of the Orf twins, Robert and Roland. "Here's a scoop for you," Christman had told a student reporter before the game. "I'll pass 'em out of the stadium by half."

« **1950:** Husker sophomore Bobby Reynolds turned a routine end sweep into a legend in NU's 40-34 win over the Tigers. The Cornhuskers faced a fourth-and-1 at the Missouri 33 in the fourth quarter, and it was no surprise when Reynolds took the handoff and began looking for running room. "I started to the right on the end run," Reynolds said later, "but it was all jammed up. So I reversed my field, then reversed it again. I guess I don't really know how many times I reversed it. I do remember faking out the last guy somewhere down near the goal line. It never dawned on me until sometime afterwards how wild of a play it really had been. During the play, I never thought about where I was or what I was doing. I just reacted to situations. It was a freakish thing that happened. It was the sort of thing where you're a goat if you get caught and a hero if you happen to succeed." Reynolds' 33-yard touchdown run probably covered 100 yards and was the game-winner. Reynolds set an NCAA record by averaging 17.4 points per game that season, a mark that stood until Oklahoma State's Barry Sanders broke it in 1988.

» **1956:** Husker back Doug Thomas (36) takes a pitch to the outside in Nebraska's 15-14 victory, its third straight over the Tigers. "But Missouri was the victim of a bad call," legendary Tiger coach Don Faurot said afterward, pointing to an official's decision on the play before the winning touchdown had scored. A Husker was hit as he dropped back to pass, and Faurot argued that the ball "traveled several yards backward and should have been ruled a fumble, Missouri recovered and we should have had possession at that point."

THE VICTORY BELL

The trophy for the annual Nebraska-Missouri game began as part of a college prank. Two University of Nebraska fraternities stole the bell from a church tower in Seward and eventually began various athletic and academic competitions for possession of it. When Missouri's athletic director later suggested that the two schools compete for a trophy, Nebraska offered up the bell.

An M was engraved on one side and an N on the other, and the first trophy game was played in 1927. Missouri won 7-6 the first year, but the Cornhuskers took the bell back in 1928.

Nebraska's Innocents Society takes possession of the bell after a victory, and Missouri's senior honor society is entrusted when it goes to Columbia.

The bell has never risen to the level of some of the storied Big Ten trophies, such as the Little Brown Jug and Floyd of Rosedale. "Never heard of it," said Nebraska lineman Ndamukong Suh when asked about the Victory Bell in 2007.

^ **1957:** Missouri scored with less than two minutes left to give the Tigers a 14-13 victory in Columbia. Winning coach Frank Broyles was generous in victory. "We were very fortunate – they outplayed us and should have won the game. ... Coach Bill Jennings really had his boys rarin' to go. They played hard all the way." Jennings said, "That No. 14 really hurt us," referring to Tiger quarterback Phil Snowden.

« **1960:** Missouri ran over the Huskers 28-0 in Lincoln. Nebraska's homecoming queen, a native of Ankara, Turkey, was asked at halftime about the game and said she knew the Cornhuskers would do better "next time." She meant "next half," but either way she was wrong. The Huskers lost the following week 31-0 to Kansas.

︾ **1961:** The Tigers won 10-0, their fifth straight in the series, but this time the Huskers showed a little more fight. The defense held MU scoreless for the first half, and sophomore back Thunder Thornton (30) rumbled for 55 yards.

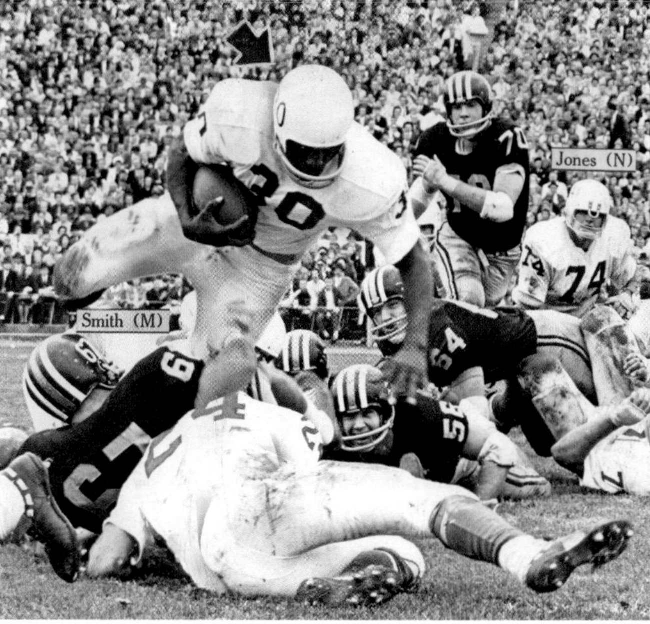

» **1962:** Missouri beat the Huskers 16-7 in a battle for first in the Big Eight. Tiger sophomore back Johnny Roland's 46-yard touchdown run helped hand Nebraska its first loss under first-year coach Bob Devaney. "All in all, the afternoon was a nightmare," said Devaney, whose team threw three interceptions and lost three fumbles. Noel Martin's 86-yard interception return gave NU its first points against the Tigers since 1957.

» **1963:** Nebraska won 13-12, ending a six-game losing streak to the Tigers, behind the play of quarterback Dennis Claridge (14). One of the key plays run by Claridge was the quarterback draw, which Bob Devaney admitted he had designed after watching films of Missouri.

TRUST BUT VERIFY

BY DAN SULLIVAN | WORLD-HERALD STAFF WRITER

⌃ **1964:** A 37-yard touchdown reception by halfback Kent McCloughan (32) sparked Nebraska to a 9-0 victory in Lincoln. "Kent really wasn't supposed to get the ball," said Husker quarterback Bob Churchich. "The pass was to Harry Wilson. Kent reached up and took it and with his speed, I guess it's a good thing he did." Pitcher Bob Gibson of the world champion St. Louis Cardinals was spotted on the sidelines talking to injured NU quarterback Fred Duda during the game.

Nebraska's Bob Devaney and Missouri's Dan Devine had been on the Michigan State coaching staff together in the 1950s before both ended up at Big Eight schools.

But their friendship didn't get in the way of a good dust-up during the 1964 game in Lincoln.

Devine complained in the first half about a measurement that gave a first down to Nebraska, arguing that the chain had been wrapped around one of the poles and was not fully extended.

He sent an observer, identified later as Missouri's freshman football coach, over to the Nebraska sideline with instructions to keep an eye on the chain gang. An irate Devaney then summoned the officials and argued that the Missourian could listen in on Husker coaching strategy.

The observer was sent back to the Mizzou sideline. Devine said afterward that he didn't wish to make any more of the incident, but added:

"This is something I've been sensitive about for several years. But if you complain too much, the next game they are in there signaling touchdowns before the ball carrier gets across."

Devine won the first meeting between the former Spartan assistants in 1962, but Devaney won their series 5-4 before the Missouri coach left for the Green Bay Packers.

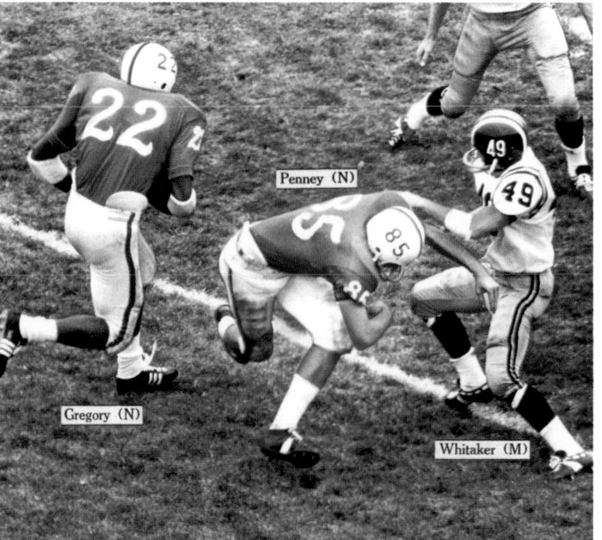

« **1966:** It's not unusual to use a quote from the opposing team to fire up a team, but the fightin' words before a 35-0 rout of Missouri weren't provided by the Tigers. UCLA Coach Tommy Prothro, when asked about Nebraska's No. 8 ranking, responded, "They ought to be forty-ninth." Devaney read the newspaper clipping with that comment to his team before the Huskers took the field in Lincoln. "While Devaney was speaking, you could have heard a pin drop," co-captain Larry Wachholtz said. "You could feel the confidence and determination of the entire squad." Ben Gregory (22) scored two touchdowns for Nebraska, which held the Tigers to 107 total yards. Missouri's Dan Devine, whose team had earlier lost to the Bruins, commented, "The Huskers are superior to UCLA."

1965: A late 26-yard field goal by Larry Wachholtz (36), who earlier had missed on an extra point try, gave Nebraska a 16-14 victory in Columbia. Missouri had gone ahead 14-0 in the first 10 minutes of the game, but the Huskers kept their poise and stuck to their plan to run the ball, grinding out 266 yards. Bob Devaney called it "probably the greatest comeback of any team I have coached."

1967: A fourth-quarter touchdown pass provided a disappointing finish for Nebraska supporters in Columbia. Devine credited his student body for a major role in the 10-7 Tiger victory, saying, "They've stuck with the team and been behind us 100 percent." The loss ended Nebraska's four-game winning streak in the series and prevented the Huskers from going to a bowl.

« **1968:** A field goal by Henry Brown (24) provided the winning margin in a 16-14 Tiger win. Nebraska lost six fumbles, including two on Tiger punts that hit unaware Huskers. Bob Devaney said he "couldn't believe the punts. They looked like they had a magnet on the ball. Our kids were trying to block, not trying to field them."

» 1969: TURNING POINT IN A LOSS

Nebraska's record dropped to 2-2 after the Huskers lost their 1969 Big Eight Conference opener to Missouri 17-7, behind the running of Joe Moore (45).

Co-captains Mike Green, a fullback, and defensive back Dana Stephenson called a team meeting following that loss.

"You have to put the situation in its proper context," Green said later. "We had just come off two 6-4 seasons. We had not been to any bowl games. It was still considered kind of a rebuilding year, and things looked pretty bleak for us.

"The seniors had to decide where do we go from here. The attitude was that . . . we would be the first senior class under Bob Devaney (to fail) to go to a bowl game. We had to turn things around."

The program made an abrupt U-turn following that meeting. The Huskers unleashed a 32-game unbeaten streak that produced three straight Big Eight championships and two national titles. The only blemish during that span was a 21-21 tie at Southern Cal in the second game of the 1970 season.

"Two men can't stand up and say this is what is going to happen – that this is what we're going to do to change directions," Green said, sidestepping credit for calling the team meeting. "Captains can be inspirational leaders, but in reality it was the whole team that made the decision to win the Big Eight championship and go to a bowl game."

– Larry Porter

1970: Nebraska won 21-7, going ahead in the fourth quarter on a touchdown that had been set up by a dazzling run by I-back Joe Orduna. "Wiggling free between left guard and tackle, Mr. Slyboots reeled off 41 yards," The World-Herald's Howard Brantz reported. "Nebraska did what they do best," said Mizzou's Dan Devine after his last game coaching against the Huskers. "When they got the ball, they stuck it to us."

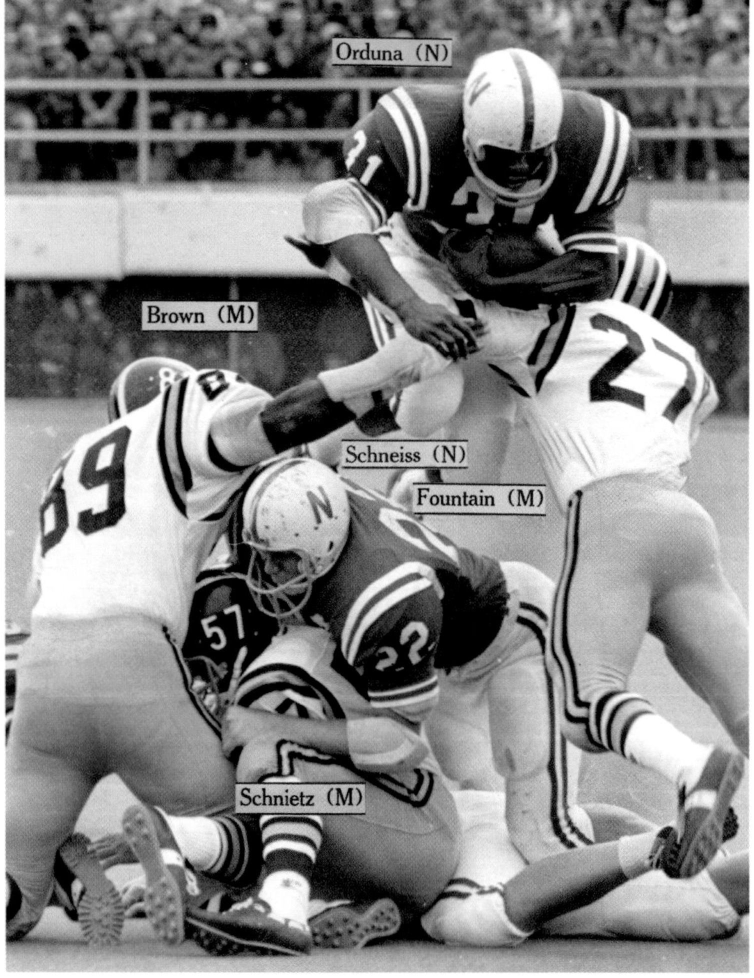

1971: Middle guard Rich Glover (79) led the Blackshirts in holding Missouri to 113 yards and seven first downs in a crushing 36-0 victory in Columbia. "This is the best Nebraska team I've seen since I've been here at Missouri the last 14 years," said Al Onofrio, who had been promoted from assistant to head coach.

« **1972:** Quarterback Dave Humm (12) threw for 267 yards and three touchdowns in a 62-0 NU rout in Lincoln.

A GAME OF CARDS

During halftime of Nebraska's home 62-0 whitewash of Mizzou in 1972, mysterious, unauthorized messages appeared from the Husker student card section, including "Screw Mizzou." NU officials said they would investigate, and six students were eventually disciplined.

Late in the game, the Missouri band started playing "Boomer Sooner," no favorite tune in Memorial Stadium. It was the visitors' reminder that a more formidable opponent would show up there on Thanksgiving Day.

Four years later, during the Nebraska-Oklahoma game, an unscheduled message once again appeared in the card section: "Screw Mizzou."

– Tom Ash

» 1973: OSBORNE WENT FOR THE WIN

Tom Osborne's first loss after four victories in his inaugural head coaching season was at Missouri, 13-12, when Randy Borg muffed a punt, and the Tigers recovered at the Husker 4 to set up the winning touchdown. Mizzou coach Al Onofrio called it "the greatest game we've ever had."

Nebraska had nearly pulled it out in the last minute when Dave Humm hit Ritch Bahe for a 24-yard touchdown to pull the Huskers within one. Faced with a PAT kick to tie or a two-point conversion to win, Osborne called a pass play that was intercepted in the end zone.

Afterward, Husker linebacker coach Rick Duval told an Omaha writer, "We're family. Stick with us. Don't get down on us now."

Osborne made the same decision in more celebrated circumstances in the 1984 Orange Bowl, when he disdained a tying kick for a national championship and went for the win against Miami. He again tried a pass, but it was tipped away.

– Tom Ash

» **1974:** Missouri delivered a crushing 21-10 defeat in Lincoln to the Huskers, including Chuck Malito (89) and Tony Davis (25). The game also was a disappointment for a 94-year-old retired farmer, C.P. Lockwood of Brock, Neb., who was attending his first NU-Mizzou game since 1899. "Back then I think there must have been only a couple of hundred people at the game," he said. The result was the same, however. The Tigers won the 1899 game 11-0.

» 1975: A GREAT CALL

The game in Columbia gave birth to the Nebraska version of a trick play dubbed the Bummeroosky, named for its creator, Bum Phillips, then the coach of the Houston Oilers.

Nebraska was leading 10-7 just before halftime and lined up to punt from the Mizzou 40. The snap went short to blocking back Tony Davis, who bent over and handed off between the legs of fellow blocker John O'Leary (14). Davis then appeared to hand off to the right to Monte Anthony and with everyone moving to the right, O'Leary remained in a crouch with the ball hidden. After the traffic cleared, he took off around left end and fled down the open field to the end zone. Nebraska won, 30-7.

Husker Athletic Director Bob Devaney called it "one of the greatest calls I've ever seen a coach make." Osborne's take: "If it works, it's a great call; if it doesn't, it's not."

– Tom Ash

1976: BOMBS AWAY

Missouri answered the Huskers' Bummeroosky the next year in Lincoln with its own stunning "roosky" surprise, which became known in series lore as the Bomberoosky.

Nebraska was clinging to a one-point lead early in the fourth quarter and had the Tigers backed up to their 2-yard-line when an improbable pair hooked up with a league-record 98-yard pass down the west sideline. Pete Woods (18), subbing for quarterback Steve Pisarkiewicz, threw it to Joe Stewart, a backup. Stewart was in for the injured Curtis Brown, the Big Eight's leading rusher, who sat out the game after one carry. The third-ranked Huskers were upset, 34-24.

– Tom Ash

» 1977: "A.O. Must Go"

Bumper stickers had started popping up in Columbia reading: "A.O. Must Go." There were rumors that Mizzou coach Al Onofrio would be dumped with a 37-39 record at the time, and old favorite Dan Devine would leave Notre Dame and come home.

"You're only as good as your last game, unfortunately," said Uncle Al. "But it's always the same people who are after your job. The guy who is spearheading the bumper sticker campaign doesn't have anything to do with the university."

Nebraska didn't help Onofrio's cause in a 21-10 victory in Columbia. He was fired at the end of the season. "All phases of our kicking game hurt us," he said after the loss.

– Tom Ash

1978: A THORN WITH NEBRASKA ROOTS

BY TOM ASH

Warren Powers was a friend and colleague when he and Tom Osborne were fellow assistant coaches under coach Bob Devaney at Nebraska, but he became a bit of an irritant after Osborne succeeded Devaney, inheriting Powers as his secondary coach.

Powers was a disciple of defensive coordinator Monte Kiffin's bend-but-don't-break coaching philosophy. Osborne, who personally directed the Husker offense, was frustrated because the Kiffin-Powers approach often allowed the opposing team to control the ball, keeping it away from his offense.

While effective in preventing touchdowns, the Blackshirt defense would often leave Osborne's offense with a long field with which to work and few turnovers in their favor.

After Kiffin left for Arkansas and Powers for Washington State, Osborne hired Lance Van Zandt, who was known for his attacking defensive style, as defensive coordinator.

When Powers left Nebraska, the irritant became a full-fledged thorn.

In his only season in Pullman, 1977, Powers brought his Washington State team into Lincoln and upset the Huskers, 19-10.

Before the game, the season opener, Osborne called his old colleague and suggested that the schools exchange spring game films. Powers refused.

NCAA rules prohibited coaches from scouting spring games at their schools' expense, so Osborne shelled out $300 from his own pocket to scout the game. Osborne's insight couldn't prevent WSU from knocking off the Huskers behind the passing of Jack Thompson, known as the "Throwin' Samoan."

The next year, Powers was at Missouri, and the Tigers were the final hurdle to the Huskers' much-anticipated national championship engagement with Penn State in the Orange Bowl. Nebraska was riding the high of its dramatic 17-14 upset of top-ranked Oklahoma the week before, was on a nine-game winning streak and was ranked No. 2 in the country. Mizzou was 6-4 and had lost two of its last three.

But these Tigers knew these Huskers. Powers' staff included former Huskers Dick Beechner, John Faiman, Bill "Thunder" Thornton, Mark Heydorff, Dave Redding and Zaven Yaralian. They would not be intimidated. Missouri had also knocked off defending national champion Notre Dame in South Bend to open the season, and MU had won its previous two games in Lincoln.

Nebraska out-yarded Mizzou 546-483, with Rick Berns (above, kneeling) running for 255 yards and two touchdowns. But Van Zandt's attacking defense was no match for Missouri muscleman James Wilder's 181 yards and four touchdowns and All-America tight end Kellen Winslow's six receptions for 132 yards. Mizzou pulled it off 35-31, sending Nebraska to the Orange Bowl for a rematch with Oklahoma.

A stunned Osborne, who had just received a double whammy when he was informed of his Orange Bowl opponent, said, "The way we played was kind of inexcusable, but not unexplainable. Football is an emotional game. It's really hard to play at a high emotional level 11 weeks in a row. That game was a classic example of that."

After the game, the goal posts were torn down in Columbia, 325 miles away.

« 1979: CALL IT EVEN

Missouri had escaped with a victory at home against Nebraska in 1973 when Tom Osborne's first team had gone for two and a win – and failed – instead of kicking an extra point for a tie. Powers returned the favor on the same field six years later.

Nebraska was ranked No. 2 in the country in 1979 and heavily favored in a game that Osborne called "particularly grueling." It came down to the final three seconds with the ball on the Husker 11-yard line and Mizzou trailing 23-20.

Powers said he would have kicked a field goal if his team was 6-1 instead of 4-3. "I really felt we had come too far not to try to score and win. When you play Nebraska, sure you go for it," he said.

He called for an underneath pass from quarterback Phil Bradley (15) to James Wilder, who was coming out of the backfield. But Wilder got hung up at the line of scrimmage, and Bradley didn't have time to find an alternate receiver. He was sacked for an 18-yard loss by NU end Derrie Nelson.

When the relieved Husker party took off from the Columbia airport, they received another scare when one of two nose wheels on their airplane blew a tire. They landed safely in Omaha, with firetrucks lining the runway, and took off for Lincoln an hour later after the flat was fixed.

– Tom Ash

^ 1980: CHANGE OF SCENERY?

Missouri coach Warren Powers thought he needed to do something differently after his first two teams were 5-7 at home and 10-2 on the road. What he decided to change was his team's lodging on the night before home games.

Under his predecessor, Al Onofrio, the Tigers had stayed in Jefferson City, 30 miles from Columbia, on Friday nights, and Powers had continued the practice until the start of the 1980 season. He then moved his team into the Columbia Holiday Inn.

"We'll try anything," Powers said. "We've been to Jeff City. That wasn't much fun. It's like going into a bar and getting the (bleep) beat out of you. You don't want to go back in there."

Powers that year brought his Tigers to Lincoln, where they had not lost since 1972. It was like a home game to him. With both teams sporting 6-1 records, Nebraska pounded the Tigers, 38-16, with Jarvis Redwine (12) scoring two touchdowns for the Huskers.

Mizzou should have stayed at the Columbia Holiday Inn.

– Tom Ash

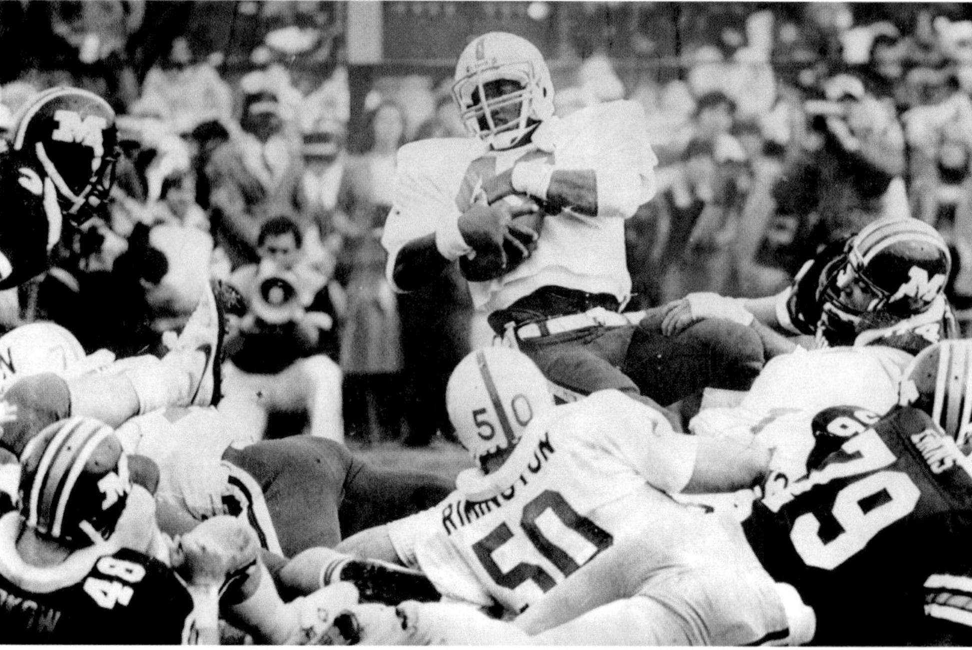

« ^ 1981: SURVIVING THE BLITZ

Defense enthusiasts got the game of their dreams when Nebraska played at Missouri. Missouri disrupted NU sophomore quarterback Turner Gill with an onslaught of blitzes by safety Kevin Potter.

Gill survived the assault to direct a clutch game-winning drive in the final minutes. Todd Brown caught passes of 24 and 21 yards to set up the game's only score with 23 seconds left: a 3-yard run by fullback Phil Bates (43) behind center Dave Rimington (50). The 6-0 win still ranks as the lowest-scoring Husker game since NU lost to Hawaii 6-0 in 1955.

– Steve Sinclair

« 1982: OPPORTUNITY KNOCKED

Bruce Mathison (19) made the most of his one big opportunity to play quarterback at Nebraska in the game at Memorial Stadium. He helped the Huskers escape an upset when he took over for Turner Gill, who had left the game after a hit by Mizzou's Randy Jostes in the second quarter. Nebraska trailed 7-3 at the time and again 13-9 in the fourth quarter.

Fullback Mark Schellen put the Huskers ahead early in the fourth quarter, and Mathison finished NU's decisive drive with a 16-yard touchdown run in the 23-19 victory.

"I thought Mathison played extremely well," Missouri coach Warren Powers said. "It was a big game, and they were behind when he came in."

Mathison went on to have more success in the NFL than he had in his Nebraska career, where he spent his time as backup to Gill, Jeff Quinn, Mark Mauer and Nate Mason.

Mathison spent five seasons in the NFL with San Diego, Buffalo and Seattle. He owns the distinction of being the last ex-Husker quarterback to throw a touchdown pass in the NFL. His last TD pass came in 1987 for the Seahawks.

"At a big school like this, that's the dream of a lot of guys, to come in and be a big star," Mathison said after the Missouri game in '82. "Sometimes it works out, and sometimes it doesn't."

Powers, who had played and coached at Nebraska, was no longer relishing his return trips to Lincoln to coach against the Huskers.

"I just love it," Powers said sarcastically when asked before the game if he liked coming back. "I'd like to do it 10 games a year. Are you crazy? Why would I want to come to Lincoln? How would you like to go to Moscow and fight the Russians?"

– Steve Sinclair

CHEAP SHOT ACCUSATIONS

BY TOM ASH AND STEVE SINCLAIR

« 1979: LOW BLOW ON AN EXTRA POINT KICK

Nebraska-Missouri relations, always tenuous, took a sharp turn for the worse in 1979, when NU star running back Jarvis Redwine (12) was injured while blocking for an extra point. Husker coach Tom Osborne didn't come right out and say Redwine was injured intentionally, but he sure leaned heavily in that direction.

Redwine, who was the No. 7 rusher in the country, had lined up as a blocking wingback, behind the right tackle, and the blocking technique called for his right leg to be extended. Tiger middle guard Norman Goodman, lining up on the left end of the Tiger line, blew in low and dropped Redwine with his full weight on the extended leg. Redwine sat out the rest of the game with a strained knee.

Said Osborne: "I'd be interested in knowing what he (Goodman) was supposed to be doing. He certainly wasn't rushing the kick. He was really whomping the I-back. In 17 years of coaching, I don't believe I've run into a situation quite parallel to it. It's not a particularly dangerous block, but when they get you all stretched out and take shots at you, it's a different situation.

"Jarvis said he heard some comments from across the line about designs to get him out of there. If there was any design to put somebody out, I'd like to call it to people's attention."

Informed of Osborne's remarks, Mizzou coach Warren Powers said the next day: "I can see why Tom was upset. I didn't realize what was going on until I saw the film, and I got all over Norman. I really feel bad about it. There's no way it fits the philosophy of the University of Missouri to play that way. There's no place in college football for it.

"I called Tom and talked to him about it. I told him we do not coach people to deliberately hurt people. We knew we had to stop Redwine. He's a great back. We intended to tackle hard, but we didn't intentionally try to take him out. A football game is not worth that."

1980: REDWINE FEELS IT AGAIN

Before the game, Osborne had downplayed the previous year's incident involving Goodman and Redwine. "I think everybody is looking forward to a good game," he told reporters who asked about lingering bad blood between the two teams.

Afterward, however, Osborne was talking about another late hit, with Redwine again the victim. The Husker I-back was driven out of bounds on the last play of the first half by a Missouri defensive back. "It looked like he threw a fist and then stuck a knee in (Redwine's) stomach," Osborne said as he narrated game film on his television show.

No penalty had been called on the play, despite Osborne's complaints. "I told the official I could see he was right on top of the play, because it was such a great call," he said sarcastically.

1981: HARD-HITTING BUT CLEAN

NU quarterback Turner Gill faced a blitzing Tiger defense in 1981, but there were no complaints about the hits he received. "Turner got smacked around so much out there, but he just kept his poise, kept coming back and he did the job," said Husker split end Todd Brown.

1982: REACTION GOES OVERBOARD

Randy Jostes, a Nebraskan who graduated from Ralston High School, became the center of controversy when his hit sidelined Gill in the second quarter. The Husker quarterback was hospitalized overnight for observation of a concussion.

Nebraska wingback Irving Fryar accused Jostes of taking a cheap shot at Gill. Osborne tried to ease the tension on the Monday following the game. "It isn't something we ought to start a civil war over," Osborne said. He added that he didn't think the Tigers played dirty football.

Jostes, a defensive tackle, said in an interview with The World-Herald's Wally Provost that his family received bomb threats and other threats of bodily harm in the hours after the game. Jostes gave a detailed account of the play and said his intent was not to make a malicious hit on Gill.

Powers said the next week that the media blew the incident out of proportion. "Without further investigating it, they hung the guy," Powers said. "It was like a lynching. The Nebraska press and ABC-TV were totally out of line."

Bruce Finlayson, the director of officials for the Big Eight Conference, reviewed the play and said he didn't think the hit on Gill was a flagrant act requiring ejection but that a 15-yard personal foul penalty should have been called. "It didn't look like he was trying to do harm to the quarterback," Finlayson said.

1983: PUTTING IT ALL BEHIND

The previous year's developments seemed as if they finally had brought an end to the hard feelings. Both Nebraska and Missouri veteran observers said after the 1983 game that they could not remember a recent Husker-Tiger battle that had less controversy.

At game's end, Osborne and Powers, often reported as the bitterest of rivals, met at midfield to shake hands. Scores of players from both teams did likewise. Powers, the former Husker player and assistant coach, then sought out Husker stars Mike Rozier and Gill. He wrapped an arm around Gill's shoulders while offering congratulations. Fans, generally, reacted likewise.

After the game, Osborne said: "Their fans were very courteous. We had absolutely no problem with them or their team. We hope this year there won't be any talk of any problems or any hassles after the game." Asked whether he thought the problems of the past were behind them, Osborne said: "I hope so. I'm tired of it."

» 1983: A PLAYER'S LONG ROAD

The Tigers had a first down at Nebraska's 1, trailing by just a touchdown, when NU senior defensive tackle Mike Keeler (61) pounced on a fumble and ended the threat in the fourth quarter. The No. 1 Huskers went on to win 34-13.

Keeler had received perhaps his greatest football honor at the beginning of the season when he was voted by his teammates as a Nebraska captain, along with quarterback Turner Gill, offensive guard Dean Steinkuhler and middle guard Mike Tranmer.

An unforgettable tragedy, however, had marked the beginning of Keeler's career as a Husker defensive tackle.

Mike was a sophomore preparing for his first major scrimmage of spring practice in 1981. His proud father, Jim, was in Memorial Stadium to watch Mike take his first big step as a Husker.

During the scrimmage, Jim Keeler died after suffering a heart attack. Three senior student trainers, along with a doctor who also was watching the scrimmage, initially administered first aid. An ambulance crew, a fire department crew and a heart team unit from a Lincoln hospital also responded, but their efforts failed to revive the elder Keeler.

The scrimmage continued while the medical teams worked feverishly to save Jim Keeler's life, but the players said they found it difficult to concentrate. Their thoughts kept swinging toward Mike, who had joined his father in the stands.

"While the scrimmage was going on, you could sense on the sideline that a lot of guys were reaching out – feeling for Mike," quarterback Mark Mauer said. "It really hit me."

Mauer said Osborne called the top units together after they had completed their work. "He asked us to kneel down and pray," Mauer said.

Mike's life took another bad turn in 1982 when he had surgery for a cancerous abdominal tumor and missed the entire season. He considered giving up football but eventually returned.

"I guess having cancer shocked me into realizing that life is so short, and I needed to get some things done," he said.

– Larry Porter

« **1984:** Linebacker Marc Munford (41) made 16 tackles, 13 unassisted, and intercepted two passes in a 33-23 win at Memorial Stadium. He didn't impress everyone, however. "Marc made some great individual plays today and undoubtedly will get a lot of individual attention," coach Tom Osborne said. "Yet in some ways he may not have played his best game in terms of tackling." Munford agreed. "On the inside run, I was kind of soft," Munford said. "I didn't bang up in there." Both schools seemed intent on putting aside some of the past animosity. Student organizations of the two schools exchanged mementos at halftime, and the NU band played the Missouri fight song for the Tiger fans.

« 1985: KICKING ASIDE THE CRITICS

Dale Klein (1) heard boos early in the season when he missed some field goals. He lost his kicking job for a time, but regained it by making a pair of 40-yarders in a win over Oklahoma State.

In his next game, he made history.

Klein, a junior walk-on from Seward, made seven field goals in as many attempts to break an NCAA record in Nebraska's 28-20 win over Missouri.

Klein made field goals of 32, 22, 43, 44, 29, 43 and 43 yards. His final field goal came with 4:16 left in the game to give Nebraska a 28-13 lead.

"There was a time not long ago when nobody had much use for Dale," coach Tom Osborne said. "He deserves a lot of credit for this victory."

Nebraska got a 199-yard rushing game from I-back Doug DuBose, but its inability to reach the end zone gave Klein his chance at a busy day of kicking. He also added an extra point on NU's lone touchdown to finish with 22 points in the game.

"I didn't really care about the record," Klein said. "I just wanted us to win the game."

– Steve Sinclair

« **1986:** Nebraska fullback Ken Kaelin (49), who grew up in Westerville, Neb., didn't want to let down the fans from Custer County. "They were having a day for me, the whole county," he said after a 48-17 win. "That was really touching." Kaelin ran for 45 yards and a touchdown, but he said he didn't deserve the credit. He borrowed a comment from Micah Heibel, Nebraska's second-team fullback. "I've got to quote Micah Heibel in that phrase he said a couple of weeks ago where any bozo could run through those holes."

» 1987: GOOD DAY TO BE A TIGHT END

Nebraska tight end Tom Banderas caught three passes in the game, and all three went for touchdowns.

"It's unbelievable," said Banderas, named the Big Eight player of the week after NU's 42-7 win. "I would rather have more receptions, but if I'm not going to get all the receptions, I might as well get them for touchdowns."

Banderas' touchdowns came on short passes of 9, 4 and 4 yards, and another tight end, Todd Millikan (43), caught a 54-yard TD pass.

For the second time in 1987, Nebraska completed five touchdown passes, four by Steve Taylor and one by Clete Blakeman. Taylor also threw five TD passes against UCLA. Against Missouri, Taylor passed for 139 yards and rushed for 75.

"You have to consider him a Heisman candidate," Missouri coach Woody Widenhofer said.

While Taylor didn't finish in the top 10 in Heisman voting that season, he was named third-team all-America by The Associated Press.

– Steve Sinclair

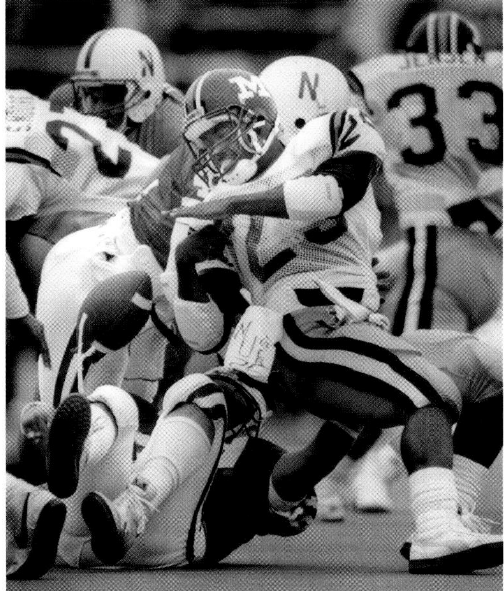

« **1988:** A heavily favored Nebraska team heard boos as it left the field trailing 6-0 at the half in Lincoln. "We get booed a lot of places," Osborne said. "But you hope when you play at home that you have some kind of an advantage. We needed it at halftime. We needed all the positive vibes we could get to win that game. We didn't need to carry boos into the locker room with us." But tough play by the Blackshirts and Missouri's three lost fumbles kept NU afloat until the offense bounced back in the second half for a 26-18 victory. At the end of the game, Nebraska fans in the north end zone continued their ritual of applauding the visiting team as it leaves the field. "We're good to the opponents here," Osborne said, noting his team had never been cheered on the road by opposing fans. "That was kind of a paradox when our fans aren't happy with us at the half and then cheer the opponent at the end."

« **1989:** Nebraska pounded the Tigers with 26 points in the first quarter and cruised to a 50-7 win. The Huskers' Mike Croel (88) blocked Mizzou's first punt for a safety, and Travis Hill (93) blocked MU's second punt for a touchdown. The crowd at Faurot Field let out its loudest cheer of the first half when the third punt was not blocked.

« **1990:** Travis Hill (93) and the Blackshirts gave up 21 points and 382 yards to Missouri, but it didn't seem to faze Nebraska defensive co-ordinator Charlie McBride. "I didn't expect minimum numbers against these guys," McBride said after the 69-21 win. "Nobody has really slowed these people down." He said Missouri had the best offensive line, passer and receivers the Huskers had faced that year. "They utilize all their players," McBride said. "They get good matchups on you."

» **1991:** Tyrone Hughes (33) caught one of three Husker touchdown passes in a 63-6 win in Lincoln. Coach Tom Osborne was asked afterward about reserve quarterback Joel Cornwell nearly scoring on the last play of the game on a quarterback sneak from the 6-yard line. "He was trying to get in, but I was hoping he wouldn't. I told (Missouri coach) Bob Stull we weren't trying to score. He said not to worry about it."

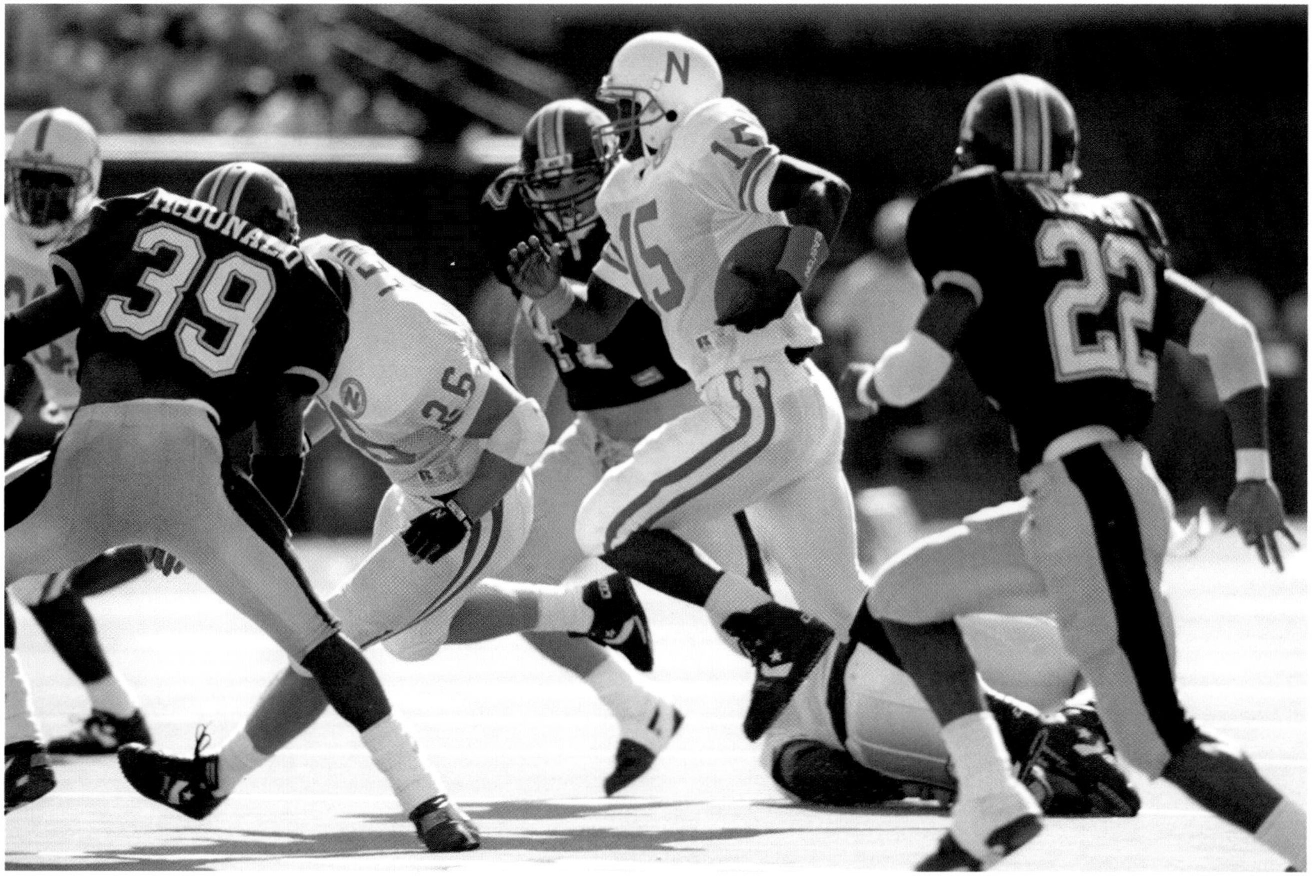

« **1992:** Coach Tom Osborne handed the keys to his team to Tommie Frazier (15), the first true freshman to start at quarterback in Nebraska football history. Frazier didn't let him down, scoring three times and accumulating 234 yards of total offense in a 34-24 win on the road. Osborne said he had decided on the Thursday before the game to start Frazier. "The thought was not to make a big deal about him starting just because of what we knew would happen with the media," Osborne said. "I know that's your business, and I'm sorry we didn't announce it earlier. I just didn't want to have him go through the hype and publicity that would surround it." Quarterbacks coach Turner Gill liked the confidence of his young starter. "He has that something you can't describe. He has an air about him. He knows how to lead. Some people have it, and some don't."

» **1993:** The Blackshirts gave an inspired performance in a 49-7 mauling of Missouri in Lincoln. Linebacker Trev Alberts (34) said the Huskers were angered by ESPN analyst Lee Corso's report on national title contenders that rapped Nebraska for its defense. "A lot of people were saying negative stuff," Alberts said. "It really hits you hard when you go out and fight every day in practice, and people don't know how hard we work."

≈ **1994:** When Nebraska needed a big play in its 42-7 win in Columbia, it came from defensive back Barron Miles (14). First the senior forced a Missouri fumble at the Huskers' 1 with the Tigers threatening in the third quarter. "I put my face on the football, and it came out," he said. "I didn't even know it until I heard everybody yelling." On Mizzou's next possession, he intercepted a pass and returned it 27 yards to set up a Husker touchdown.

≈ **1995: THANKS FOR WRITING**

The unsigned letter arrived in Christian Peter's mailbox. The Nebraska defensive tackle (55) said he didn't know for sure where it came from, other than someplace in Missouri. The message wasn't fit to print, but it in effect said that Missouri's offense was going to run the ball right at and through the Huskers' defense. "I was seething," Peter said. "It was just a couple of sentences, but it said a lot, an awful lot. It made everyone mad. It was an insult to the defensive line." A reporter suggested to Peter in the locker room after the game that the letter could have just as easily been a joke. After all, the Huskers were facing a Missouri offense that had generated just 118 yards in a 30-0 loss to Kansas State the week before and was 87th nationally in total offense. "You've got a point there," Peter said. "But we took it to heart." Peter's response to his Missouri correspondent came in the form of a 57-0 shutout.

≈ **1996:** NU I-back Ahman Green (30) overcame a turf toe injury to run for 161 yards in a 51-7 victory, as the two teams played again in Lincoln because of the changeover to a Big 12 schedule. "I made some pretty good cuts, and it didn't aggravate it or bother it at all," said Green, who had not been able to practice at full speed. The Husker special teams scored once and set up two other TDs; the defense also set up two scores. "I said all along," MU coach Larry Smith said, "that Nebraska's strength is their defense and special teams."

1997: THE MIRACLE IN MISSOURI

BY STEVEN PIVOVAR | WORLD-HERALD STAFF WRITER

The play that made Matt Davison (3) a Nebraska football legend almost didn't get called.

Trailing by seven points with seven seconds to play, the Huskers were down to their last shot in their epic 1997 battle at Missouri. Nebraska needed 12 yards to get into the end zone, and Husker coach Tom Osborne considered running an option play out of the shotgun.

Instead, Osborne, at the urging of quarterbacks coach Turner Gill and quarterback Scott Frost (7), opted for "Shotgun, 99, Double Slant." It was a play the Huskers ran every day at practice but had not used in a game that season.

The rest is history. Frost tried to get the ball to wingback Shevin Wiggins (5) near the goal line. Wiggins appeared to have the ball in his hands but it popped out as Missouri safety Julian Jones pulled him to the ground.

Just as the ball was about to hit the turf, Wiggins kicked it, sending it sailing into the end zone. Davison, a freshman and one of four Nebraska receivers on the play, caught up to it as he broke across the end zone.

"It was floating like a punt, kind of end over end," Davison said. "I dove and I guess the Lord was watching over me. I was in the right spot at the right time. It was probably a few inches off the ground when I caught it."

The catch allowed Nebraska to tie the game and send it into overtime. The Huskers pulled out a 45-38 victory and went on to finish unbeaten, earning a share of the national championship.

Osborne summed up the wild finish when he met Missouri coach Larry Smith at midfield.

"He said, 'We got lucky,'" Smith recalled after the game. "He's right. They did."

THE FINAL TOUCH

Missouri natives Mike Rucker (84) and Grant Wistrom (98) finished off the 1997 Miracle in Missouri by sacking Tiger quarterback Corby Jones on fourth down in overtime. Mizzou coach Larry Smith summarized the game in three words: "One stinking play."

» **1998:** Quarterback Monte Christo (9), a fifth-year senior from Kearney, had watched from the sidelines on many occasions but never had taken center stage in Memorial Stadium until the 20-13 victory. But with starter Bobby Newcombe slowed by a knee injury, Christo produced, pulling the Huskers from a 7-point halftime deficit by scoring the first two touchdowns of his career. Christo said his teammates got behind him after first-year coach Frank Solich and fullback Joel Makovicka ripped into them when they went into the locker room trailing 13-6 at halftime. "Joel and Coach Solich both had a little fire in their breath," Christo said. "They really tried to get people going. I think that was a difference in the second half."

« **1999:** Correll Buckhalter (36) led Nebraska to a 40-10 victory with 132 yards and a touchdown. Most important to Husker rover back Mike Brown was that the win came in a fashion that would quiet Missouri's players and fans. "Since I've been here, Missouri has always talked a lot and said what they're going to do," Brown said. "I said today that they were going to see the real Nebraska – the past two years they really haven't gotten our best game. Today, we really wanted to come out and play well against them. I don't like Missouri. I wanted to come out and prove to them that we're a great team. I think we did that today, and they can't say anything about it now."

» **2000:** The top-ranked Huskers were able to extend their mastery of Missouri, as their 42-24 victory stretched their winning streak in the series to 22 straight games. Bobby Newcombe (12) provided an electrifying moment when he returned a punt 94 yards for a touchdown, breaking the school record set in 1971 by Johnny Rodgers. Coincidentally, the 1972 Heisman Trophy winner was honored at a pregame ceremony for his induction into the College Football Hall of Fame. The punt-return record was broken again in the 2010 Texas game, with Eric Hagg racing 95 yards for a score.

» 2001: CROUCH'S GREATEST RUN

It's said that a player needs a defining play in order to win the Heisman Trophy. Nebraska quarterback Eric Crouch had his "Heisman moment" during a 36-3 victory at Faurot Field. Crouch took what was supposed to be a pass play designed to pick up a first down on a third-and-8 play from the Nebraska 5-yard line and turned it into his signature play. He rolled to the right, stepped out of a tackle by Missouri defensive end Nick Tarpoff 3 yards deep in the end zone and scooted upfield. He made several rapid course adjustments to avoid Missouri tacklers near the 10- and 25-yard lines, then rocketed into the clear and raced untouched to the end zone. Has a quarterback ever avoided a sack in his own end zone and ended up running the length of the field to score? "It was phenomenal," NU assistant coach Dan Young said. "We were looking at how many guys he beat one-on-one (five). It was a heck of a play."

» **2002:** The Blackshirts, led by linebacker Barrett Ruud (38) and lineman Le Kevin Smith (66), held Missouri quarterback Brad Smith (16) to 157 yards of total offense in a 24-13 win in Lincoln. "Without question, a great deal needs to be given to (the Blackshirts) because they took ownership and took possession of that football game," said defensive coordinator Craig Bohl.

« 2003: THE STREAK ENDS

Missouri ended the frustration of a 24-game losing streak to the Huskers with a 41-24 win in Columbia, but the postgame chaos ended up overshadowing the game. About 50 fans were arrested after rushing the field, and coach Frank Solich said he had to cut short the traditional postgame prayer out of concern for his players' safety. A Nebraska player, Kellen Huston, punched a Missouri fan who ran onto the field. He later pleaded guilty to a misdemeanor charge of public disturbance by fighting. Missouri coach Gary Pinkel was conciliatory and said a similar scene had taken place a couple of weeks earlier when Kansas had knocked off his Tigers. "I know that can happen," Pinkel said, "because it happened to us." Husker lineman Jake Andersen (71) showed his reaction to the loss.

« **2004:** Nebraska's defense put on a dominating performance in a 24-3 win in Lincoln. Benard Thomas (5), Le Kevin Smith (66) and the Blackshirts kept quarterback Brad Smith (16) out of the end zone, sacking him four times. On the night before the game, former Nebraska defensive coordinator Charlie McBride had chatted with the Blackshirts about "throwing the bones" and playing with excitement. "He told us to show the world that we're not down and out," Thomas said. "I don't know about everybody else, but it (motivated) me. That man practically originated the Blackshirts."

^ **2005:** The Huskers went scoreless in the second half and again lost at Faurot Field, 41-24. The Huskers set a record for fewest rushing attempts in school history. The 19 carries, which included six by quarterback Zac Taylor (13), broke the previous record of 25, set in 1947. "We thought we'd run better than we did, obviously," Taylor said. "I don't know how many yards we had. It couldn't have been a lot." The answer was minus two.

« **2008:** Nebraska coach Bo Pelini took the blame for a 52-17 loss in Lincoln, criticizing his own defensive game plan. Pelini said efforts to simplify and be aggressive backfired against Mizzou, which scored at will for three quarters. "Sometimes you try too hard as a coach," he said. "We weren't able to execute what we wanted to do . . . and that equates to a bad plan." NU defensive tackle Ndamukong Suh commended Pelini for taking the blame but said the Huskers should execute no matter what they're asked to run. "It's on our shoulders as well, especially more for our mistakes we made," he said. "You have to own up to those."

^ **2006:** Nebraska beat the Tigers 34-20 in Lincoln to take the inside track in the race for the Big 12 North title. Up by 17-0 in the second quarter, the Huskers resolved not to let this lead slip away as others had earlier in the season. "Everybody just said, 'Keep going, keep pounding,'" said Husker cornerback Cortney Grixby (2), who returned three punts for 24 yards and broke up two passes on defense. "That was about it. Nobody made too much of that."

» **2007:** Missouri fans didn't bother to rush the field after their 41-6 victory in Columbia. Tiger quarterback Chase Daniel (10), who threw for 401 yards, later criticized the Huskers' defensive schemes, saying they were "like high school stuff." Daniel can say what he wants, NU defensive coordinator Kevin Cosgrove said. "I'm going to say just one thing. With what they do, the way they spread the field, there's only so much you can do."

» **2009:** If there's such a thing as a "Heisman moment," then maybe there's also an "Outland moment" for the nation's outstanding lineman. Ndamukong Suh's (93) season of highlight-reel plays would have to include tossing Missouri quarterback Blaine Gabbert to the turf in the Huskers' 27-12 victory in a rainstorm in Columbia. Gabbert, who originally had committed to Nebraska before changing his mind, fumbled and injured his ankle when Suh grabbed him and threw him. The big defensive tackle later intercepted a pass to set up the go-ahead touchdown.

STILL HAVING NIGHTMARES ABOUT . . .

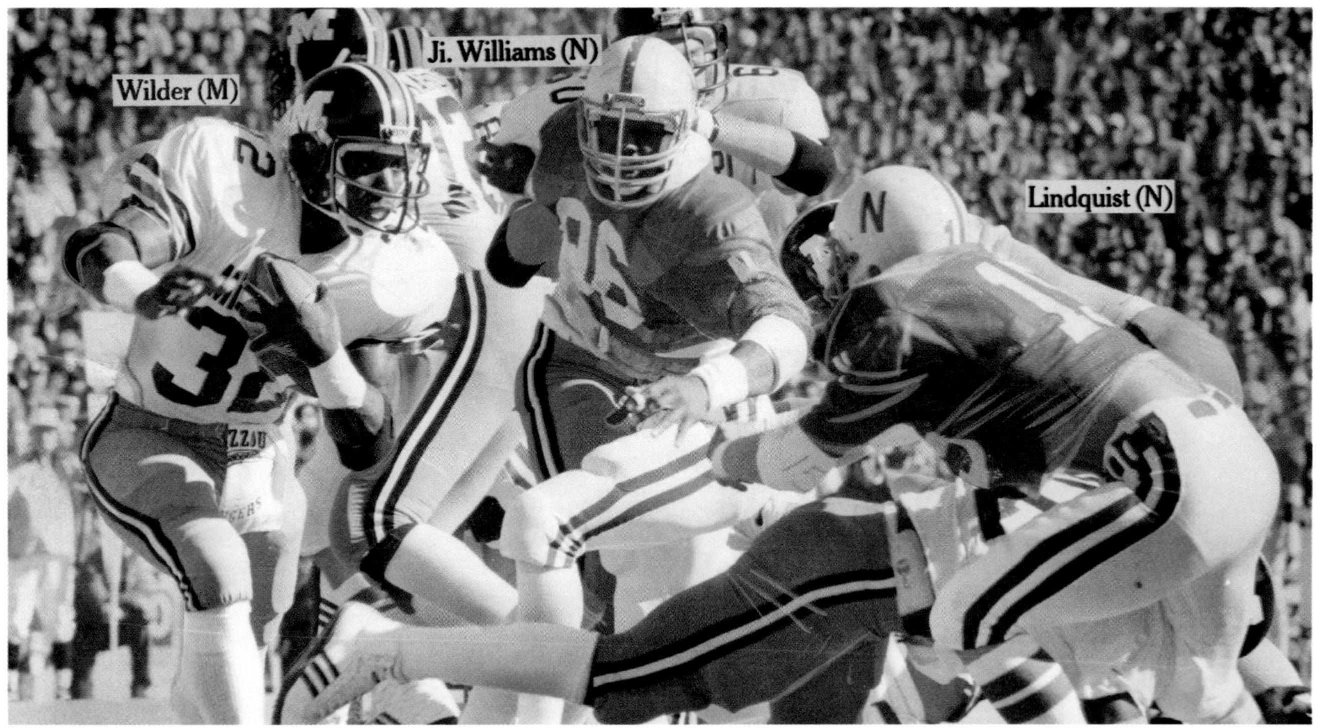

^ JAMES WILDER

Running back

Former NU coach Tom Osborne recalls James Wilder as a beast of a running back.

"He hit you as hard, probably harder than just about anybody," Osborne said, "but I don't know if you'd put him in the same category as a Billy Sims."

On Nov. 18, 1978, Wilder was every bit as good as Billy Sims, the Oklahoma Heisman Trophy winner whom the Huskers had defeated a week earlier.

Wilder rushed for 181 yards and four touchdowns, including the 7-yard game-winner with less than four minutes to play, as Mizzou dashed the Huskers' national title hopes with a 35-31 win at Memorial Stadium. It was a devastating defeat that sent the Huskers to an Orange Bowl rematch with the Sooners, who exacted revenge with a 31-24 win.

Blame it on Wilder. He ran with the same punishing style during nine years with the Tampa Bay Buccaneers. He is still the franchise's leading career rusher.

While the Huskers kept Wilder out of the end zone in victories in 1979 and 1980, he remained a force.

"Nebraska is a physical team, and you have to get nasty with them," he said.

"James was just a great ballplayer," said John Faiman, the Missouri offensive coordinator in 1978 who coached at the school for six years. "He was built like Superman." Faiman, a former Nebraska quarterback and kicker now coaching at Bellevue West, worked at Mizzou under former NU assistant Warren Powers.

The Huskers were ranked No. 2 nationally at 9-1 before the 1978 game, but Missouri was far from outclassed.

Notably, the Tigers had Wilder, tight end Kellen Winslow and quarterback Phil Bradley. On that memorable day, Wilder inflicted the most damage, piled upon the residual damage left from Sims and Co.

"It wasn't that we didn't want to get up for Missouri," Osborne said. "We were ready to play, but that Oklahoma game was one of the hardest-hitting we'd ever had." It took a toll, the coach said, and Wilder showed up to make the Huskers pay.

– Mitch Sherman

JOHNNY ROLAND

Running back/defensive back

Earned All-America honors at defensive back in 1965, but the two-way star beat Nebraska just once in three years.

STEVE PISARKIEWICZ

Quarterback

Directed three touchdown drives in the fourth quarter of the Tigers' 1974 win, a 21-10 upset of No. 5 NU.

KELLEN WINSLOW

Tight end

Caught touchdown passes in 1976 and '78 wins over Nebraska in Lincoln before going on to NFL stardom.

BRAD SMITH

Quarterback

Started for four years, with his 2005 production in a 41-24 MU win worth a double take: 246 yards rushing and 234 passing.

CHASE DANIEL

Quarterback

Tormented Huskers with a total of 654 passing yards in consecutive 35-point Tiger wins in 2007 and '08, the largest Mizzou margins over NU since 1947.

The road to Manhattan has become a familiar one for Nebraskans over the years, and the visitors made their presence felt again in the 2010 game.

KANSAS STATE

ROAD WAS NORMALLY ONE WAY, WITH A FEW TWISTING TURNS

BY MICHAEL KELLY | WORLD-HERALD STAFF WRITER

NEBRASKA'S CLOSEST NEIGHBOR in the Big 12 Conference, Kansas State sits in the city of Manhattan, only 137 miles from Memorial Stadium in Lincoln. And since the two schools first met in football in 1911, K-State has acted downright neighborly in winning only about one of every six games against the Cornhuskers.

But in one of the most amazing turnarounds in major-college football, Kansas State went from being the worst team to one of the best. You could say that under coach Bill Snyder, the Wildcats turned heads. But what happened on a night in 1998, when K-State ended Nebraska's 29-year series winning streak, was the most head-turning of all – and the most memorable, if grisly, image in the border-state rivalry. With the Huskers trailing by four and mounting a fourth-quarter drive, a Wildcat linebacker accidentally grabbed the face mask of quarterback Eric Crouch, twisting his head and neck like an image from "The Exorcist." To the horror of Husker fans, no penalty was called, and Kansas State went on to win 40-30. Their drought over, fans tore down goal posts and carried them to the menagerie of shops and restaurants known as Aggieville, the shouts heard far into the surrounding Flint Hills. Ding-dong, the witch was dead. The devilish streak was over, and K-State had performed a football exorcism of its own on a night unforgotten in Manhattan.

Before they became good in the '90s under Snyder, the Wildcats mostly endured losing, starting with games in the other '90s – the 1890s. They did have some good teams in the 1950s, defeating Nebraska five times. After a 10-7 K-State win over Nebraska in 1956, a World-Herald scribe said the only pleasant feature of the dark and dreary afternoon was a group of coeds marching with the band. "The loss," he wrote, "could call for an emergency meeting of the Monday morning quarterbacks." After NU lost in 1959, Husker trainer Paul Schneider observed: "I've never seen so many bloody noses in my life."

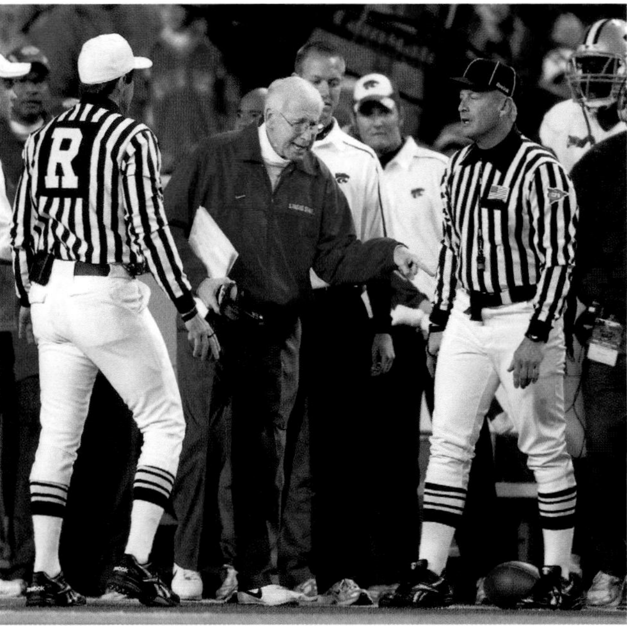

Bill Snyder expects perfection, even from the officials.

With the arrival of Bob Devaney as NU coach in 1962, the Huskers posted some easy wins and then a close one, 16-14 in 1967, when sophomore Bill Bomberger of Columbus, Neb., kicked a 31-yard game-winning field goal on a muddy field. "I was so scared," he said. "I was praying it would go through but I didn't look up to see it." Things were looking up for K-State, which defeated NU 12-0 the next year in Lincoln behind quarterback Lynn Dickey. Coach Vince Gibson had enlisted female students as "Gibson Girls" to welcome recruits and relentlessly pursued good players. Though he had some good teams, that would be K-State's last victory over Nebraska for nearly decades.

ROAD TRIP TO

MANHATTAN

Kansas State University

Founded: 1863

Enrollment: 23,500

Colors: Purple and white

Conference history:
Founding member of Big Six in 1928

Stadium:
Bill Snyder Family Stadium, capacity 50,000

History of "Wildcats":
Originally called the "Aggies," a new coach began using "Wildcats" in 1915 and the name eventually stuck.

Distance from Memorial Stadium in Lincoln:
137 miles

Worth remembering:
Willie Wildcat, a student in an oversized Wildcat head, can put on a show if Kansas State is having a good day. Among his popular antics are crowd surfing and push-ups after his team scores. The school's Powercat logo, introduced by coach Bill Snyder shortly after his arrival in Manhattan, is a familiar sight, and "Purple Pride" is the KSU equivalent of "Go Big Red." Wondering why the KSU band is launching into "The Wabash Cannonball"? After a 1968 fire in the music department, it was the only piece of music salvaged (it was in the band director's briefcase). With a game coming up, the band took to playing it frequently and its popularity grew. It's now an unofficial fight song.

Quote:
"I feel very good about this win. I'm humbled by it in all honesty because of how long it took."

– Bill Snyder after ending Nebraska's 29-game streak against the Wildcats (1998)

The Huskers often ran up big scores, and hordes of NU fans made the short drive to the college town near the confluence of the Kansas and Big Blue Rivers.

As head coach, Tom Osborne warned fans not to take the Wildcats for granted. "Kansas State is for real," he said in 1976, just before Nebraska won 51-0. K-State is no pushover, he said before a 48-14 Husker win in 1978.

In the late '70s, Manhattan began calling itself "The Little Apple," after the other Manhattan, the Big Apple in New York. But in football, little changed. In 1986, snow and sleet turned Memorial Stadium into a rink, and NU skated to a 38-0 win. In 1987, odds-makers named NU a 52-point favorite, and the Huskers beat KSU by 53. But in 1989, Bill Snyder arrived.

At first he suffered as a string of other K-State coaches had at the hands of the Huskers, including a 58-7 loss. But the Wildcats were no longer the Mildcats and started playing NU closer.

The Huskers scored two touchdowns in the final seven minutes in 1991 to escape with a 38-31 win. In 1992, the teams traveled to Japan for the regular-season Coca-Cola Bowl at the Tokyo Dome, where NU won 38-24. Chad May set a Big Eight record against NU in 1993 by passing for 489 yards, but the Huskers won 45-28.

In 1994, third-string quarterback Matt Turman of Wahoo, Neb., started for the Huskers at K-State because of the top guys' health problems, and Nebraska won 17-6. "Nebraska is still Nebraska," said Husker linebacker Ed Stewart, "and Kansas State is still Kansas State."

But in 1998, Kansas State was a different Kansas State. Yes, TV replays and newspaper photos showed Crouch's head twisted at an unnatural angle. But the 'Cats at long last had outplayed NU, and Snyder became the national coach of the year.

The Huskers won easily the next year, but lost 29-28 in the 2000 return to Manhattan, and 49-13 there in 2002. The next year in Lincoln, a 38-9 K-State victory no doubt hastened the end of coach Frank Solich's proud NU career as a player, assistant and head coach. Bo Pelini, then an assistant coach, charged across the field and accosted Snyder at the end of the game, screaming at him for leaving his starters in to score again at the end.

Nebraskans have left a dent in Purple Pride with victories in the last three games at Bill Snyder Family Stadium.

Bill Callahan became the NU coach and lost 45-21, K-State's fifth win over Nebraska in seven seasons. Nebraska won on a field goal the next year, and Snyder announced his retirement.

In 2007, with the Huskers not winning regularly as in past decades, even a 73-31 rout of K-State – and a school-record 510 passing yards by NU's Joe Ganz – couldn't save Callahan's job. He was soon replaced by Pelini. A year later, K-State brought Snyder back for an encore as head coach at Bill Snyder Family Stadium. And before long, the longtime neighbors would say good-bye.

THE MEDIUM WAS THE MESSAGE

Kansas State's student section was so excited about a Wildcat touchdown in a 1959 victory over Nebraska that they threw their flash cards into the air in celebration. While what goes up must come down, it doesn't necessarily come down in the right spot, and the students couldn't get their act together for the halftime show. "Due to circumstances beyond our control, there will be no flash card display today," the public address announcer informed the crowd.

YESTERYEARS

» **1937:** Nebraska wrapped up a Big Six title at Manhattan in coach Biff Jones' first season at Nebraska. Lowell English's field goal in the snow beat the Wildcats 3-0 in the final game of the regular season.

» **1948:** High school bands from across the state took part in the annual Band Day game, a tradition that began in 1939 and ended in the 1970s after the Memorial Stadium sellout streak began. And who better to schedule for Band Day than Kansas State, which finished last in the conference from 1943 to 1952? The Cornhuskers marched to a 32-0 victory.

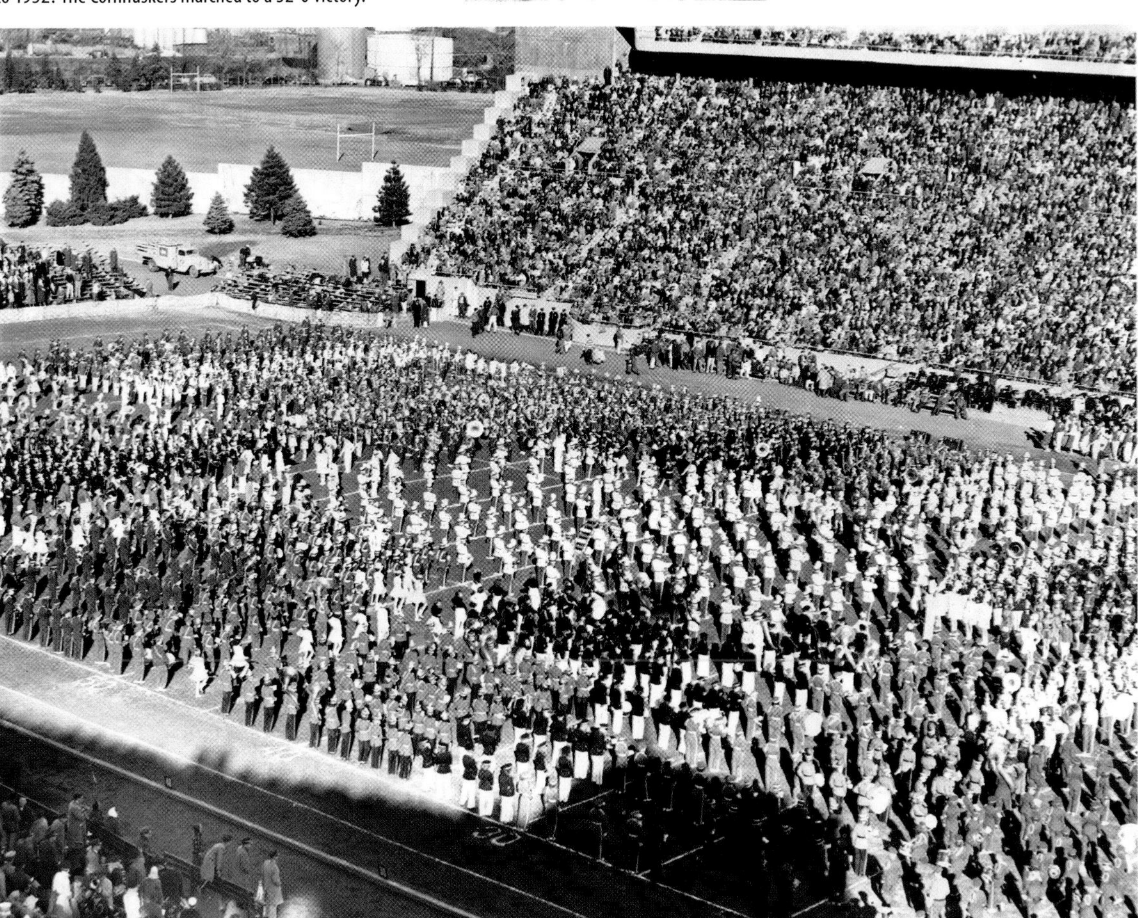

» **1953:** Kansas State won 27-0 at Manhattan's Memorial Stadium, its first win over the Huskers since 1942 and only the fifth victory in 38 meetings. Nebraska coach Bill Glassford announced after the game that he was abandoning the newfangled platoon system with its separate units for offense and defense. "I'm going to pick the best 11 football players and let 'em go," Glassford said. The best 11 would have included Rex Fischer (13), an All-Big Seven halfback in 1955.

» **1957:** NU had four players out with injuries for coach Bill Jennings' first Big Seven game. But as The World-Herald reported after the 14-7 NU win, "Fortunately full speed wasn't necessary, as the K-State offense had little hustle and no finesse." Husker back Doug Thomas rushed for 47 yards, and the Huskers claimed their only conference victory that season and one of just two against the Wildcats during a seven-game stretch from 1953-59.

« **1960:** Nebraska won 17-7 in a dull game featuring turnovers and mistakes. "The first half was so sad most of the musicians participating in the sensational halftime Band Day spectacular left for home during the intermission," The World-Herald's Gregg McBride reported.

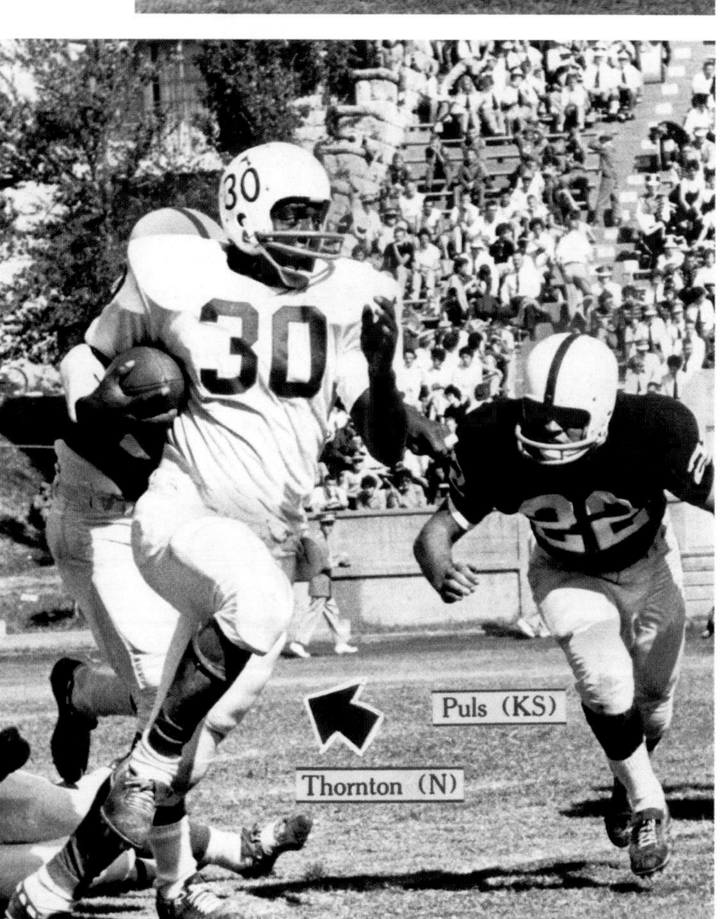

« **1961:** Tough defense and a running game featuring powerful fullback Thunder Thornton (30) led Nebraska to a 24-0 win.

« **1962:** Nebraska fullback Gene Young and his running mates rumbled for 317 yards in a 26-6 win under first-year coach Bob Devaney. It was the first NU team to start off 5-0 since 1933.

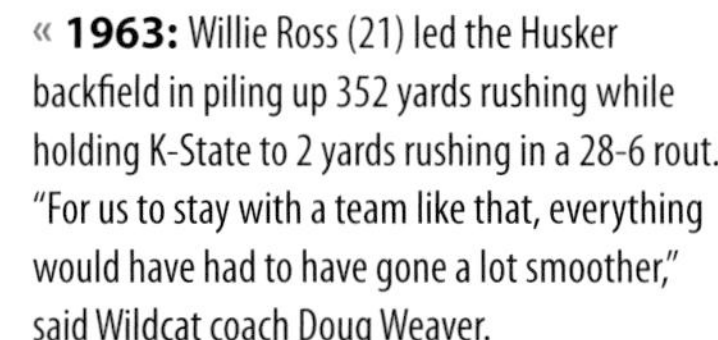

« **1963:** Willie Ross (21) led the Husker backfield in piling up 352 yards rushing while holding K-State to 2 yards rushing in a 28-6 rout. "For us to stay with a team like that, everything would have had to have gone a lot smoother," said Wildcat coach Doug Weaver.

⌃ **1964:** Quarterback Bob Churchich (15) ran for two touchdowns in a 47-0 romp in Lincoln, as the Blackshirts held K-State to just 36 yards of total offense. "Kansas State lived up to only one of its reputations – that of owning the Big Eight's poorest offense," The World-Herald reported.

« **1965:** Quarterback Fred Duda (10) led an attack that rushed for 250 yards and threw for 184, as Nebraska again blew out the Wildcats, 41-0. "In spite of what it might appear, we are not trying to run up scores to impress for the polls," Bob Devaney said. "We just had more and better players than Kansas State."

≈ **1966:** NU middle guard Wayne Meylan (66) blocked his third punt of the season, recovering it for a touchdown in a 21-10 win. Like most of his teammates, Meylan didn't feel the team had given its best effort. "Nobody seemed to be playing as we should have," he said. "We are just not playing up to our potential."

» **1967:** Bob Devaney gave the game ball to end Dennis Richnafsky (82) after a tough 16-14 win in Manhattan. Richnafsky caught 14 passes, the last one at the K-State 15-yard line to set up the game-winning field goal by Bill Bomberger. Wildcat fans chanted "We got pride" during the game, inspired by first-year Wildcat coach Vince Gibson.

« **1968:** Nebraska fans suffered through a dismal homecoming game, losing 12-0 to a K-State team that had lost 14 straight conference games. It was no fluke, however. The Wildcat offense featured three future NFL players: quarterback Lynn Dickey and backs Mack Herron and Larry Brown. Nebraska quarterbacks completed just 7 of 28 passes, and Bob Devaney called his team's passing "the worst it has ever been."

^ **1969:** Fullback Dan Schneiss (left) and tight end Jim McFarland celebrated after NU held on for a 10-7 win in Manhattan. Schneiss, who had 92 yards rushing and 44 receiving, got a key block from McFarland on a 34-yard run that set up Nebraska's only touchdown. A K-State receiver was brought down on the Nebraska 5 in the closing seconds, and time ran out as the Wildcats scrambled to line up for one last play.

≋ **1970:** The Huskers wrapped up a share of the conference title with a 51-13 stomping in Lincoln, as running back Joe Orduna (31) scored four touchdowns. Nebraska intercepted seven passes in the game, for which the Big Eight had assigned an extra official. "With all the passing that was expected, necessitating a lot of running up and down the field, it would have been impossible for four officials to cover everything if the fifth in the game was injured," explained the extra one. The Big 12 now has seven officials on the field.

≈ **1971:** Nebraska blasted the Wildcats 44-17, as Jerry Tagge threw three touchdown passes, including two to Johnny Rodgers (20). "That Johnny Rodgers can do everything," KSU's Vince Gibson said. "We don't have enough speed in the secondary to cover a guy like Rodgers."

« **1972:** NU bowled over K-State 59-7 in Lincoln, with Johnny Rodgers again plaguing the Wildcats. His 52-yard punt return for a touchdown in the first quarter was the seventh of his career. KSU lost five fumbles and threw three pass interceptions in the worst beating since the schools' first game, which NU won 59-0 in 1911.

» **1973:** The Huskers raced to a big lead early but had to recover from a K-State rally before winning 50-21 in Manhattan. Nebraska went ahead 23-0 at the half, marching 66 yards for its last score after Blackshirt lineman John Dutton (90) crunched KSU quarterback Steve Grogan on a fourth-down pass attempt. But the Wildcats pulled back to within 9 points in the second half.

≈ **1974:** Quarterback Dave Humm threw two touchdown passes, the second to reserve Brad Jenkins (92), as NU won 35-7 in Lincoln. "I couldn't believe how open I was, and I thought, 'What if I drop it?'" Jenkins said. "The crowd was all excited, and I could just hear them going, 'aaah.'"

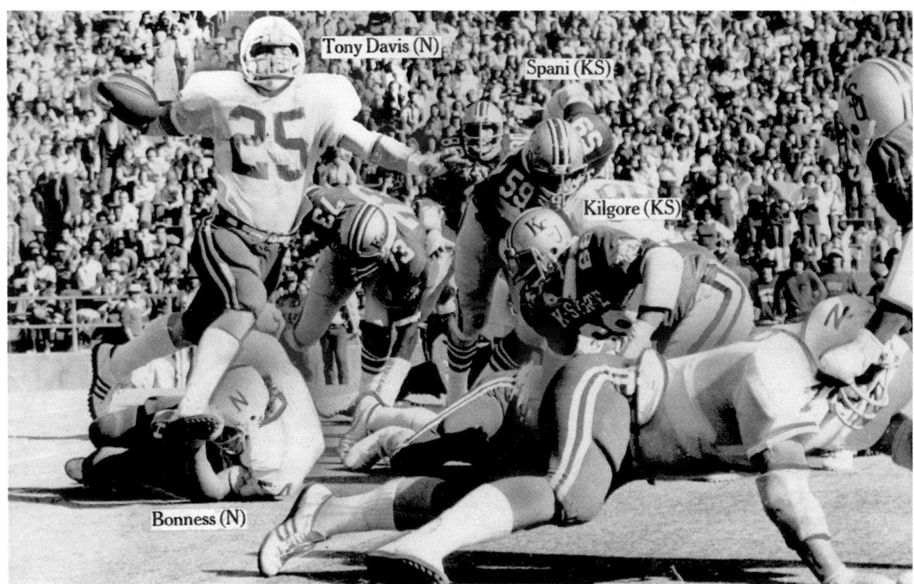

« **1975:** Tony Davis (25) scored the only touchdown in third-ranked Nebraska's 12-0 win. The locker room was subdued afterward until word arrived that Kansas had just upset Oklahoma and that highly ranked Penn State, Florida and USC had also lost. "It helps when you can play poorly and still win," coach Tom Osborne said.

A THUMBS-UP PERFORMANCE

The Nebraska team holed up in its customary Friday night digs at the Kellogg Center on East Campus prior to the 1976 Kansas State game. The players fidgeted the next morning as the departure time came and went and no team buses showed up.

Showing youthful initiative, groups of three or four players marched out onto Holdrege Street and started flagging down cars headed for Memorial Stadium. The entire team managed to hitch rides to meet up with the Wildcats. The KSU offense never did show. The Huskers won 51-0.

– Tom Ash

» 1976: NOWHERE TO RUN, OR HIDE

Defensive tackle Ron Pruitt (91) took a look at the tackle chart and laughed. "I didn't have much to do today," said Pruitt, who logged only one unassisted tackle during Nebraska's 51-0 victory. "Every time I looked up, Mike Fultz was jumping all over the guy."

The shutout was memorable because the Wildcats were held to minus-45 yards rushing.

Fultz did play well, logging a team-leading 10 tackles (six solos, four assists). The defensive tackle led a Blackshirt charge that resulted in eight sacks for losses totaling 95 yards.

"That may be a record," Pruitt said of the eight sacks. "It probably is. I believe, at least, that it's the most since I've been here."

Nebraska's record-keepers in 1976 did not keep track of sacks. Since then, the most ever recorded by the Blackshirts in one game was 11, in 1989 against Oregon State and in 2005 against Maine.

– Larry Porter

« 1977: I.M. CONFIDENT IN ABILITIES

Celebrated walk-on I.M. Hipp (32) unleashed his second straight 200-yard rushing performance – the first Nebraska running back to forge back-to-back 200-yard games – during Nebraska's 26-9 conquest of Kansas State in 1977.

Meeting with reporters following the game, the sophomore sensation heard his name linked with the Heisman Trophy and found himself compared with Oklahoma State's Terry Miller.

Then a sportswriter asked this hypothetical question: "If I wrote that you were the best running back in the Big Eight, would you believe it?"

Hipp pondered the question for a moment. "I wouldn't find that hard to believe," said Hipp, who was not recruited by a single college or university and walked on unannounced from his hometown of Chapin, S.C. "But I don't believe that I am."

"Wait a minute," the reporter said. "How can you say you don't find it hard to believe, but you don't believe you are?"

"Well," Hipp replied, "you can say I'm the best back. You can write what you want. But within myself, I know there are a lot of good backs in the Big Eight. I'm not a bragger."

The topic of discussion then turned to OSU's Miller, a leading candidate for the Heisman Trophy. "I'm better on a given day," Hipp said when asked who of the two was the best runner. "It's hard to say. He has good moves and good speed, too. I don't know how I'm better."

Miller finished second to Texas' Earl Campbell in the 1977 Heisman Trophy balloting. Hipp never finished in the top 10 among those receiving votes for the Heisman, but he still ranks among NU's all-time career rushing leaders with 2,913 yards.

Hipp's full name was Isaiah Moses Walter Hipp. Don Bryant, NU's sports information director, shortened his name to the eye-catching I.M. Hipp in the belief that some sportswriters had trouble spelling Isaiah.

Mike Corgan, Nebraska's gruff running backs coach, never had trouble with Hipp's first name, especially when Isaiah needed to be corrected. Whenever Isaiah made a mistake, Corgan called him Ezekiel.

– Larry Porter

COULD THE BLACKSHIRTS HAVE BEEN A LAUGHING MATTER?

BY TOM ASH

Tom Osborne called North Carolina defensive coordinator Jim Dickey in 1977 to see if he would be interested in the same job at Nebraska after Monte Kiffin moved on to Arkansas. They had known each other from Dickey's previous stops at Oklahoma, Oklahoma State and Kansas.

Dickey turned down the job, which eventually went to Kansas assistant Lance Van Zandt, because Dickey didn't want to uproot his son Darrell (4) before his senior year in high school. Darrell, who was named for former Texas Coach Darrell Royal, was the top quarterback in North Carolina and was also being recruited by Nebraska. "But I don't think he wants to get too far away from his mother," Jim Dickey said.

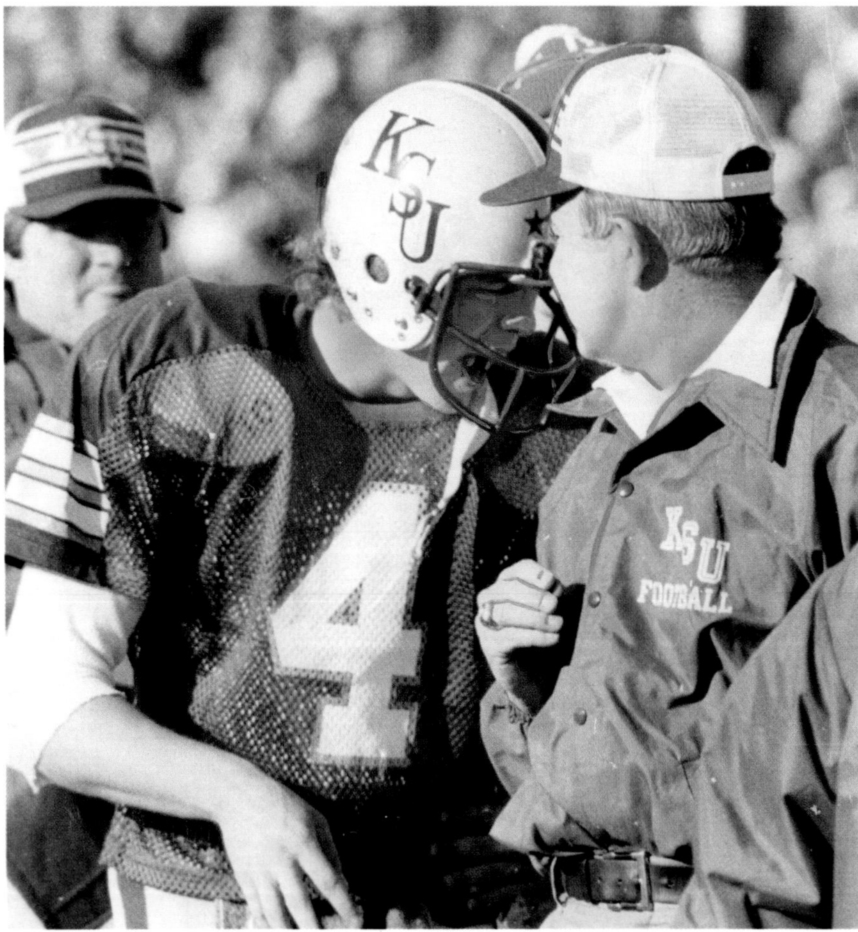

The next year, the elder Dickey took the Kansas State head coaching job, and Darrell didn't leave his mother. He lived at home during his redshirt freshman year at K-State. The next year, he got an apartment while trying to win the starting position for his dad's team.

"He sneaks home to see his mother when I'm not there," his dad said. "He'll play if he's good. If he's mediocre, he'll sit on the bench with me and test my loyalty."

Asked about recruiting his son, Dickey said, "I think if they'd check me real close, I'd be illegal. He's driving a car of mine."

Dickey came back into the league with an endless supply of one-liners. At the Big Eight coaches' luncheon in Kansas City his first year, he said, "I looked at the agenda, and it said I get five minutes. I thought I was looking at my contract."

And, "My president told me he wants a clean program, but he wants to win. I told him, 'Kansas State hasn't won a championship in 40 years. If I don't win one in that amount of time, I'll resign.'"

And, "My daughter came home from her first date and started reading the Bible. You never know what that means."

While Darrell sat, Dickey's first team was 4-6, including a 48-14 loss to Nebraska. The next year, Dickey said a good friend had told him before the previous season: "If you can win twice as many games as last year's team (two), I'll think you're a good coach." After he won four games in his debut, Dickey said the friend told him the same thing. "I don't like his math. He's not quite as good a friend now," he said.

With his son battling for a starting job, Dickey said, "He's going to sulk for a while. He's not going to play until he's ready." By the Nebraska game, Darrell was starting for the 3-5 Wildcats against the 8-0 Huskers. Nebraska lost five fumbles but still won, 21-12, while Dickey completed 10 of 23 passes for 128 yards and a touchdown. He went on to set a K-State passing record that season.

In 1980, Darrell's sophomore season, an unusually somber Jim Dickey greeted the Big Eight Skywriters tour. He said, "I got several letters last year from people who said they wanted a football coach, not a comedian."

Nobody in Manhattan was laughing that year when Nebraska won 55-8 in Lincoln. Darrell went out with an injury in the second quarter without completing any of his five passes.

Darrell Dickey completed his eligibility two years later and remains the only Wildcat in history to lead his team in passing and total offense four straight years. He is still the No. 2 passer in school history, but he was 0-4 against Nebraska.

» **1978:** Tight end Junior Miller (89) caught his first touchdown pass of the season in NU's sixth game, a 48-14 victory. "Sure, it was beginning to bother me that I haven't scored a touchdown," said Miller, who ended up with six for the season.

PICK YOUR POISON

Nebraska opponents in 1978 had a difficult task in preparing for the Huskers' running game. During one three-game stretch, a different I-back rushed for more than 100 yards in each game.

Tim Wurth (25) started the unusual streak by gaining 102 yards against Iowa State. I.M. Hipp exploded for 183 yards in a 48-14 win over Kansas State, and the following week Rick Berns gouged Colorado for 132 yards.

Quarterback Tom Sorley said he was unaware in the huddle when a fresh I-back entered the game. "I don't have any idea when they come in," Sorley said. "They all have their heads down (in the huddle) so the linemen can hear what I'm saying. The first time I know is when I hand off. Then it's, 'Hey, look who's here.'"

– Larry Porter

TOUCHDOWN
Wurth (N)

« **1979:** Tim Wurth's (25) third-quarter touchdown put the Huskers ahead for good in a 21-12 battle in Manhattan.

» **1980:** Todd Brown (29) hauled in a 7-yard touchdown pass in the Huskers' 55-8 rout of K-State. Nebraska led 48-0 after three quarters before clearing the bench. "For the crowd's sake, I wish they had started that bunch they let us play against at the end," said KSU coach Jim Dickey, whose team put up its only points against the subs.

« 1981: THE GAMBLE WORKED, TO A POINT

Coach Dickey gambled in 1981 that his program would benefit long-term by redshirting eight of its best senior football players.

The Wildcats struggled to a 2-9 record, including a 49-3 loss to Nebraska in a game that featured a 93-yard run by I-back Mike Rozier and the Blackshirts holding KSU to just 136 yards.

The redshirt decision paid dividends with a more experienced squad the next year, when the 3-1-1 Wildcats prepared to play Nebraska. "They're the superior team in the conference," Dickey said. "I'd like to see if we've closed the gap any."

The gap remained wide, and Nebraska won again, 42-13, the next year.

But the Wildcats finished 6-5-1 – their first winning season since 1970 – and played in a bowl game for the first time in school history. KSU lost to Wisconsin 14-3 in the 1982 Independence Bowl, the first live college football game televised by ESPN.

Kansas State slipped back to mediocrity in 1983 with a 3-8 season.

Dickey got only the one winning season out of his redshirt gamble in 1981. He closed his K-State career with a 3-7-1 mark in 1984 and a 1-10 record in 1985.

– Steve Sinclair

« 1982-1983: GOOD EYE FOR TALENT

Every Husker football fan raves about the "Scoring Explosion" that set the 1983 team apart from all others. But Kansas State Coach Jim Dickey saw it coming a year early.

"I've been up here many times with many ballclubs – Oklahoma, Oklahoma State, Kansas and this one," Dickey said in 1982 following Nebraska's 42-13 victory over K-State. "I believe this is the best offensive team I've ever seen Nebraska have."

"The Triplets" – quarterback Turner Gill, I-back Mike Rozier (30) and wingback Irving Fryar (27) – were juniors. Senior Roger Craig moved to fullback that year.

And the offensive line? Oh, my! It may have been the best ever assembled at Nebraska. For starters, it was anchored by senior center Dave Rimington, who won both the Outland Trophy and Lombardi Award in 1982. Rimington also won the Outland as a junior.

Next to him at offensive guard was junior Dean Steinkuhler, who in 1983 also would rake in Outland and Lombardi honors.

Also on the 1982 all-Big Eight team were tight end Jamie Williams (80), who would spend 12 years in the NFL, offensive tackle Randy Theiss and offensive guard Mike Mandelko. Three-year letterman Jeff Kwapik was the other starter at tackle.

Rounding out the offensive lineup was senior split end Todd Brown, who finished his career with 65 receptions for 1,092 yards.

Dickey said the 1982 NU offense was unusual "because they have so much speed in so many positions – at quarterback, running back and receivers. I hope I live long enough to see them run out of material. They look like they can put about anybody in the backfield and he'd be good. Their backs all look really good. But their offensive line is something. They're one of the finest I've ever seen. I could run the ball in some of those areas, and I'm 95 years old."

Rozier, who the following year would win the Heisman Trophy, hammered Dickey's Wildcats for 204 yards rushing on 21 carries behind the blocks of that splendid offensive line.

The 1982 Huskers would finish 12-1 – the only blemish was the controversial loss at Penn State – and wind up ranked No. 3 in both polls. The most infamous play of that game – and one of the most in Husker history – was a 15-yard toss from quarterback Todd Blackledge to tight end Mike McCloskey, who caught the ball out of bounds at the NU 2-yard line to keep the drive alive. Penn State scored the winning touchdown with four seconds left.

The next year, the Scoring Explosion blew up the Wildcats 51-25.

– Larry Porter

» **1984:** Chris Spachman (76) and the Blackshirts held K-State to just 53 yards rushing and 190 total yards in a 62-14 romp. Wildcat quarterback Randy Williams (5), who was sacked five times, was impressed by the Huskers. "Their ability to get to the ball, their strength and their pursuit," Williams said when asked about NU's strengths. "And they had a lot of gang tackles, too."

» **1985:** Nebraska registered its 600th football victory with a 41-3 victory over Kansas State. Husker fans who made the trip to Manhattan yelled their loudest when freshman quarterback Steve Taylor (11) ripped off a 32-yard run with 2:10 left in the game. Quarterbacks Travis Turner and McCathorn Clayton combined to hit 6 of 17 passes for 75 yards and two interceptions in the game, and Osborne didn't rule out the possibility of more varsity action for Taylor.

« 1986: WHITEOUT IN LINCOLN

Nebraska and Kansas State battled the elements as the Huskers won 38-0 in a snowstorm.

"Those were the worst playing conditions we've ever had in my 24 or 25 years here," Nebraska coach Tom Osborne said.

The Nov. 1 snow covered the field in the second quarter, and it took 40 minutes at halftime to blade off the artificial turf. An inch and a quarter of snow fell during the game.

"I've always been able to tell recruits, particularly from the South and West Coast, that it gets cold, but we never play in snow," Osborne said.

– Steve Sinclair

» **1987:** Steve Forch (38) and the Blackshirts shut down the Wildcats 56-3, beating the oddsmakers' 52-point spread by one, with 105 players seeing action at Memorial Stadium. Fans stood and cheered as an offense that included numerous members of the scout team drove to the KSU 1-yard line late in the game but came up short. "When everybody gets involved, it makes all the guys feel good," said backup quarterback Clete Blakeman. "Who wants to come down here and not play?"

» **1988:** Tyreese Knox (34) had four touchdowns in a 48-3 victory with which the Huskers assured themselves of a 27th straight winning season. That broke the NCAA Division I-A record that Nebraska had shared with Penn State (1939-64) and Alabama (1958-83). The streak ended at 42 seasons in 2004.

⌃ **1989:** The Kansas State "Powercat" logo made its appearance in Lincoln under first-year coach Bill Snyder, who spent several minutes talking to the players after their 58-7 loss to Nebraska. He compared the game to a 57-0 defeat Iowa suffered at Memorial Stadium in 1980, when he was a Hawkeye assistant. "I told them I had been in two of these in my lifetime and both of them were right here," Snyder said. "I told them we have two directions to go, and it was up to them which way we went. If this football team truly believes all the things we've been talking about – about not giving up and learning how to play hard and not making mistakes and all those things you do to beat yourselves, but in particular about not giving up, then the true test was right here." Ken Clark (32) ran for 166 yards and two touchdowns in the game.

» **1990:** Linebacker Mike Petko (99) had seven tackles and broke up a pass attempt in Nebraska's 45-8 victory in Manhattan. "Nebraska has two exceptional linebackers in (Pat) Tyrance and Petko," said Wildcat center Quentin Neujahr, a freshman from Ulysses, Neb. "They're kind of the key to their defense."

» **1991:** Nebraska I-back Derek Brown (21) scored two touchdowns in the final seven minutes of a 38-31 win, but the game wasn't secured until linebacker Travis Hill jarred Paul Watson's pass loose from tight end Russ Campbell on fourth down and goal from the NU 7. "Kansas State is good," coach Tom Osborne said. "Nobody will give them any credit because they're Kansas State."

1992: FRAZIER "GREAT" IN ANY LANGUAGE

Nebraska locked up its second straight trip to the Orange Bowl with a 38-24 win in the Coca-Cola Bowl at the Tokyo Dome. Sports Nippon reported, "Tommie Frazier was the most outstanding player. He is a great, great player." I-back Calvin Jones helped out, rushing for 186 yards on 30 carries to go over 2,000 career yards as a sophomore. The Huskers went ahead 21-0, but the Wildcats outplayed them in the second half to tighten the game. Actually, coach Tom Osborne said, that might have been a good thing. "We've got to ride back on the plane with these K-State guys," he noted. While Osborne said he thought his players probably benefited culturally from the trip to Japan, Trev Alberts begged to differ. "For two or three nights it was like solitary confinement in this little room that has nothing but CNN the whole night. It's a nice country, but it would be better just to come and visit."

« **1993:** KSU junior quarterback Chad May (5) threw for a Big Eight-record 489 yards in a 45-28 loss but complained afterward about Huskers taunting him. Tom Osborne said he talked to the players who were alleged to have been involved, but both denied saying anything. May also said he thought Husker outside linebacker Trev Alberts might have hit him late on a couple of occasions. "He took a blow to my head," May said. "I got up and told the ref. He told me it was one step Alberts took (after the throw). I said, 'How can you take one step when I'm standing for two seconds watching the play and he hits me in the back of the head?' It happened a couple of times."

≈ **1994:** NU linebacker Troy Dumas (4) blocked an extra-point kick and intercepted a Chad May (5) pass to highlight the Huskers' defensive effort in a 17-6 victory in Manhattan. "We don't have a slouchy defense," Dumas said. "There were a lot of people doubting us . . . but we showed up and played a great game." May felt the pressure all afternoon from Donta Jones (84) and the Blackshirts. The K-State quarterback again complained about dirty play, saying a Husker defensive lineman had gouged his eye after the whistle had blown. Speculation about the identity of the alleged culprit this time centered on Christian Peter, who denied it was him. "A lot of us guys have been talking about it, and no one knows who did it," Peter said.

THE "TURMANATOR"

BY DAN SULLIVAN | WORLD-HERALD STAFF WRITER

When leaders were needed in 1994, an unlikely one appeared.

Nebraska headed into its game against unbeaten Kansas State with starting quarterback Tommie Frazier out with a blood clot. His backup, Brook Berringer, hadn't been allowed to have contact in practice because of a recurrence of a collapsed lung from an injury in an earlier game.

Next down the depth chart was Matt Turman (11), who had walked on at NU in 1992 as a defensive back but asked to be switched to offense. He started out as a receiver, then moved to quarterback, the position at which he had starred at Wahoo Neumann High School. Along the way he picked up the nickname "The Turmanator."

Turman, who had seen only mop-up duty, had his teammates' backing as they prepared for the game in Manhattan, even if he lacked his coach's ringing endorsement. "He's not the worst," coach Tom Osborne had said in 1993, when injuries first put Turman in position to see action. "But he'll have to get good in a hurry."

Osborne still wasn't exactly brimming with enthusiasm in 1994. "Turman is one of those guys who, when you look at him, you don't think he ought to be very good. But he seems to get the job done." It was an accurate assessment.

The sophomore quarterback mostly gave the ball to I-back Lawrence Phillips (1), who handled it on 14 of the Huskers' first 15 plays. Turman also completed 2 of 4 passes – both screens to Phillips – and ran four times for 10 yards.

Berringer, who had been cleared on a limited basis, took over at the end of the second quarter and played most of the rest of the 17-6 victory.

Asked to evaluate his first collegiate start, Turman said, "It was a W, so I can't complain." Berringer was able to start again for the rest of the games in NU's Big Eight title run, and Frazier returned for the Orange Bowl victory in January that wrapped up the Huskers' national championship.

"I don't think the feeling will ever wear off," Turman said after he was awarded a scholarship the next semester. "I started against a ranked team for the team that won the national championship."

« **1995:** Jason Peter (95) and the Blackshirts stuffed No. 8 Kansas State 49-25, logging nine sacks and posting the fifth-best rushing defense total in school history, minus-19 yards. Did Kansas State resemble other Top 10 teams Nebraska had played in recent years? "Uh, that's a hard question," NU middle linebacker Doug Colman (46) said as he backed toward the interview room door. "You've got to remember it's hard to play us here."

≈ **1996:** The Huskers held the Wildcats to 86 total yards in a 39-3 victory. Linebackers Terrell Farley (43) and Jon Hesse (44) were part of a charge that yielded zero yards in the first half. "They're pretty doggone good," coach Tom Osborne said of the Blackshirts, though he added some caution. "Ask me again at the end of the season because about the time you start bragging on them, they goof up."

« **1997:** I-back Ahman Green (30) ran for four touchdowns and 193 yards in Nebraska's 56-26 victory, its 29th straight over the Wildcats. "Those guys still don't know if they can beat us or not," NU co-captain Jason Peter said. "They still have that in the back of their mind. When we jumped out on them early there, I think that was a real positive thing."

» **1998:** K-State took a head-turning 40-30 victory in Manhattan, giving the Wildcats their first over Nebraska since a 12-0 victory in 1968. One regret Eric Crouch had from the loss had nothing to do with his performance, which included 247 yards of total offense: "I should have gotten some ice on my neck after the game," he said later. Crouch's pain in the neck was caused by Kansas State linebacker Travis Ochs, who sacked the Husker quarterback in the closing minutes by grabbing his face mask. The referee did not throw a flag on the play, although Ochs admitted he was a little nervous about possibly being called for an infraction. A face-mask call would have kept alive the hopes of Nebraska, which trailed by just 4 points at the time. "I knew I got face-masked, and I knew I got ripped down," Crouch said, "but I didn't know the extent of just how bad it looked. When I saw the replay, I said, 'Man!' I didn't know I got flung around like that. I was surprised that I got up." The game twice was delayed in the final seconds by fans storming onto the field in premature celebration, and the goal post at the north end of the field eventually was carted off by the fans. "I'm happy, I can assure you of that," said Bill Snyder, reserved as usual. Husker cornerback Ralph Brown said the Wildcats should savor the sweet taste of a victory over the Huskers. "This is a one-year deal," Brown said. "We won't lose to K-State next year. You can put that one on me."

« **1999:** Kyle Vanden Bosch (83) had one of five Husker sacks, as Nebraska dismantled the unbeaten Wildcats 41-15 in Lincoln. NU forced Kansas State into four turnovers – three fumbles and an interception – and blocked a punt and a field-goal attempt. Eric Johnson (27) returned one of the fumbles 15 yards for a touchdown.

» **2000:** Kansas State put Nebraska's conference championship hopes on ice with a 29-28 victory in the cold and snow in Manhattan. Wildcat players slid for joy on the snow-covered field when the game was over, and fans tore down the north goal post.

» **2001:** I-back Dahrran Diedrick (30) had 108 yards to give Husker fans something to cheer about in a 31-21 victory. "Everybody in purple got hit today," he said. "We knew they wanted to come in and play smash-mouth football. We wanted to show that we are the power team. We're the ones who play smash-mouth football. We wanted to wear them down, and in about the third quarter, their guys didn't want to get hit anymore."

« **2002:** It was hard to imagine, but Nebraska's coach was asked if he felt the opponent ran up the score on his team. That's what Frank Solich faced after a 49-13 Wildcat victory. It was pointed out to him that K-State kept its starters in the game for four quarters, even after the Wildcats had taken a 29-point lead with 5:04 left. They scored again, with starting tailback Darren Sproles (43) running 70 yards for the final touchdown with 2:11 to play. "They're conditioned to play four quarters of football," Solich said, "so I have no problem with that. In fact, we were keeping our players in and battling to come back. They have every right to do the same thing."

» **2003:** Ell Roberson (3) passed for 313 yards and two touchdowns, and the Huskers gave up 24 second-half points in 15 minutes in a 38-9 loss. It was the Wildcats' first win in Lincoln since 1968. First-year Nebraska defensive coordinator Bo Pelini thought KSU's Bill Snyder ran up the score by playing his top offensive unit in the final two minutes of the game. "I did, and I told him about it," Pelini said of their encounter on the field after the game. "That's not the way I've gone about things in the organizations I've been a part of." Snyder's account of the meeting: "I don't think I would care to repeat what he called me." It was reported after the game that NU Athletic Director Steve Pederson had gone to the skyboxes in Memorial Stadium assuring boosters that he would "do something." Pederson denied discussing with any booster the status of coach Frank Solich, who was fired about two weeks later.

» **2004:** The Huskers said after the 45-21 loss that they had prepared all week for KSU's option game, but backup KSU quarterback Alan Webb (8) still managed to run for 147 yards and four touchdowns. The Wildcats won for the third straight season, their longest winning streak in the series. "I'm accountable," first-year NU coach Bill Callahan said. "I offer no excuses. Just understand that. There are no excuses, none whatsoever."

» **2005:** Freshman kicker Jordan Congdon (29) drilled a 40-yard field goal with 1:05 left in the game, giving NU a 27-25 win in Lincoln. NU quarterback Zac Taylor, who had set the single-season school passing record in the third quarter, was knocked out early in the fourth quarter and was relieved by Harrison Beck. The freshman threw an interception, but a later completion and a roughing-the-passer call led to the winning field goal. KSU coach Bill Snyder announced his retirement several days after the game.

2006: A CHANGE OF HEART

BY RICH KAIPUST | WORLD-HERALD STAFF WRITER

Josh Freeman (1) punched Nebraska in the gut once – pretty hard, too – but never again.

The Huskers were banking on the rifle-armed, big-bodied quarterback out of Kansas City to be their signal-caller of the future when he committed over the summer of 2005. Six months later, Freeman changed his mind, opting for Kansas State in one of those de-commitments that force you to remember that nothing is official in recruiting until signing day.

Freeman had the kind of talent that would make him a first-round pick in the 2009 NFL draft. And Nebraska was left with a hole in its 2006 recruiting class that it wasn't going to be able to fill at such a late date.

NU coach Bill Callahan chose to take the high road in discussing Freeman before Husker-Wildcat games in 2006 and '07. His one swipe came during a speaking engagement in the spring of 2006 – at, of all places, a Special Olympics promotional luncheon in Omaha.

"We want players who want us, because we feel Nebraska's a special, special situation," Callahan said. "If you're a prima donna, if you're a drama queen, there's no room for you at Nebraska. You can go to Kansas State."

Hmmm, wonder whom he was talking about?

Alas, Freeman went 0-3 against Nebraska and was pulled in the last of those against a Bo Pelini defense that completed the Huskers' payback. Freeman completed a combined 56 of 109 passes (just 51.4 percent) with three touchdowns and two interceptions in those games. He was sacked 12 times in the three meetings – often by NU defenders who knew well the Freeman story and took satisfaction in any pain inflicted.

One last footnote to the story: It is believed that Freeman alerted Callahan of his de-commitment with a text message that read, "We're not coming."

True or not?

"Next question," Callahan said during NU-KSU week in 2006.

The Blackshirts sparked a 21-3 win in 2006 by sacking Freeman four times, including once by Ndamukong Suh (93), and forcing him into two interceptions.

» **2007:** Quarterback Joe Ganz (12) was named Big 12 offensive player of the week for his school-record 510 passing yards and seven touchdowns in a 73-31 rout of Kansas State. "He's a product of the system," said coach Bill Callahan, who coached his last game in Memorial Stadium in the win. "This is a player that we've developed and you could see his development ooze all over the field on Saturday."

« **2008:** Nebraska punished K-State in a 56-28 win in Manhattan, running for 340 yards and leaving behind a string of battered and bruised Wildcats. I-back Quentin Castille (19) put an exclamation point on the mauling when he rumbled past the line and straight at a KSU defensive back in the fourth quarter. Castille won the fourth-quarter collision, leaving the victim on the ground for several minutes before he could be helped from the field.

2009: Nebraska beat Kansas State 17-3 to clinch the Big 12 North title in a hard-hitting but ugly game that fit the season. "It's become our identity," said NU coach Bo Pelini. Ndamukong Suh (93) and the Blackshirts made it a long night for Wildcat quarterback Grant Gregory (6), who completed only 11 of 31 passes.

STILL HAVING NIGHTMARES ABOUT . . .

^ **DARREN SPROLES**

Running back

Even at 5-foot-7, Darren Sproles was a big headache.

He helped Kansas State beat Nebraska three straight years, the longest such Wildcat streak in the series, totaling over 400 yards and six touchdowns in the 2002, 2003 and 2004 games.

The speedy Sproles was a tough runner who could take advantage of his size.

"He has good footwork and he's short, so it's hard to see him in the hole," Nebraska safety Josh Bullocks said. "He has some pretty good offensive linemen, and some big guys, so it can be pretty hard to spot him in the backfield."

His Wildcat teammates didn't even like practicing against him. "We figured that out our freshman year," K-State defensive end Scott Edmonds said, "and I don't think we've caught him since."

Sproles, whom bowl game stadium workers once asked about equipment bags and where the team bus was parked, let his play do his talking. "I don't like this," he was heard muttering while moving from one interview spot to the next at Big 12 Media Days.

He frequently heard people compare him to Oklahoma State Heisman Trophy winner Barry Sanders but shrugged off such talk. "He was one of my idols," Sproles said. "But there is only one Barry Sanders."

Nevertheless, like Sanders, he proved that a little man could succeed in the National Football League.

Kansas State coach Bill Snyder, not one to exaggerate, provided high praise for Sproles.

"He's as capable as any player I've ever known," Snyder said. "He's a very humble young man. You have to love him to death, just because of who he is."

LYNN DICKEY

Quarterback

Directed a 12-0 win in 1968, the last time K-State would beat the Huskers in Lincoln until 2003.

MICHAEL BISHOP

Quarterback

Engineered the 1998 victory that stopped NU's 29-game win streak in the series, running for 140 yards and passing for 306.

MARK SIMONEAU

Linebacker

Logged a 14-tackle game in 1999.

QUINCY MORGAN

Wide receiver

Caught seven passes for 199 yards in the 2000 game, including the game-winner with 2:52 remaining.

ELL ROBERSON

Quarterback

Threw two TD passes, ran for another score, and accounted for 403 yards of total offense in the 2003 game.

Fans at the Nebraska-Oklahoma Big 12 championship game in 2006 at Arrowhead Stadium in Kansas City, Mo., weren't quite ready to let go of the past.

OKLAHOMA

THE BROTHERHOOD OF BIG-TIME FOOTBALL PROGRAMS

BY MICHAEL KELLY | WORLD-HERALD STAFF WRITER

FOR MOST NEBRASKA FANS, the biggest regret in Nebraska's leaving the Big 12 Conference is saying goodbye to Oklahoma – a respected rival whose "Sooner Magic" has served as a most worthy adversary to "Husker Power." Oklahoma created Husker headaches and heartbreaks but also bowed to the jubilation of Husker Nation. NU and OU are "frenemies," friendly enemies: The Big Red of the North vs. the Big Red of the South. They met many times in crucial games, none bigger than "The Game of the Century" in 1971, a classic whose advance hype was equaled by the magnificence of the contest itself, the No. 1-ranked Cornhuskers edging the No. 2 Sooners, 35-31. Nothing can say more about the civility and esteem between two of the greatest college football programs in history than a 2008 reunion of that game – in Norman, Okla., where the noble hosts were none other than the men who had played on the losing side. With few exceptions, it was that kind of series – like Ali and Frazier, Nebraska and Oklahoma stood their ground as heavyweight champions who pounded away furiously at each other but made their opponent better.

Fans of both schools, for the most part, emulated that mutual respect. That's not to say there weren't a few knuckleheads in the stands who taunted and cursed. But overall, the series was conducted with class. That includes sportsmanship and good humor by the coaches. OU coach Barry Switzer arrived on the set of NU athletic director Bob Devaney's TV show and presented him with a bag of tacos – because of a Devaney prediction that Oklahoma would play in the Sun Bowl, where he said they could eat a lot of tacos. Devaney returned the favor by surprising Switzer on his TV show with a sombrero. Years later, at a 76th-birthday tribute for Devaney in Kearney, Neb., Switzer surprised him by wearing a chef's apron and hat and carrying a cake into the room as the audience sang.The Nebraska-Oklahoma series has produced memorable names, from OU's J.C. Watts to NU's I.M. Hipp. From Oklahoma's Carl "Sheepdog" McAdams, Elvis Peacock and Buster

The ponies Boomer and Sooner pull the Sooner Schooner around Owen Field when the home team scores.

Rhymes to Nebraska's "Choo Choo" Charlie Winters, Thunder Thornton and Wonder Monds. The rivalry started in Lincoln in 1912, the Huskers winning 13-9. OU publicist Harold Keith years later wrote that Nebraska's "mighty football Romans of the prairies ignored the slow stumblings of the forward pass," and had defeated teams of that era "with a ground offensive of epic sweep and savagery." In defeat, the '12 Sooners completed a pass thrown 50 yards that Keith said must have been the first long pass a Nebraska team had ever seen. In 1919, the teams played to a 7-7 tie – in Omaha. Nebraska dominated the early decades of the rivalry, including the 24-0 inaugural game at Memorial Stadium in 1923. The 1940 Rose Bowl team from Nebraska beat OU 13-0. But starting in 1942, things changed and Oklahoma won regularly. The 1950 Big Seven championship game featured a duel in Norman between halfbacks Bobby Reynolds of NU and Billy Vessels of OU, the Sooners prevailing in spite of Bobby's three touchdowns and five extra points. Despite a 55-7 thrashing by the Sooners in 1954, the Huskers went to the Orange Bowl because of an odd rule that

ROAD TRIP TO

NORMAN

University of Oklahoma

Founded: 1890

Enrollment: 30,000

Colors: Crimson and cream

Conference history:
Founding member of Big Six in 1928

Stadium:
Gaylord Family-Oklahoma Memorial Stadium, Owen Field, capacity 82,112

History of "Sooners":
Participants in the Oklahoma land rush of 1889 who got the jump on the others, racing ahead to stake their claim, were known as Sooners. Oklahomans came to associate the word with ambition.

Distance from Memorial Stadium in Lincoln:
425 miles

Worth remembering:
Visiting fans get a kick out of watching the Sooner Schooner, a covered wagon pulled by white ponies named Boomer and Sooner, race around Owen Field whenever Oklahoma scores. However, visitors often find that the OU band plays the fight song "Boomer Sooner" way too much, with the annoyance linked directly to the score of the game. While the tune is stolen from Yale's "Boola Boola," the lyrics have been changed to include the memorable, "I'm a Sooner born and Sooner bred and when I die, I'll be Sooner dead."

Quote:
"You never think about losing. You're just thinking about moving the football, and we felt we could do that. There wasn't a word said in the huddle on that drive. We just knew what we had to do."

– Nebraska quarterback Jerry Tagge describing the winning drive in the Game of the Century (1971)

Oklahoma's fans, like Nebraska's, always have their favorite team on their minds.

the conference champ couldn't go there in consecutive seasons. (NU lost the bowl game to Duke, 34-7.)

Oklahoma had a 74-game conference unbeaten streak over 13 years under coach Bud Wilkinson – but then came Halloween in 1959, one of Nebraska's greatest upsets. NU's Ron Meade intercepted a third-down pass in the end zone with 25 seconds left to seal the 25-21 victory in Lincoln. The goal posts ended up on the lawn of the Governor's Mansion, and someone said NU coach Bill Jennings could become governor. Commentators said the OU loss pumped new life into a league that had been a one-team show. The next year, Jennings told the team to "go out and shuck 'em up," and Nebraska won by a field goal despite a second straight 4-6 record. With Devaney's arrival as head coach in 1962, Husker fortunes took a historic turn for the better that would last four decades, but his first NU team lost to OU 34-6. In spite of that blowout, Devaney met an enthusiastic fan response days later in Omaha. "We're trying to win the championship," he told the lunch crowd. "With this tremendous interest, there must be a way to have that kind of football team here."

The day after President John F. Kennedy was assassinated in 1963, the Nebraska-Oklahoma game went on in Lincoln as scheduled. Wilkinson, the president's national adviser on physical fitness, spoke against postponing the game. After a contentious six-hour meeting, the Nebraska Board of Regents gave the go-ahead. Nebraska won 29-20, giving the Huskers their first conference title since 1940. NU captured the Orange Bowl game over Auburn in Miami, and Devaney, 48, was courted for the head-coaching job at the University of Miami. Fortunately, he decided to hang his hat for good in Nebraska. After NU's two decades in the football wilderness, Scarlet fever was raging and fans referred to the team as the Big Red. Longtime World-Herald writer Gregg McBride called that "thievery," saying that "Nebraska lifted the 'Big Red' slogan from Oklahoma." But after OU upset unbeaten NU 17-7 in 1964, McBride wrote that the Oklahoma faithful took the victory in stride and Nebraska fans didn't beef. He predicted that "the two Big Reds" would become "one of the hottest rivalries on the collegiate battlefront."

The mid-'60s were heady days for Husker fans. In 1965, NU went 10-0 for the first time in a half-century after defeating OU, but lost to Alabama in the Orange Bowl. Nebraska was undefeated the next year until losing to Oklahoma by a point, and again lost to 'Bama in a bowl. Then came a couple of 6-4 records for Nebraska, including a 47-0 pasting by the Sooners in '68, with no bowl games either year and a petition circulating in Omaha to fire Devaney. Who could have known what lay ahead – an improbable run that catapulted Nebraska to the top? The '69 team turned the tables on the Sooners, 44-14, and went 9-2, setting the stage for national championships the next two years. In 1970, the Nebraska win over Oklahoma ended as the 1959 game had, with an interception in the end zone, this time by co-captain Jim Anderson. That was a big game, but 1971 was the biggest – and the buildup reached a pitch previously unseen.

Besides the tanker-loads of ink spilled in newspapers and magazines, broadcast media and fans in general went all out. President Richard Nixon, who had appeared in Lincoln in January for a celebration of the 1970 national title, wrote to Devaney that he hoped both teams played their best. Western Union in New York announced it would spread the telecast around the world. The game at OU didn't disappoint. The Nebraska I-formation and the Oklahoma wishbone provided a visual feast on Thanksgiving Day. But the signature play of this signature game, and perhaps the most famous play in Cornhusker football history, was the 72-yard punt return for a touchdown by Johnny Rodgers of Omaha, who twisted and eluded tacklers at the start, sped down the left sideline, received a welcome final block from teammate Joe Blahak and sped to the end zone. As KFAB's Lyell Bremser described the end of the run, an audio that has been replayed many times: "To the 20, to the 10, he's all the way home! Holey-moley! Man, woman and child, did that put 'em in the aisles! Johnny 'The Jet' Rodgers just tore 'em loose from their shoes!" But it was a final 74-yard drive engineered by quarterback Jerry Tagge that brought NU from behind to win. Jeff Kinney of McCook, his tear-away jersey in shreds, bulled across for the touchdown, his fourth of the day. In the bedlam of the NU locker room, it took a half-hour for President Nixon's congratulatory call to get through. In the Orange Bowl game, Nebraska again played Alabama – and this time Devaney and the Huskers were loaded for Bear – rolling over coach Bear Bryant and the Crimson Tide, 38-6.

Devaney coached one more year before handing the reins to 35-year-old Tom Osborne, and the final game at Memorial Stadium for the Bobfather of the modern era of Nebraska football came against Oklahoma, a 17-14 loss. In 1973, the first game between Osborne and OU coach Barry Switzer, the Sooners blanked NU 27-0. Larry Lacewell, the OU defensive coordinator, said of his charges: "I would take this defense and go fight Russia." The Nebraska-Oklahoma rivalry wasn't a cold war, but the president of the Nebraska Medical Association said there was a strong relationship between Husker football success and good health for the average Nebraskan. When the team did well, he said, it tended to sell the idea of physical fitness. But OU beat NU six in a row in the '70s, and a World-Herald reader implied that Nebraska needed a psychiatrist. The team couldn't relax against OU, he said, because "We have Okie-phobia!" The president of the university felt compelled to say Osborne's job was not in jeopardy. Said Osborne: "I know of the grumbling that I can't win the big one and I can't beat Oklahoma, but football players win games. Regardless, I knew I'd better beat them pretty soon. And I also know that a bad year around here is 7-4, and if that happened there would be a lot of sentiment to get rid of me." The coach's first victory over Oklahoma came against one of the Sooners' best teams, 17-14 in 1978, when NU recovered a Billy Sims fumble at the Nebraska 3-yard line. Switzer said it was his most disappointing defeat, but he added that Nebraska would represent the Big Eight Conference well in the Orange Bowl. Nebraska had to swallow a bitter pill when the bowl picked NU's opponent – Oklahoma, which won the rematch 31-24. In between those two Oklahoma games came a 35-31 NU loss to Missouri, and criticism led Osborne to travel to Boulder to look into the Colorado head-coaching job. But he stayed at Nebraska, his best days ahead.

The Nebraska-Oklahoma rivalry had become so huge that Switzer lamented: "The guy who invented this game didn't mean for it to get this big." Osborne put it another way: "I do sometimes resent the fact a little bit that it almost becomes a one-game season." After a couple of close Sooner victories, Nebraska won three in a row, 1981 through '83. That was the era of the Husker trio that Switzer nicknamed "The Triplets" – Turner Gill, Irving Fryar and Mike Rozier. In the '83 game in Norman, fullback Mark Schellen put No. 1-ranked Nebraska ahead for good with a 17-yard touchdown run, and the victory was sealed when NU's Neil Harris broke up a pass in the end zone with 32 seconds to play. Oklahoma won the next four against Nebraska. This was the height of Sooner Magic, and OU won on a field goal with six seconds left in 1986. Osborne called the next year's game his most disappointing loss to date – No. 2 Oklahoma beat No. 1 Nebraska 17-7 in Lincoln. NU got revenge the following year in Norman, a 7-3 win that Osborne called the greatest defensive coaching job he had ever seen. The teams traded lopsided scores the next two years before Osborne ended his coaching career with seven wins in a row over Oklahoma, the last two by 73-21 and 69-7. He retired as head coach after going 60-3 his last five years, including national championships in 1994, 1995 and 1997.

Nebraska's Carl and Bo Pelini and longtime friend Bob Stoops of OU have matched wits in recent years, bringing mutual respect back to the rivalry.

Nebraska and Oklahoma had moved in 1996 from the Big Eight Conference to the Big 12, and that helped dilute the storied rivalry. Because they played in different divisions, the schedule meant that instead of playing annually, the Huskers and Sooners played each other for two years but not the next two. Oklahoma became Oklahoma again under coach Bob Stoops, splitting two games against NU coach Frank Solich. In 2001, the magic belonged to the Huskers – quarterback Eric Crouch, who would win the Heisman Trophy, handed off to a running back, who pitched to backup quarterback Mike Stuntz. The left-handed true freshman threw a pass true to its mark – Crouch, who had slipped out of the backfield, got behind OU defenders and scored on a 63-yarder in a 20-10 win. OU won all three games when Bill Callahan coached the Huskers, including the 2006 Big 12 championship game in Kansas City. Bo Pelini, a former Husker assistant coach who was spurned for the NU head coaching job that Callahan got in 2004, was hired as the Nebraska coach by the new athletic director – former coach and ex-congressman Tom Osborne, who returned to clean up a mess and a Husker downturn. Pelini's Huskers lost 62-28 to Oklahoma in 2008, but won 10-3 in 2009 behind a Blackshirt defense anchored by Ndamukong Suh, the Associated Press college football player of the year. After a one-point loss to Texas in the Big 12 title game and a 33-0 victory over Arizona in the Holiday Bowl, Pelini declared that Nebraska was back.

The Nebraska-Oklahoma rivalry was one of college football's classics. The teams may play each other again, but in future seasons not in conference games. Some day, though, gray-haired men from both teams might embrace, tell stories and raise toasts – to a noble rivalry known not just for a great Game of the Century, but for a century of great games.

BOOMER T.O.?

Barry Switzer introduced Tom Osborne at a 2007 event in Oklahoma City when the Nebraskan was made an honorary Oklahoman. T.O. revealed that while growing up in Hastings, Neb., he was a big Sooner fan. "I really wanted to go to Oklahoma," he said. "If Oklahoma had called, I'd have come here."

A VIEW TO A DRILL

A story was floating around the Big Eight in 1975 that a Sooner fan, apparently a friend of OU defensive coordinator Larry Lacewell, had spied on Nebraska's practices before the 1971 Game of the Century. Reports said the alleged spy, Lonnie Williams, claimed that he had camped out in a Memorial Stadium tower restroom overlooking the field. He said he got cramps in his hands, fingers and back from standing on a urinal so he could get up to a ledge to look out a window. When told of the reports, Nebraska's Bob Devaney said, "He probably smelled pretty bad. He should have come down and gotten comfortable. We had open practices at the time."

– Tom Ash

YESTERYEARS

» **1935:** Lloyd Cardwell (24) led Nebraska to a 19-0 victory in Lincoln in an October game matching the league's two best teams. The Cornhuskers' Big Six title was the first of three straight.

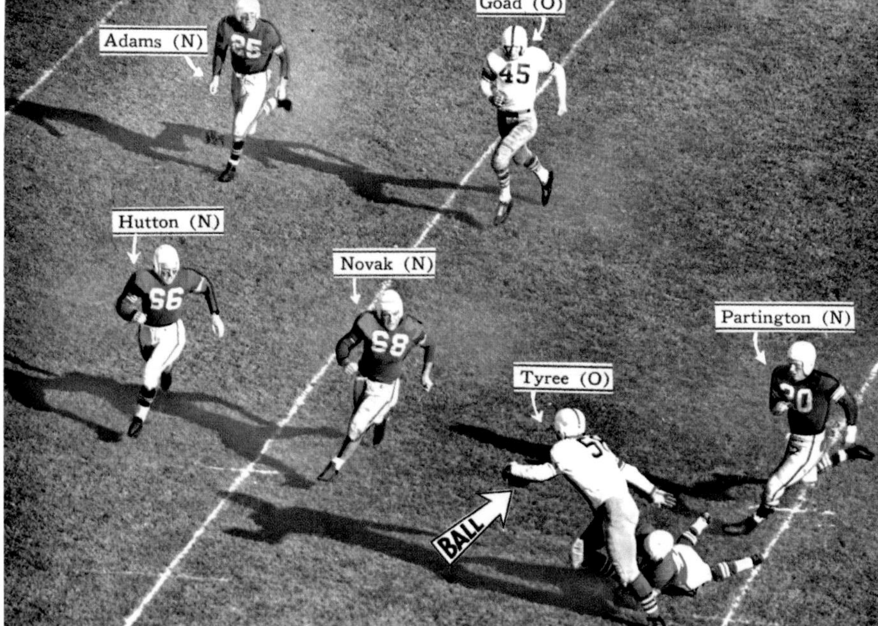

⌃ **1947:** Oklahoma beat the Huskers 14-13 in Lincoln in coach Bud Wilkinson's first season with the Sooners. His first team tied with Kansas for the Big Six title. His next 12 won outright league championships. Wilkinson's Sooners did not lose a conference game until 1959 against Nebraska.

« **1950:** An estimated 5,000 Nebraskans traveled to Norman for a season-ending game for the Big Seven championship. While the Sooners, the eventual national champions, won 49-35 for their 30th straight victory, NU fans were pleased with the effort. "Around five hundred fans – from tiny toddlers to grey-haired matrons – welcomed the Nebraska football team home Sunday afternoon," The World-Herald reported. "The crowd broke into 'There Is No Place Like Nebraska' as the Huskers alighted from their four-motored chartered plane at Municipal Airport." The game matched two star sophomore backs – Nebraska's Bobby Reynolds (12) and OU's Billy Vessels (lower left), who went on to win the Heisman Trophy in 1952. Each scored three touchdowns, and the game was so exciting that Bud Wilkinson and Nebraska coach Bill Glassford agreed to have the schools face each other in the final conference game again. The tradition of Nebraska facing Oklahoma in its final league game lasted until 1959, when the game was scheduled in late October.

1959: "Nebraska 25, Oklahoma 21! Yeeeeooooooooooowww! Multiply that exuberant yell 34,000 times and you have a sample of Cornhusker reaction to the sweet taste of victory," The World-Herald's Tom Allan wrote after the Cornhuskers handed OU its first defeat after 74 straight conference wins stretching back to 1947. Nebraska first went ahead on a blocked punt by Jim Moore (54) that was picked up by a teammate and run in for a score, then had to rally again in the second half for the win. Moore, Harry Tolly and Mick Tingelhoff (51) carried Bill Jennings off the field after the win, the biggest during the coach's time at Nebraska. Fans poured onto the field at Memorial Stadium and the goal posts came down, ending up that night on the lawn of the Governor's Mansion. "It couldn't happen to a finer bunch of guys," Harold Keith, OU's sports publicist, said after the game. The two schools had maintained good relations through periods when each school had made a habit of mauling the other. "While some other schools were growling that Bud Wilkinson poured it on, there was little complaining from the Cornhuskers," Gregg McBride wrote. "(And) Oklahomans didn't beef when Nebraska was winning by lopsided scores in the 1920s."

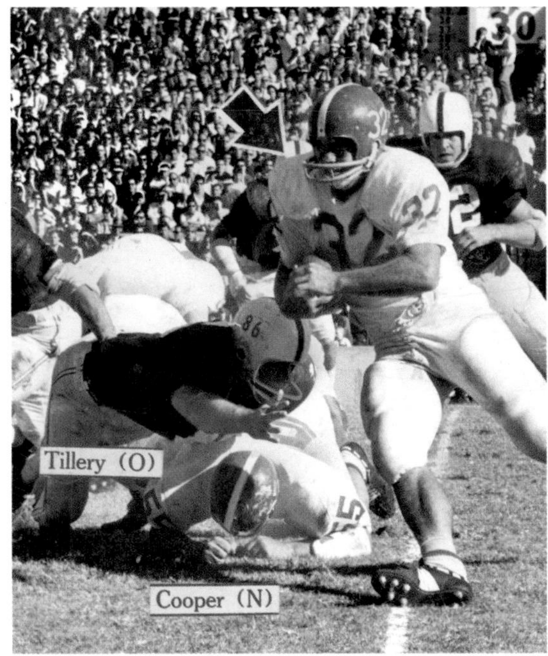

≈ **1960:** Fullback Noel Martin (32) helped the Huskers follow up their 1959 shocker with a 17-14 win in Norman. While this series has been known for its mutual respect, there have been moments of animosity. When Nebraska visited Norman in 1960, four policemen were assigned to the NU bench because of threats against NU coach Bill Jennings. Some Oklahomans believed Jennings had turned in the Sooners over a recruiting slush fund, leading to probation, but the NCAA later cleared his name. In spite of the tension, Jennings said Bud Wilkinson "was very generous" in his praise for NU when the two met on the field after the game. The game was noteworthy in that it was the last time that both teams finished in the bottom half of the conference standings. OU was fifth at 2-4-1, while Nebraska tied for sixth at 2-5.

« **1962:** Nebraska's magical first year under Bob Devaney came crashing down as the Sooners punctuated their return to the top of the conference with a 34-6 win in Norman. NU senior fullback Thunder Thornton promised his teammates in the locker room afterward, "OK, you guys, we missed our chance this year and I'm telling you this: You all are going to the Orange Bowl next year, and I mean it and wish you the best of luck." Thornton was accurate in assessing the program under Devaney. The Huskers won the Big Eight the following season and defeated Auburn in the Orange Bowl.

» **1961:** Oklahoma rallied for a 21-14 victory, helped by a controversial call on a fourth-quarter plunge by OU's Jimmy Carpenter. NU's Bill Jennings insisted that Carpenter had lost a yard on the play and that the official had placed the ball in the wrong place after cleaning it. The spot gave the Sooners a first down on the Husker 3, and they went on to score the winning touchdown. "The measurement should be from where the ball has come to rest and before it has been moved around," Jennings said.

THE DAY AFTER JFK DIED

BY DAN SULLIVAN |
WORLD-HERALD STAFF WRITER

Nebraska and Oklahoma brought unbeaten conference records into the 1963 game, and the anticipation for the game drove ticket prices as high as $40 for a $4 ticket.

Excitement built in Lincoln during the days ahead of the game. About 3,000 NU students made an impromptu march from campus to the Governor's Mansion on Thursday night and, discovering that Gov. Frank Morrison was gone, marched back again.

The next day, Nov. 22, President John F. Kennedy was assassinated in Dallas, and erroneous radio and television reports said that the Saturday game had been canceled.

The Nebraska Board of Regents held a special meeting that Friday, taking six hours to make the decision to play after consulting with the governor, a Big Eight official and the presidents of the eight conference schools.

"The Board of Regents of the University of Nebraska, deeply sorrowful of the death of President Kennedy, believe the people of Nebraska would have the Nebraska-Oklahoma game played as scheduled," a statement read.

Gov. Morrison later related that he had tried to convince OU coach Bud Wilkinson, the president's consultant on national fitness, that the game should be postponed. But Wilkinson, a friend of Kennedy's, thought the game should go on.

Morrison added that before he departed for the president's funeral in Washington, he had told NU coach Bob Devaney to show "what a group of really physically fit young men could do."

Flags flew at half-staff at Memorial Stadium that Saturday, and a moment of silence was observed after the national anthem was played. Military jets flew over the stadium just after the start of the game, which Nebraska won 29-20.

« ˄ **1963:** Nebraska scored twice after OU fumbles to win 29-20, claim its first conference championship since 1940 and earn a trip to the Orange Bowl. Fans at Memorial Stadium pelted the field with oranges as NU went up by 29-7 in the fourth quarter. The north goal post came down with 42 seconds still left on the clock, injuring a student, and the south goal post followed after the game ended as fans stormed the field. The Nebraska band left the stadium as the mayhem subsided and led a parade through downtown Lincoln, where the crowd was reported to be "orderly but high spirited."

˅ **1964:** Although Nebraska already had the conference title wrapped up when it visited Norman, the Sooners' 17-7 victory ruined hopes for an undefeated season. NU led 7-3 at halftime after a 56-yard touchdown reception by Freeman White (85), but OU went ahead with 6:16 to play and added another touchdown 3 minutes later. When it was suggested that Nebraska might have been looking ahead to its Cotton Bowl game, Nebraska quarterback Bob Churchich responded, "Cotton Bowl? Oklahoma is the game we really wanted."

» **1965:** Coach Bob Devaney and the Huskers celebrated a 21-9 victory that wrapped up the Huskers' first unbeaten regular season since 1915. The Sooners, who had provided NU's only regular-season loss in 1930 and 1964, led early, but a 29-yard touchdown by "Choo Choo" Charlie Winters narrowed the gap to 9-7 before halftime. Harry Wilson scored twice in the third quarter, and the Blackshirts shut down OU the rest of the way. The game had been changed to Thanksgiving Day in order to get national TV coverage, making it the first Big Eight game to be televised nationally. Conference schools had played teams outside the league in national TV games before, but never against each other.

⌃ **1966:** OU's victory came before anyone had heard of "Sooner Magic" but provided the recipe followed in later games. "An orphan with a turkey drumstick couldn't have had more fun on Thanksgiving Day than Oklahoma's Sooners, who kicked Nebraska's perfect football record into limbo, 10-9, with a 21-yard field goal in the final minute," The World-Herald's Wally Provost wrote. It was reported that "Bob Devaney accepted an engraved Sugar Bowl invitation in the Cornhusker dressing room . . . as though it were an invitation to his own funeral." The despair was shared by defensive lineman Carel Stith (72) and fullback Dick Davis (45).

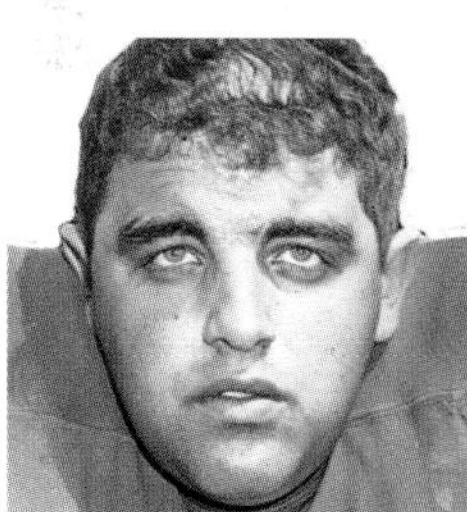

⌃ » **1967:** Underdog Nebraska put up a tough fight in losing 21-14 to fifth-ranked OU. Husker quarterback Frank Patrick (10) ran for one touchdown and threw for 290 yards and another score, but the Sooners once again went ahead in the fourth quarter and held on. "The thing that hurt us most was they made the most of their third-down plays," said NU linebacker Barry Alvarez (right).

1968: OU bullied a Nebraska team that failed to receive a bowl bid for the second straight year. Bruising tailback Steve Owens scored five touchdowns for the Sooners, who led 28-0 at halftime and won 47-0 in Norman. Nebraska halfback Joe Orduna (31), reminded afterward that he had predicted an unbeaten season for the Huskers, said, "If I wasn't optimistic, I shouldn't play." Asked if the whipping had hurt his outlook heading into the next year, the Omaha Central grad responded, "Oh, no, I'm used to it. I lost 22 games like this in high school."

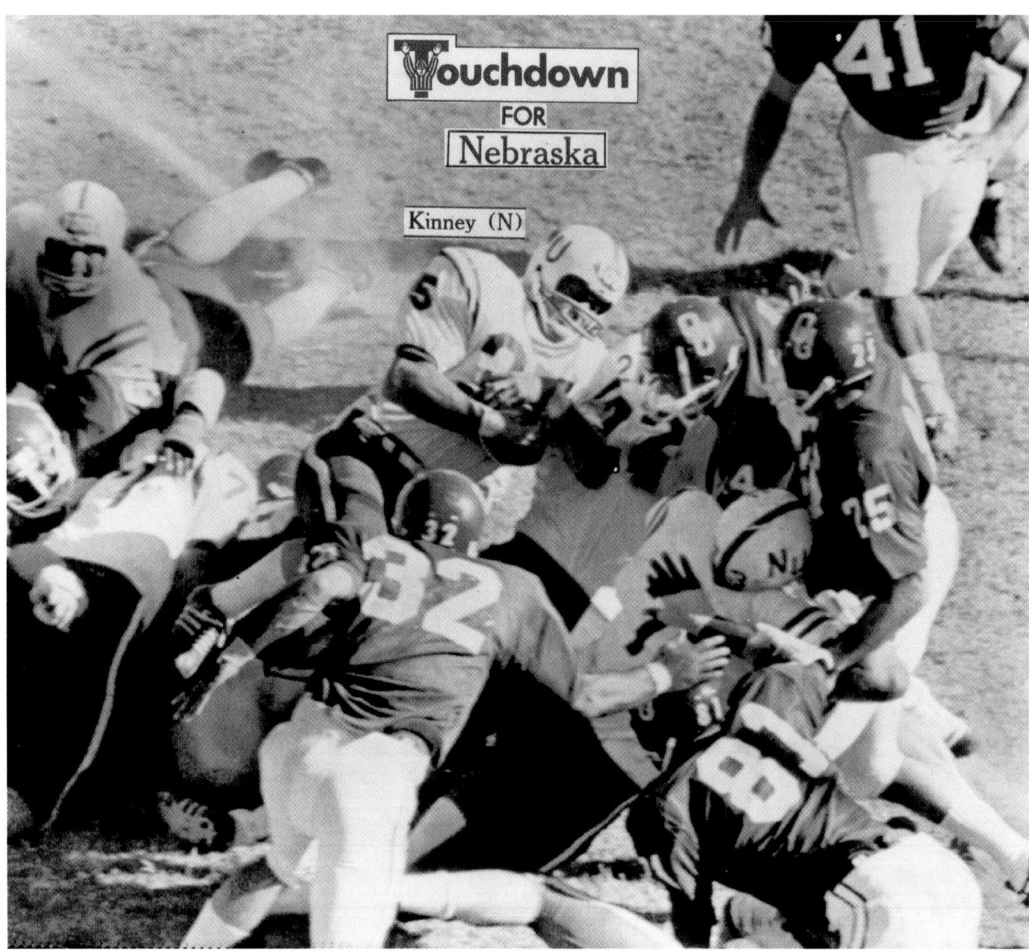

1969: Oklahoma scored first, then watched NU run off 37 straight points in a 44-14 rout that wrapped up a share of the conference crown with Missouri. Sophomore running back Jeff Kinney (35), recruited as a quarterback, led the Huskers with three touchdowns and 127 yards rushing and another TD passing. OU's All-American Steve Owens was held without a touchdown for the first time in 16 games and without at least 100 yards rushing for the first time in 19 games. "You couldn't tell the Heisman Trophy candidates without a program," The World-Herald's Wally Provost wrote. Owens, who was named the Heisman winner in December, was gracious in defeat. "When they put in their second team, one guy kidded me with 'Hey, you are not getting (100 yards) today.' I told him big deal. It's not that important."

⌃ 1970: WRAPPING UP AN UNDEFEATED SEASON

NU wrapped up a 10-0-1 regular season for its first outright Big Eight championship in four years, twice coming from behind to grab a heart-stopping 28-21 win in Lincoln. Nebraska finally went ahead for good with 7 minutes left, but the Sooners refused to quit. A pass from Jack Mildren to Greg Pruitt carried Oklahoma to the NU 27 in the closing seconds, but defensive back Jim Anderson intercepted a pass in the end zone as time expired to preserve the victory. "I'm very proud of our players for the way they kept their poise and fought back throughout the game," coach Bob Devaney said. "Those are the real lessons of football – you never give up in life or anything else, no matter how tough the odds." The undefeated team presented Devaney and his staff with the game ball in the locker room, then tossed the coaches into the showers.

1971: LASTING MEMORIES OF THE GAME OF THE CENTURY

THE BUILDUP

BY DAN SULLIVAN | WORLD-HERALD STAFF WRITER

The 1971 Nebraska-Oklahoma matchup had all of the ingredients needed to generate interest not just in Big Eight territory, but across the nation:

• Both teams came in unbeaten, with NU ranked first and OU second.

• Nebraska, the defending national champion, hadn't lost in 29 games, while Oklahoma's only loss in its last 15 had been to Nebraska.

• Both teams not only were winning, they were destroying their opponents. Colorado, which ended up ranked third in the country, lost by 24 to Nebraska and by 28 to Oklahoma.

• Nebraska entered the game with the nation's No. 1 defense, while Oklahoma boasted the nation's top offense.

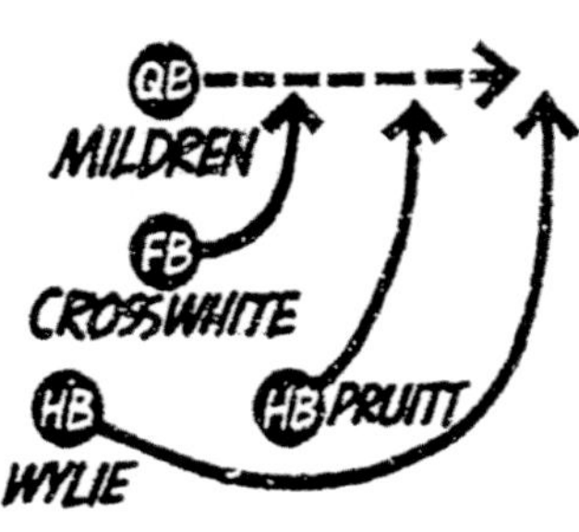

• Oklahoma featured the new triple-option wishbone offense in which the ball could end up in the hands of any one of four backs, who one writer described as "Oklahoma's answer to the Olympic track team." The World-Herald carried a diagram showing how the wishbone worked, and former Sooner coach Bud Wilkinson demonstrated it on the ABC pre-game coverage.

• Nebraska countered with a defense with a name that carried its own national reputation: the Blackshirts.

• Sports Illustrated immortalized the game before it had been played with its cover, "Irresistible Oklahoma Meets Immovable Nebraska."

• There was no shortage of personalities, such as Oklahoma running back Greg Pruitt, whose T-shirt read "Hello" on the front and "Goodbye" on the back. Pruitt had told Oklahoma's 1969 Heisman winner, bruising runner Steve Owens, "You'd play second string here now if you couldn't get more than four yards a run."

• In addition to Pruitt, who averaged 9.49 yards per carry, there was plenty of other star power, especially Nebraska wingback Johnny Rodgers, who had caught 10 touchdown passes coming into the game and was the most dangerous kick returner in the country.

• You can't have a big game without great quarterbacks, and this one had two: NU's Jerry Tagge was the nation's pass-efficiency leader and on pace to set a Big Eight record for total offense. OU's Jack Mildren, the master technician of the wishbone, had run for nearly 1,000 yards.

• Some of the individual matchups alone were worth the price of admission. On the line, for example, Husker middle guard Rich Glover, the 1972 Outland Trophy winner, was to butt heads with OU All-American center Tom Brahaney.

• A total of 97 writers from 65 newspapers, two magazines and two wire services received press credentials for the game. "I hope everyone sends their skinniest guys," said OU sports information director Johnny Keith, fearful that they wouldn't all fit in OU's press box.

• The game was scheduled for Thanksgiving Day, guaranteeing that it would be watched by huge numbers of viewers who were home for the holiday. ABC estimated that 55 million people watched the game, and the 13.6 million sets tuned to the game beat the previous record for a college football game set by Notre Dame and USC in 1970.

• Even President Nixon got into the excitement, proclaiming it the "game of the decade – or century" in a letter to coach Bob Devaney. "I am hoping that I may be able to see the game," Nixon added, "hopefully in person but certainly on television." The president wasn't able to make it to Norman, however. Nixon, a big sports fan, had been in Lincoln in January (at right) to present the 1970 national championship plaque to Devaney and co-captains Dan Schneiss and Jerry Murtaugh.

• Talk was tough from both sides ahead of the game. "If anyone should be favored, we should," Devaney said. "We're the No. 1 team." There also was no shortage of confidence on the other sideline. Asked if the Huskers would be able to stop the wishbone, Mildren gave a simple "no."

• Everybody likes a teacher-pupil story line: Devaney, as an assistant at Michigan State, had coached Sooner coach Chuck Fairbanks.

• Both teams had the previous weekend off ahead of the Thursday game, allowing for 12 straight days of attention.

• Reports said tickets, which sold for $6, were going as high as $100. To put that in perspective, that markup would mean an $85 ticket to the 2010 Nebraska-Texas game would have cost more than $1,400.

• The primitive computers of the day got into the act, with one in Oklahoma predicting a Sooner win, countered by a Union Pacific machine in Omaha that favored the Huskers.

• Both teams lay claim to the title "Big Red." A billboard on Interstate 35 in Oklahoma proclaimed to Nebraskans coming to the game, "There's only one Big Red in the Big Eight – Boomer Sooner."

After all of that, many wondered how the game could live up to the buildup. Previous games of this stature, Notre Dame-Army in 1946 (0-0) and Notre Dame-Michigan State in 1966 (10-10), had ended in ties.

But the 1971 Nebraska-Oklahoma game not only lived up to the hype, it surpassed it.

THE KICKOFF

By the time the game was ready to start, traffic lights were unnecessary at the intersection of 72nd and Dodge Streets in Omaha.

1971: LASTING MEMORIES OF THE GAME OF THE CENTURY

THE PUNT RETURN

Johnny Rodgers (20) gave the Huskers a 7-0 lead just a little more than 3 minutes into the game, with his 72-yard punt return. While the entire run was spectacular, three moments stand out. First, after fielding the ball under pressure, he had to elude OU's offensive star, Greg Pruitt (30), before ducking out of a crowd and heading upfield. At about the NU 35, he dipped a shoulder and changed direction, a move that left an official scrambling to get out of the way. And finally, teammate Joe Blahak (27) provided the block on OU's Jon Harrison (12) that got Rodgers into the end zone. Harrison claimed he was clipped on the play. Blahak disagreed and said in 2010 that he regretted missing a "Game of the Century" reunion two years earlier in Norman. "I wanted to go and find Jon Harrison," Blahak said. "And have him admit that was not a clip."

1 2 3

7 8 9

4

5

6

10

11

12

1971: LASTING MEMORIES OF THE GAME OF THE CENTURY

THE MAN IN THE MIDDLE

Nebraska middle guard Rich Glover crouched, facing Tom Brahaney, Oklahoma's All-America center, in a pose for television cameras before the kickoff. Brahaney smiled, but Glover did not. "I had my game face on," Glover (above) said later. "I said to myself, 'He just doesn't know what he's in for today.'" Glover had 22 tackles as Nebraska held the nation's leading running team to its lowest production of the season.

THE PASSING SOONERS

In spite of all the attention given to the Sooners' wishbone, it was quarterback Jack Mildren's passing that burned the Huskers. He completed only six passes, but they went for 188 yards and two touchdowns, both to Jon Harrison. NU's Bill Kosch (above), a safety forced to line up at cornerback because of a defensive adjustment, was burned twice by Harrison. Husker coaches weren't ready to let Kosch take the blame for the scores, however. "You're still the best safety man in the Big Eight Conference," assistant coach Monte Kiffin told him afterward.

THE DRIVE

Oklahoma went ahead 31-28 in the fourth quarter on Jon Harrison's second touchdown reception. "Nebraska then took the kickoff and embarked on a championship drive that should be accorded space in football anthologies for many decades to come," The World-Herald's Wally Provost wrote. Starting from the NU 26 with just 7:05 to play, quarterback Jerry Tagge directed the Huskers down the field through a light rain under darkening skies of the late November afternoon. The ball repeatedly went to halfback Jeff Kinney, with Tagge also hitting a key third-down pass to a diving Johnny Rodgers to keep the drive alive.

1971: LASTING MEMORIES OF THE GAME OF THE CENTURY

THE DECISION

Nebraska assistant Mike Corgan (above) had kicker Rich Sanger on his feet and ready for a field-goal attempt as the Huskers drove into Oklahoma territory late in the game and trailing by 3 points. "We want to go for the win," coach Bob Devaney (top) told Corgan after seeing Sanger on the sideline, and the matter was settled. However, another Corgan idea was a winner: the "tear-away" jerseys worn by Nebraska's main ball carriers. The NU assistant had noticed that earlier opponents had been slowing Tagge by pulling on his shirt and decided to put in an order before the OU game. "It's a real cheap shirt that they put some chemical on," Corgan explained.

THE WARRIOR

For all the excitement that the game provided, Nebraska running back Jeff Kinney (35) was the "show-stealer," The World-Herald's Wally Provost wrote. "Kinney does have outstanding talent, but most of all he had old-fashioned Husker dedication." The senior from McCook finished with 171 yards rushing and four touchdowns, including the game-winner with 1:38 left on the clock.

» 1972: SAD ENDING FOR DEVANEY

In his swan song in the Big Eight, future Hall of Fame coach Bob Devaney and his Cornhuskers took a 14-0 lead in the third quarter against OU in 1972, only to fade in a 17-14 loss, thanks largely to four lost fumbles and three Dave Humm interceptions.

Oklahoma coach Chuck Fairbanks, who was on the losing side in the previous year's Game of the Century and was also leaving after the season, said, "If Bob Devaney had been playing anybody else, I wish he would have won his last Big Eight game."

It was also Devaney's final game before Nebraska fans at Memorial Stadium.

– Tom Ash

1973: Nebraska didn't cross midfield in a 27-0 shellacking in Norman. The Sooners, who were on probation and ineligible for a bowl game, held the Huskers to just 174 yards of total offense behind a dominating defensive line anchored by Big Eight defensive player of the year Lucious Selmon. "How can they beat you if they can't score?" crowed OU coach Barry Switzer after his first matchup with Tom Osborne.

» 1974: OUT OF THE LIMELIGHT

The annual Big Red showdowns were played in relative obscurity in 1974 and 1975 – both OU victories sparked by quarterback Steve Davis (5) – because OU was on probation and ineligible for television coverage or bowl games. The sanctions were the result of a 1972 case in which Oklahoma recruit Kerry Jackson's high school transcript was altered. Nebraska and the other Big Eight schools were also penalized to the tune of $200,000 each in lost TV revenue. Still, Oklahoma received its customary one-eighth share of TV and bowl income from conference members in good standing.

Nebraska Athletic Director Bob Devaney voted to give OU its full share. "It was a pretty general feeling that Oklahoma got nailed pretty good. We decided that Oklahoma had been penalized enough," he said. But he had second thoughts later. "I believe I would vote for (cutting off the Sooners) if I had it to do over, or if it ever comes up again," he said.

There was talk in 1974 about Oklahoma possibly leaving the Big Eight and going it alone, like Notre Dame, but Devaney scoffed: "Oklahoma couldn't draw flies to play if it left the conference."

– Tom Ash

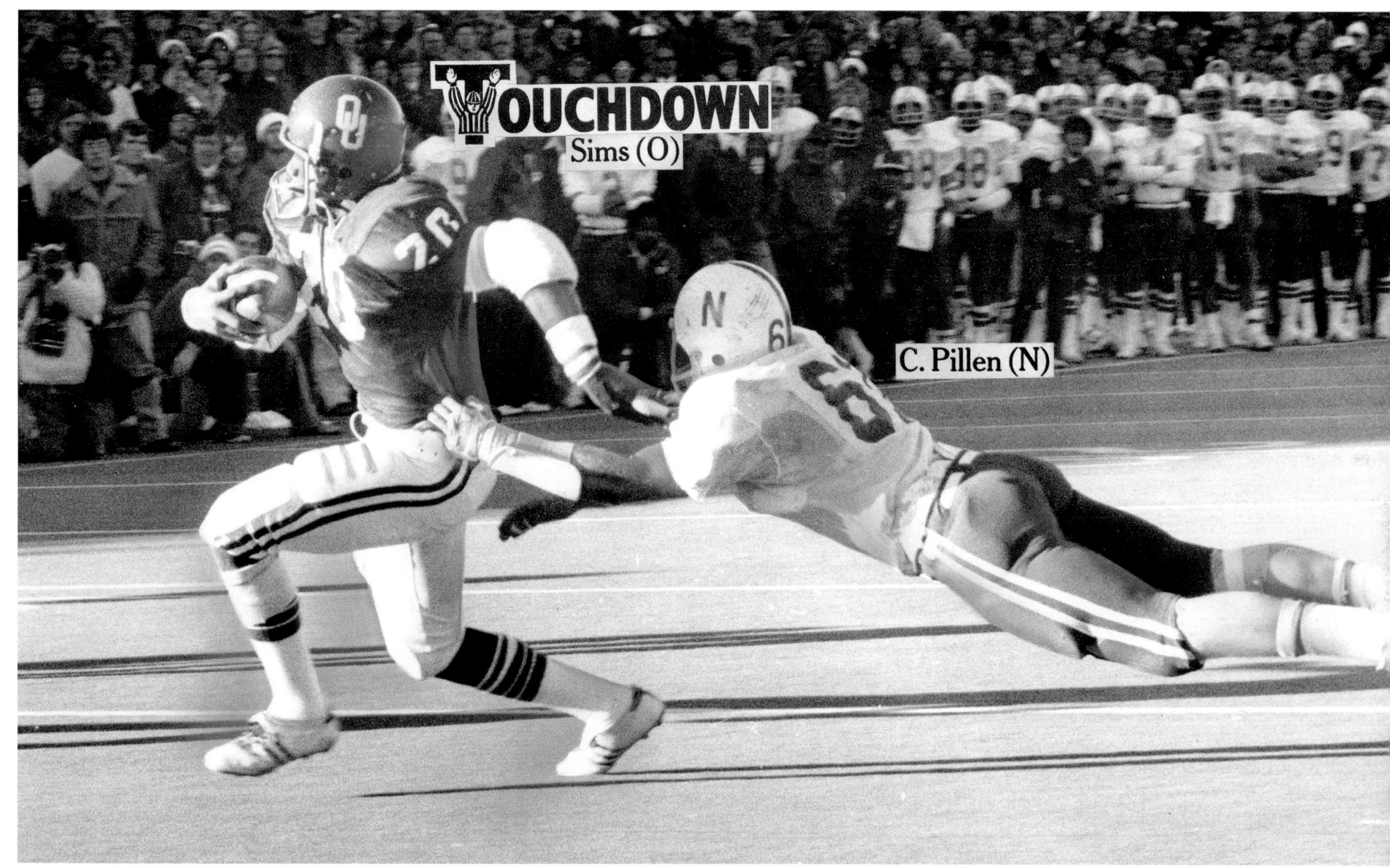

1975: Nebraska led 10-7 in the third quarter, but the Sooners came out on top again, 35-10, by cashing in on six Husker turnovers. Coach Barry Switzer gave an honest assessment of his team's victory: "We were awfully lucky! If Nebraska hadn't made some of those mistakes, we would have had a hard time winning." The Sooners, who wrapped up an Orange Bowl bid with the win, got a late touchdown from heralded freshman running back Billy Sims (20).

⮝ » 1976: OU FORCED TO THROW . . . OH!

Iowa State coach Earle Bruce was in the Nebraska press box for the 1976 Oklahoma game, cheering on the Huskers as they tried to protect a four-point lead in the final minutes.

A Nebraska victory would be Osborne's first over Switzer, and the Huskers would head for the Orange Bowl while the Cyclones would make it to Houston and the Astro Bluebonnet Bowl.

Said Bruce: "If Oklahoma has to throw, I'm going home because I know we've got it won."

The Sooners had attempted just two passes in their previous two games, both incomplete. But in their final drive, OU reserve halfback Woodie Shepard took a pitchout and heaved a 47-yard completion to Steve Rhodes. Then reserve quarterback Dean Blevins hit Rhodes again, this time on a hook pattern. As he was about to be hit, Rhodes pitched to Elvis Peacock, who fled 32 yards to the NU 2. Peacock scored on the next play to pull out the 20-17 shocker, and the Sooners had a wild celebration on the field at Memorial Stadium.

Nebraska wound up in the Astro-Bluebonnet Bowl, while ISU stayed home.

– Tom Ash

FOX

THE GETTYSBURG ADDRESS II

BY LARRY PORTER

Tom Osborne was only four seasons into what would become a College Football Hall of Fame coaching career, and already the dogs were nipping at his heels.

It was the week of the Oklahoma game. Nebraska had lost to Iowa State 37-28 in the previous game, but that loss was not on the minds of many fans. They were focused on Osborne's 0-3 record against Barry Switzer's Sooners.

"I have heard people say that we – specifically me – have not been able to win the big ones," Osborne said prior to the 1976 clash with OU. "Personally, I feel every game is a big one. Lose to Kansas State and I guarantee it soon becomes a big game."

Osborne said the idea the average fan has of motivating a team is the locker room scene at halftime in which actor Pat O'Brien, portraying Knute Rockne, implores Notre Dame to "win one for the Gipper."

That, Osborne said, is nonsense. "You don't turn on motivation the day of the game," Osborne said. "It builds all week. Our preparation for Oklahoma began 10 days ago. If oratory would do it, there would be a heck of a lot more winning coaches."

A case in point, Osborne said, was the recent loss to Iowa State.

"The worst chewing out I've ever given a team came at halftime of that game," he said. "And the second half was probably the worst this team has ever played. There is no correlation whatsoever between fire-and-brimstone speeches and winning."

A fuming D.B. "Woody" Varner appeared at the Extra Point Club luncheon following Nebraska's 20-17 loss to Oklahoma.

Smoke was coming from the ears of the university president, who had heard ABC sports commentator David Diles say that Nebraska fans were up in arms following the loss to the Sooners and that a coaching change might be made.

But in a short speech directed at Diles and others who might demand a coaching change, Varner gave his full support to Osborne.

"On behalf of the Board of Regents," Varner said, "I would like to say that David Diles does not hire and fire University of Nebraska football coaches."

Varner said his appearance at the luncheon "was to quell the Monday morning quarterbacks and fair-weather fans. We're going to hear a lot of people saying things have gone to hell and some changes must be made.

"But," Varner continued, "I don't know of a coaching staff I would be willing to trade for anywhere in the United States."

Osborne was grinning when he took over the podium following Varner. "That was one of the finest talks I've ever heard," Osborne said. "That ranks right up there with the Gettysburg Address. But I must confess I was a little worried when I saw him (Varner) walk in."

Two weeks later, the regents gave Osborne a three-year extension of his contract and hiked his yearly salary from $30,918 to $34,000.

« 1977: SOONERS "GOING TO THE BEACH"

The Nebraska-Oklahoma series departed from its usual nail-biter ways in 1977 when the Sooners, a 9-point favorite at home, scored three second-quarter touchdowns en route to a 38-7 breeze. Oklahoma went back to the Orange Bowl as Big Eight champs, while Nebraska settled for the Liberty Bowl in Memphis.

Switzer chortled afterward, "We're going to the beach; we're not going to the river."

OU defensive coordinator Larry Lacewell mentioned the criticism of Osborne and his coaching staff after they lost their first five games against the Sooners.

"Frankly, I'd like to see them get rid of that whole bunch up there, but putting pressure on them is the most unfair thing I've ever seen," Lacewell said. "Nebraska, Oklahoma, Michigan and Ohio State have been the most consistent winners in the country the last few years.

"Nebraska has the best coaches in the league. We've had the best athletes, and we've been so lucky against Nebraska you wouldn't believe it."

Among the "best athletes" was quarterback Thomas Lott (6), who ran for 143 yards and a touchdown.

– Tom Ash

SUPPORT FOR NU MOVE

Long before Nebraska left the Big 12 Conference to move to the Big Ten, there were reports that the Big Ten was wooing the Huskers. Rumors floated around in 1977 that Northwestern was thinking about pulling out of the Big Ten, and a couple of University of Nebraska regents said they had received phone calls from an unnamed Big Ten source inquiring if Nebraska would be interested. Longtime NU regent and former Cornhusker player Ed Schwartzkopf said he "hadn't heard any rumors of Big Ten overtures since 1938, '39 and '40." Switzer opined: "I wish Northwestern would get out, and Nebraska would get in."

– Tom Ash

1978: A TURNING POINT FOR NEBRASKA FOOTBALL

BY TOM ASH

The 1978 Nebraska-Oklahoma game in Lincoln set off an improbable chain of events that may have been the most pivotal in Nebraska football history. Those events included Tom Osborne's finally slapping that 0-5 Sooner monkey off his back, a crushing downer the next week against Missouri, a courtship, renewed vows and a do-over in the Orange Bowl.

The term "Sooner Magic" germinated in the first five years of the Osborne-Barry Switzer crusades, with Switzer's boys doing all the pillaging. Osborne's fortunes didn't appear to be much brighter when Switzer brought what he considered to be his best team to Memorial Stadium that November Saturday in front of ABC's national TV cameras.

The Sooners were unbeaten and ranked No. 1. Nebraska was 9-1, with only an opening loss to Alabama, and ranked No. 4. Said OU quarterback Thomas Lott from under his bandana: "The only thing that can stop us is us."

But Oklahoma had delivered an omen in its previous game while fumbling eight times and losing five in a win over Colorado.

Another omen appeared in a telegram on the Husker locker room message board. The challenge from former Husker firebrand Tony Davis, then with the Cincinnati Bengals, read: "You're here once in a lifetime. It's a nasty game for nasty boys. Kick their ass!"

The Nebraska nasties pulled it off, 17-14, when OU fumbled nine times and lost six. It would have been 10 and seven if the officials had seen what 76,000 in the stands and a national TV audience had witnessed. Husker John Ruud drilled Sooner kickoff returner Kelly Phelps after Nebraska had taken the lead with 11:51 remaining, and NU recovered at the Sooner 11. The officials ruled there was no fumble.

No Sooner Magic this time, however. Heisman Trophy winner Billy Sims (20) was tooling along on his way to another Husker heartbreak when Jeff Hansen (48) ended his 17-yard journey with a thud, and Jim Pillen recovered OU fumble No. 9 three yards from another Husker devastation.

The final 3½ minutes ran off, all that pent-up Husker emotion was unleashed and the Memorial Stadium goal posts finally came down, costing the university $6,000.

Quarterback Tom Sorley (12) and his teammates got a ride from the fans who swarmed the field.

The celebration lasted until the following Saturday, when Missouri strode onto the same Memorial Stadium turf and sobered the Husker faithful by knocking NU out of the national championship game with Penn State. Instead, Osborne was informed in the somber NU locker room that he'd get to play Oklahoma again in the Orange Bowl.

Orange Bowl President Robin White said, "The Nebraska-Oklahoma game was the greatest game played this year, and we think Nebraska will get up for another classic in the rematch." But Osborne knew that beating Switzer's best team twice would be a tall order.

The Huskers got up enough for a valiant effort, but they could not overcome a 31-10 deficit in the rerun, falling a touchdown short.

At least they still had their coach.

A disheartened Osborne was wondering during the depression following the Missouri game if that was the best he could do. Could he do better elsewhere? Colorado had just fired Bill Mallory, and Osborne sent out a feeler. Colorado Athletic Director Eddie Crowder called and invited Tom and Nancy to come out for a visit.

Osborne said later that he was "pretty close" to taking the offer to coach near good trout streams. He didn't think he was getting the statewide support he needed, particularly from Omaha business leadership, as evidenced by cancellation of his TV show by an Omaha station because of a lack of advertisers. "A couple of things like that bother me. Oklahoma's coaches have about 50 airplanes at their disposal, and we have two."

Colorado offered "more money, a little more security and not as much pressure." But he was not convinced that he could win more games in Boulder and, bottom line, his heart was in Nebraska.

And so he stayed. The Nebraska Board of Regents rewarded Osborne by raising his salary from the bottom of the Big Eight to the top and gave him the title of assistant athletic director.

» 1978: EVERYBODY SAW WHAT HAPPENED, EXCEPT . . .

John Ruud (46) might have unleashed Nebraska's most celebrated special-teams tackle. Nebraska had just moved into the lead on a 24-yard field goal by Billy Todd (14) with 11:51 remaining. The Sooners' Kelly Phelps (7) fielded the ensuing kickoff near the west sideline, took a couple of steps and was nearly belted out of his shoes by Ruud's violent tackle. "I went down there, he came across and I hit him with everything I had," Ruud said.

The ball skipped loose, NU's Dan Lindstrom pounced on it and the Memorial Stadium crowd of 76,015 went delirious with the prospect of the Huskers setting up shop on the Sooner 11-yard line.

But that joy turned to boos when an official wiped out the fumble and placed the ball at the 19. "No one could believe it," Ruud said. "But an official told me (Phelps) stepped out of bounds when he caught the ball. I think now he wishes he had stayed out of bounds."

– Larry Porter

GIRDLE WEATHER

The temperature at game time was a chilly 35 degrees, but I-back Rick Berns (35) was fully prepared right from the kickoff. The delirious Huskers celebrated in their locker room for a full 30 minutes following their 17-14 victory over OU that ended a six-game losing skid against the Sooners.

A patient Berns waited for the bedlam to die down, then he waited some more until most of his happy teammates had showered, dressed and left. "Don't laugh," Berns said, glancing furtively around the nearly empty locker room. Berns tugged at his football pants. They dropped to the floor and revealed the fact that Berns was wearing a girdle.

"I wore one when I was a sophomore," Berns said, breaking into a shy grin. "My muscles have been tight lately, and since it was a cold day I put it on again."

The girdle, along with an overpowering Husker offensive line, put some snap into Berns' ground game. ABC's offensive player of the game scored the first touchdown from 5 yards out and finished with 113 yards on 25 carries, most of which were aimed at the heart of the Sooner defense.

– Larry Porter

THE SOONER WAX MUSEUM

Johnny Keith, Oklahoma's sports information director, was invited to say a few words at the Extra Point Club luncheon – a weekly gathering of Nebraska fans – prior to the game. Keith described the Sooner coaches as they viewed film of NU's 63-21 victory over Kansas, during which the Huskers gained 799 yards of total offense. "I know y'all are familiar with a wax museum," Keith said. "Those figures look just like real people, except the complexion is a little paler. That was the way the OU coaching staff looked after seeing the films of the Kansas game."

– Larry Porter

≈ 1979: REMATCH IN THE ORANGE BOWL

Nebraska's frantic attempt to rally fell short in a 31-24 loss. Coach Tom Osborne said the game's key play was when a tired OU defense stopped Craig Johnson in the fourth quarter on a fourth-and-one from the Sooner 6. "If we scored that time, we knew we had a chance to get the ball back and score again," Husker quarterback Tom Sorley said. Nebraska's David Clark (63) recovered Oklahoma's only lost fumble in the rematch of two teams that had played only about a month before.

≈ 1979: FUTURE CONGRESSMEN SQUARE OFF

Nebraska entered the 1979 Oklahoma game unbeaten, while OU was 9-1. As had become custom, the Big Eight championship and Orange Bowl were on the line in Norman, and the nation was tuned in on ABC-TV. "The guy who invented this game didn't mean for it to get this big," Barry Switzer said.

The Sooners coach was worried because he did not have his best team, and his Heisman Trophy-winning halfback, Billy Sims, was off his 1978 pace. He also was missing quarterback Thomas Lott, who had embodied the Sooner swagger and nonconformity with one of his 80 bandanas flying out the back of his helmet as he turned the corner.

The departed Lott was replaced by Julius Caesar Watts, who went by J.C. and was not as fleet as Lott, averaging about a yard-and-a-half less per carry. But Watts did not lack spunk. After he had been booed by Sooner fans earlier in the year, he had replied: "Those people who boo know as much about football as a pig knows about Mother's Day."

Nebraska led the nation in rushing offense and defense, but Tom Osborne was concerned about the Husker passing game. Turned out he should have been more concerned about the rushing offense and defense. The Huskers were consistently denied on third-and-short and resorted to introducing the "Fumblerooosky" to the nation. First, guard John Havekost picked up an intentional fumble on the center-quarterback exchange and trucked 11 yards for a first down. Then guard Randy Schleusener did it again for a 15-yard touchdown.

Sims returned to Heisman form by averaging 8.8 yards on 28 carries against the No. 1 defense, and OU won for the eighth time in nine years, 17-14.

Watts would go on to become a U.S. congressman from Oklahoma and serve alongside Rep. Tom Osborne of Nebraska.

– Tom Ash

^ 1980: SOONER MAGIC, OR "A SPELL"?

Although NU owned a 390-275 advantage in total yards, a 43-yard run by freshman Buster Rhymes fueled an OU drive that produced the winning touchdown with 3:16 remaining. "It seems like somebody put a spell on us," Husker cornerback Andy Means said after the 21-17 loss – the ninth in the past 10 games against the Sooners. "Maybe we're not supposed to beat Oklahoma. It's unbelievable."

"I've got a feeling they feel something big is going to happen, and it does," agreed Oklahoma offensive lineman Louis Oubre (66). NU finished with a 10-2 record after defeating Mississippi State 31-17 in the Sun Bowl.

The Huskers' other loss was also by four points against Florida State. Linebacker coach John Melton mentioned the loss to the Seminoles in the fourth game of the season, then shook his head and muttered: "Eight points cost the best coach in the nation the national championship."

– Larry Porter

IT'S NOT POLITE TO POINT

Nebraska I-back Jarvis Redwine got the Huskers off to a good start in 1980 with an 89-yard run on a first-quarter sweep. But some of the celebration was muted when he was flagged for unsportsmanlike conduct for turning and pointing at pursuing Sooner defender Ken Sitton. Redwine's day didn't get any better after the game. The Sooners said in the locker room that coach Barry Switzer had fired them up by reading a newspaper clipping quoting the Huskers' star runner. "Nebraska players talked a lot before the game and Redwine said in that clipping earlier this season he didn't feel we were in Nebraska's class and were in the class with Iowa State and Kansas State," said defensive tackle Richard Turner. "We feel we are in a class by ourselves."

1981: FINDING REDEMPTION IN NORMAN

BY STEVE SINCLAIR

Mark Mauer's senior season as a Nebraska quarterback started with jeers and ended with cheers. Mauer received the brunt of criticism from fans after the Huskers opened the 1981 season with a 10-7 loss to Iowa in his first career start. He heard barbs from hecklers as he walked off the field at Iowa City, and several fans called him at his home the next day to express their displeasure at his performance, which included a pass interception and a drive-killing fumble in the fourth quarter.

Nate Mason started the next two games before Mauer made his second start against Auburn. The Huskers struggled in that game and heard boos as they left the field trailing 3-0 at halftime.

Turner Gill replaced Mauer against the Tigers and took over as the starter against Colorado the next week. The sophomore directed the Huskers to six straight wins before a leg injury against Iowa State ended his season. So Mauer returned as the starter for the season's biggest game, on the road at Oklahoma. Mauer (17) performed like a champion in a 37-14 win, completing 11 of 16 passes for 148 yards and a touchdown. Mauer, a co-captain who spent most of his final season on the bench, said he had no regrets about his career. "I've been nothing but grateful for the experience," he said. "There are things that I'll treasure."

Nebraska coach Tom Osborne got a victory ride on the shoulders of his players after the game. "I'm not a very flamboyant guy," said Osborne, whose teams had been frustrated by beating the Sooners only once in his first eight seasons as coach. "But I'm pleased that our players thought enough of me to do that."

The victory was NU's first in Norman since the Huskers won the Game of the Century in 1971. "Everybody is really happy," Osborne said. "We have taken so much guff over this game."

A WIN WORTH CELEBRATING

A crowd estimated at 2,000 jammed into the Lincoln airport in November 1981 to welcome Nebraska's football team after it had brought a decade of frustration to an end.

"We should beat Oklahoma more often," defensive captain Jimmy Williams said as he took in the cheering fans.

Tom Carlstrom, an offensive guard from Polk, Neb., looked around in amazement at the turnout.

"There are more people here than in the town of Polk," Carlstrom said. "I never thought anything like this would happen."

Dr. Pat Clare, the Huskers' team physician, was squeezed into a corner as the players snaked their way through the crowd.

"This is one of the biggest (welcoming crowds) I've seen," said Clare, a former Cornhusker running back and team captain. "It's the biggest in the last 10 years. It's quite a response. It's just as flamboyant now as it was quiet after the Iowa game (a 10-7 loss to open the season)."

– Larry Porter

"OUR KIND OF PLAYERS"

Oklahoma coach Barry Switzer liked Nebraska's Mike Rozier and Roger Craig (21) as a 1-2 punch at I-back. "I think they are better I-backs than they've ever had," Switzer said. "I was a Rick Berns fan because he reminded me so much of Steve Owens (OU's Heisman Trophy winner in 1969). He was a north-south slasher. Those two guys they've got now are our kind of players." Rozier rushed for 105 yards on 24 carries and Craig gained 102 on 18 carries in the Huskers' 1981 victory.

In 1982, Rozier was walking with the aid of a cane on the Monday before the Oklahoma game because of a sprained ankle. He started the game against the Sooners, but didn't play in the second half after gaining 96 yards. Craig, who switched to fullback in 1982 so the Huskers could get both backs on the field at the same time, rushed for 56 yards and a touchdown in his final game against the Sooners.

– Steve Sinclair

HUMILITY VS. HYPERBOLE

BY STEVE SINCLAIR

Part of the intrigue of Nebraska's rivalry with Oklahoma was the coaching matchup between Tom Osborne and Barry Switzer. Osborne said he and Switzer performed their jobs with different personalities. "He's more flamboyant than I am," Osborne said. "He's more outgoing. That's not to say I'm not outgoing at times.

"He's more apt to say this guy is dynamite. This guy is E.T., or he's from outer space. I don't very often say that. The reason I don't do that is that I don't want to get a guy out on a limb too far, too fast. The next year, he may have problems."

Osborne and Switzer said they liked each other and got along fine.

"Tom is a super gentleman," Switzer said. "He's a little different than most coaches. He's got a Ph.D. That qualifies him to be a helluva lot smarter than the rest of us."

After the Sooners got off to a slow start in 1982, the Daily Oklahoman newspaper wrote an editorial that suggested it might be time for Switzer to move on. Osborne responded by writing Switzer a letter of support.

"I just thought it was a real commentary on the instability of the coaching profession," Osborne said. "Here was a guy who had won as many games as he did, and all of a sudden, they were calling for his resignation. It just seemed like it was a little premature."

Switzer said he appreciated Osborne's letter. "Tom's been very supportive," Switzer said. "And I don't understand why anyone would think we're not friends. I have a great deal of respect for Tom and his program."

BARRY'S 'JAB'

The differences in the two coaches' personalities showed in Osborne's objections to some of Switzer's comments about heralded running back Marcus Dupree (22).

Dupree was the nation's most highly recruited football player after his senior season of high school at Philadelphia, Miss., in 1981. Switzer changed offenses from the wishbone to the I-formation to take advantage of Dupree's talent after the Sooners started the 1982 season with a 1-2 record.

"He loves to jab at us," Osborne said. "He said it's a good thing he (Dupree) is at Oklahoma because if he was at Nebraska he wouldn't play. He said they won't play freshmen at Nebraska. I suspect if Marcus

Dupree was up here, we'd find a place for him to play somewhere," Osborne said.

The Husker coach described Switzer's comment as a psychological ploy. "He's a great one for trying to get an edge," Osborne said, "one-upmanship and that kind of thing."

The Blackshirts got to face the magic of Dupree just one time before the hyped Oklahoma running back's career flamed out.

By the time Oklahoma played Nebraska that November, the freshman Dupree had gained 756 yards despite playing little in Oklahoma's first three games, and the Sooners had won seven straight to get in position to play Nebraska for the Big Eight championship and an Orange Bowl berth.

"There are four great running backs in college football," Switzer said before the game in Lincoln. "They are Herschel Walker, Dickerson, Rozier and Marcus." SMU's Eric Dickerson was a senior. Georgia's Walker and Nebraska's Rozier were juniors.

Dupree didn't disappoint against the Huskers. His 86-yard touchdown – the longest run in the conference that season – on the third play of the second half cut Nebraska's lead to 21-17. Nebraska escaped with a 28-24 win, but Dupree finished with 149 yards on 25 carries.

After running for a Fiesta Bowl record of 239 yards against Arizona State, Dupree figured to be a contender for the Heisman Trophy as a sophomore.

But he was slowed by injuries to start the 1983 season and disappeared for a week after suffering a concussion against Texas. When he resurfaced, he announced his plans to transfer to Southern Mississippi but never played there. Injuries kept him from doing much as a pro in the United States Football League and the National Football League.

Despite Switzer's earlier "jab," Osborne was critical of a Sports Illustrated story after Dupree had left about the troubles between Switzer and the running back. Osborne said that he wouldn't return any phone calls to the Sports Illustrated writer and that he would tear up any messages he had to call the writer.

SHIFT IN TALENT

Whether a player was "E.T." or not, Osborne and Switzer shared an eye for talent. Switzer said that during the years Oklahoma dominated Nebraska – winning eight of 10 games from 1972 until 1981 – the Sooners had the better players. Nebraska started to close the talent gap in the late 1970s, he said, and the Huskers took the lead in talent in the early '80s. "I really marvel at the people they have playing for them on their offensive football team," Switzer said after the series had turned the Huskers' way.

One reason for the shift was that Switzer had failed to wrap up Turner Gill (12) in a recruiting battle with Nebraska in February 1980. When asked how close he came to deciding on Oklahoma, Gill snapped his fingers to indicate how he nearly became a Sooner. "It was real close," Gill said.

Nebraska's recruiting win for Gill turned out to be huge, as the Texan led the Huskers to three straight Big Eight Conference championships. He joined I-back Mike Rozier and wingback Irving Fryar to form one of the most explosive backfield combinations in the history of college football. Switzer gave Gill, Rozier and Fryar their nickname: The Triplets.

RIMINGTON 'THE BEST'

When talking about the Huskers' playmakers, the Oklahoma coach didn't overlook the big man in the trenches – Husker center Dave Rimington. "Rimington is the best center that's been in college football," said Switzer, who played center, guard and linebacker for Arkansas in the late 1950s. "He's the best center I've seen since Arkansas of '59."

Rimington ended his career as a two-time consensus All-American, the only player to win the Outland Trophy back to back, NU's second Lombardi Trophy winner and the fifth-place finisher in the Heisman Trophy voting as a senior.

Rozier went on to win the Heisman Trophy and became the first pick in the USFL draft. Fryar became the first pick in the NFL draft. Switzer said the wingback Fryar could have been the best tight end in the Big Eight because of his speed, size and blocking ability.

He also admired Rozier's toughness. "Rozier is a tank," Switzer said. "He bites you in the face when he's going down."

But Switzer said Gill was the player that made the Huskers go.

"As good as Rozier is, and as good as Fryar is – they're the best in the country – the guy is Turner Gill," Switzer said before the 1983 NU-OU game. "You've got to win over him."

Typically, Osborne had a more simple take on Gill in 1981: "Turner's a good football player."

« ⌃ 1982: ANOTHER TRICK PLAY

Nebraska added the Bounceroosky to its collection of memorable trick plays in the 28-24 win.

In the playbook, it was called Bounce Pass Left. In Husker legend, it became known as the Bounceroosky to go along with two other famous trick plays of the past – the Bummeroosky and the Fumbleroosky.

Coach Tom Osborne called for the Bounceroosky after Oklahoma had taken a 10-7 lead in the second quarter. The play started with quarterback Turner Gill throwing a long lateral pass to wingback Irving Fryar (27) that one-hopped off the AstroTurf. Fryar then threw a pass to tight end Mitch Krenk, who made a one-handed grab on the 37-yard play to the Sooners' 14. Two plays later, fullback Doug Wilkening (34) scored on a 3-yard run to give NU the lead.

"It's just something we put in for the game," Osborne said. "It's a little deceptive because when the ball hits the ground, people tend to relax."

– Steve Sinclair

BLACKSHIRTS SHINE . . .

Defensive coordinator Charlie McBride was proud of his unit after it turned back an Oklahoma threat late in the game. "Maybe these kids know they are worth something now," he said. "They hung together all year on character when people criticized them. We kept telling them if they would stay together no matter what, they were going to come out on top." Safety Bret Clark (10) listened. "Our defense is so close-knit," he said. "We just had the feeling they weren't going to score." Cornerback Dave Burke (33) didn't start, but ended up with 12 tackles against the Sooners.

AND SO DO THE LIGHTS

The 1982 Oklahoma game was the first to be played under lights at Memorial Stadium. Portable lights were turned on as the November sky darkened for the afternoon game, and the stadium's electronic scoreboard read "first night game ever." The portable light system consisted of truck-mounted hydraulic cranes that extended to 150 feet.

A SOUR VICTORY FOR OSBORNE

Nebraska coach Tom Osborne was furious with fans who celebrated excessively during NU's 28-24 victory over Oklahoma in 1982. Husker fans, in anticipation of a trip to the Orange Bowl, rained oranges onto the field after Nebraska's first touchdown in the first quarter. They later celebrated NU's remaining touchdowns by throwing more oranges. A security officer was injured during the game when he was struck in the back of the neck by a frozen orange.

Hundreds of fans swarmed the field after Scott Strasburger's interception with 26 seconds left clinched the victory. NU received a 15-yard penalty for unsportsmanlike conduct. The field was cleared so the game could be ended. Then fans swarmed the field again after the final play and tore down the goal posts.

Oklahoma coach Barry Switzer was knocked down during the postgame celebration.

Osborne, who apologized to the OU coaches after the game, said he was upset by the mob scene and the throwing of oranges. Osborne said orange throwing "is one of the most idiotic customs I've ever seen. And then to run out there on the field and get us penalized."

Strasburger hugged a football as he made his way through the mass of humanity that rushed onto the field. "I'm taking it home," said Strasburger, a sophomore walk-on from Holdrege who hadn't played much in the 1982 season. He did against the Sooners as a third defensive end who was stationed as a linebacker in a special defense put in for the game.

"Oh, thank goodness that young man decided not to go to Dartmouth," said George Darlington, NU defensive ends coach, during the wild celebration in the locker room that followed the Husker win.

Strasburger declined a scholarship offer to Dartmouth to walk on at Nebraska and fulfill a childhood dream of playing for the Cornhuskers. "I made that play in front of 76,000 fans," said Strasburger, now a team physician for the Huskers. "At Dartmouth, it would have been in front of 6,000. I'm glad I'm here."

– Steve Sinclair

SOONERS
80
SKOAL

» 1983: IN THE PENTHOUSE

Nebraska cornerback Neil Harris (11) ended his junior season of ups and downs with the highlight of his career.

The Huskers' perfect regular season was on the line. Nebraska led 28-21, but the Sooners were driving with time running out and the rain falling in Norman. They got deep into Husker territory when Danny Bradley completed a 27-yard pass to Derrick Shepard over Harris.

With OU facing fourth-and-nine on the Husker 10, Harris batted away a Bradley pass intended for Buster Rhymes (4) in the corner of the end zone with 32 seconds left. The play wrapped up a third straight undisputed Big Eight Conference championship and NU's first unbeaten and untied regular season since the 1971 national championship team.

Harris, who had been bothered by a hamstring injury, lost his starting job to Todd Fisher two weeks before the OU game. He had struggled in pass coverage against Kansas State and Iowa State.

"One minute you're in the outhouse, and the next minute you're in the penthouse," said Bob Thornton, NU secondary coach. "Neil Harris just put us in the penthouse."

– Steve Sinclair

« **1984: PROUD IN DEFEAT**

Nebraska coach Tom Osborne told his players that he admired the way they played in their 17-7 loss – a defeat that ended NU's 27-game Big Eight Conference winning streak.

The fourth-ranked Sooners upset the No. 1 Huskers with 10 points in the fourth quarter and a defensive effort that stopped NU twice inside the OU 10 in the second half, including the game's biggest play when I-back Jeff Smith came up three inches short of the goal line on a fourth-down run with 5:32 remaining.

"I think that was about as much effort and contact as I've been around in a long time," Osborne said. "I told the players I was very proud of them."

Nebraska and Oklahoma shared the Big Eight title. The Huskers ended the game with a big edge in statistics – 19 first downs to nine and 373 total yards to 201 – but the Huskers had four costly turnovers.

– Steve Sinclair

» 1985: NO MAGIC NECESSARY

Oklahoma tight end Keith Jackson made his first big splash against Nebraska in OU's 27-7 blowout victory. Less than four minutes into the game between the second-ranked Huskers and the third-ranked Sooners, quarterback Jamelle Holieway (4) optioned left but handed to Jackson on a reverse that he took 88 yards for a touchdown.

"I think I should be nominated for the Heisman now," Jackson said after his impressive performance. Jackson led the Sooners in rushing with 136 yards on three carries – all reverses – and made Oklahoma's only pass reception of the game with a 38-yarder on third-and-4 that set up Holieway for the Sooners' second touchdown.

Defensive tackle Chris Spachman allowed Nebraska to avoid its first shutout in 147 games when he picked up a fumble and returned it 76 yards for a touchdown with only 26 seconds remaining. Nebraska had not been shut out since 1973 when Oklahoma beat NU 27-0.

"I felt like crying," said Oklahoma All-America middle guard Tony Casillas, who watched Spachman's play on the sidelines. "When I saw the guy running down the field, I was in shock. I felt like tackling him."

Casillas had gotten to experience Nebraska hospitality off the field in the summer of 1985 before his senior season when he was invited to North Platte to participate in the community's Nebraskaland Days celebration. "It was really exciting," Casillas said. "When I got off the plane and walked into the little terminal in North Platte, all of these people were packed in there and they started playing music. It was really a great welcome.

"When I think of Nebraska, I think of a bunch of people with a lot of hospitality. Of course, playing Nebraska in a football game is a different story."

– Steve Sinclair

HANGIN' WITH THE BOZ

BY STEVE SINCLAIR

The Boz's final prediction in the Nebraska-Oklahoma series didn't come true, but he did come out a winner in the three games he played against the Huskers. Brian Bosworth (44), Oklahoma linebacker and college football's Mr. Outrageous, predicted that the Sooners would shut out the Huskers in 1986, his final game against NU. But Oklahoma needed last-minute heroics to pull out the victory.

Nebraska linebackers Marc Munford and Kevin Parsons said before the game that they admired Bosworth's play on the football field but not certain aspects of his public personality.

"He's a great player," Munford said. "He's got all the tools and great linebacker instincts. When we've watched film while preparing for other teams, he sticks out. You can't miss him."

Bosworth's antics on and off the field were also hard to miss.

"Generally people who have a lot to say about themselves don't think very much of themselves," Parsons said. "I wouldn't say Brian Bosworth shouldn't do the things he does, because that's his business.

"But that's not my style. And I don't think it's right to handle the game or your private life in that way either."

Oklahoma coach Barry Switzer described Bosworth as an actor.

"It's as simple as that," Switzer said. "Football is just his stage. It doesn't matter to me how a kid wears his hair or if he wears an earring or any of that stuff. It's all hype and cosmetics. All that matters is attitude."

Bosworth made his debut against the Huskers with 19 tackles in the Sooners' 17-7 win in 1984. In the fourth quarter, he made the first tackle in a goal line stand that ended with NU three inches from the end zone.

Bosworth said before the 1985 game – a 27-7 OU win – that he had great respect for the Huskers.

"Tom Osborne, the way he keeps putting the players out there, year in and year out," Bosworth said, "with the kind of caliber he's got, it's unbelievable."

Bosworth said he views Nebraska differently than teams like Texas and Oklahoma State.

"It's more respect toward Nebraska," he said. "I respect their program. I respect what they do. They don't show me anything that would aggravate me. I see that in Texas. I see that in Oklahoma State. You can look at somebody, and you just don't like it. I like Nebraska. I like Tom Osborne."

1986: SOONER AIR RAID

BY STEVEN PIVOVAR

Brian Davis was a pretty fair defensive back at Nebraska, a second-team all-conference pick who went on to play eight seasons in the National Football League. But Davis was no match for Oklahoma tight end Keith Jackson (88) when the pair found themselves lined up opposite each other on the key play of the Sooners' 1986 showdown with the Huskers.

With a Big Eight title and a trip to the Orange Bowl on the line, Nebraska led 17-10 when Oklahoma took over on its 6-yard line with four minutes to play. Sophomore quarterback Jamelle Holieway, who had thrown just 54 passes in the first 10 games, completed three on the gut-check drive that produced the tying points.

The last was a 17-yarder to Jackson on a play in which just about everyone at Memorial Stadium, Davis included, knew the ball was going to Jackson. Why? Because the tight end had yelled at Holieway moments before the center snap to throw him the football.

Split wide on the play, Jackson blew past Davis, then outwrestled the Husker for the football in the end zone.

"I was supposed to lob the ball to Keith," Holieway said after the game, "but if I'd have thrown a lob, they had a guy coming over who would have had a chance to knock the ball down. So I threw the ball behind Keith, on a line, and he came up with a nice catch.

"He's amazing. I'm glad Keith is on my side."

The touchdown tied the game with 1:22 to play. Jackson, though, wasn't through. After Oklahoma's defense held on downs, Oklahoma got the ball back at its 35-yard line with 50 seconds to play.

Four plays later, Holieway tossed a ball just over the fingertips of Nebraska defensive end Broderick Thomas (89) to Jackson for a 41-yard play that ended when Jackson was knocked out of bounds at the Nebraska 14. Moments later, Tim Lashar came on to kick a 31-yard field goal that sent Oklahoma to Miami with a 20-17 win.

Holieway completed six passes in the game, four in the final two crucial drives.

"We know Jamelle can throw the ball," Jackson said amid the celebration in the Sooner locker room. "Nebraska didn't. Nebraska prepared all week to stop our running game, and they did a great job. But everyone knows Oklahoma doesn't throw the football."

Jackson paused, then let out a hearty last laugh.

"Well, they think Oklahoma can't throw the ball," he said. "The one thing Nebraska didn't prepare for was the pass, and it ended up beating them."

Iceman

1987: GAME OF THE CENTURY II

BY STEVE SINCLAIR

Nebraska didn't match up physically with Oklahoma in the 1987 game billed as Game of the Century II. The Huskers won the first Game of the Century 35-31 in the 1971 showdown of unbeaten No. 1- and No. 2-ranked teams – a game remembered as one of the greatest ever. The unbeaten Huskers and Sooners ranked No. 1 and No. 2 again in 1987, but the game didn't reach epic status as OU dominated for a 17-7 win.

"I'm not in any way making excuses," Nebraska coach Tom Osborne said. "We flat got knocked around."

Oklahoma beat Nebraska several times in the 1970s and 1980s with Sooner Magic, what seemed like miracle comebacks. Sooner Magic became the name of the ability OU had for pulling out those wins.

"Talk about Sooner Magic," Oklahoma coach Barry Switzer said after the '87 win. "We didn't need it today. We dominated from start to finish. This was a dominating win."

Oklahoma, ranked No. 1 all season, had fallen to No. 2 behind Nebraska the week before the game after playing poorly in wins over Oklahoma State, 29-10, and Missouri, 17-13.

The Sooners had lost star quarterback Jamelle Holieway, an All-Big Eight selection the previous two seasons, and fullback Lydell Carr to injuries. Even Switzer was on the injured list for the game after he tore a knee ligament when a player rolled into him on the sideline in the Missouri game.

A 25-yard run by Keith Jones (6) gave the Huskers an early lead, but redshirt freshman quarterback Charles Thompson filled in impressively for Holieway, directing the Sooners to 444 yards in total offense. OU rushed for 419 yards against an NU defense that ranked No. 2 nationally against the run, allowing only 68 yards per game. Nebraska had talked a big game before playing Oklahoma.

"The flat-out truth is Oklahoma can't play with us," said Husker quarterback Steve Taylor (9). "They're not good enough. Let me tell you, it might not even be close, and I mean that." Taylor's comment was reproduced on 8-by-10 paper and taped on all the doors in the OU locker area.

The Sooners also took note of boastful comments during the season by defensive end Broderick Thomas, who came up with some memorable phrases: The 1987 Hell-Raisin' Tour. Bring the wood. The Sand Man. Our house.

Oklahoma's Keith Jackson said he admired Thomas for his athletic ability, but he objected to one thing. "I think he has a big mouth," Jackson said. "I think he's a great athlete, though. He's quick-footed. He's big. He's strong. He's a great defensive end. But I think he talks too much. I don't think you should brag about all you're going to do before you get on the football field."

While the Huskers had to eat their words after the loss, they did so in a classy manner. "I'd like to wish Oklahoma a whole lot of luck in Miami," Thomas said.

Oklahoma went to Miami for the Orange Bowl. In another battle of unbeaten teams ranked No. 1 and No. 2, the University of Miami beat OU 20-14 to win the national championship.

Osborne said he didn't discourage the Huskers' bold talk before the Oklahoma game. "I felt sometimes in the past that they had lacked confidence for this game," Osborne said. "Since they seemed to be confident, I didn't want to pour cold water on it. So we'll take our lumps on that deal, I'm sure."

SOONERS
40
SOONERS
98

» 1988: HOLIEWAY CAN'T BACK IT UP

Sooner quarterback Jamelle Holieway had said during the Big Eight Skywriters tour that Nebraska wouldn't beat the Sooners, because the Huskers choked in big games.

"There's no way Nebraska can beat us," the OU senior said. "Let me tell you why. It's just Nebraska. It seems like they choke during the fourth quarter. It seems like they just choke during big games, when it's time to play somebody big." Holieway, recognizing the interest of the Big Eight Skywriters in his statement, added, "You guys are just eating this up."

The Sooner quarterback didn't have the opportunity to back up his words, however, since he was injured for the game in Norman in November, won 7-3 by Nebraska.

The Huskers scored on their first possession on a 1-yard run by quarterback Steve Taylor (9) and then turned the game over to the defense.

The Blackshirts, using a defensive wrinkle installed in August but saved until the OU game, limited the 438-yards-a-game Sooner wishbone to 137 total yards.

But Oklahoma still hung around in the driving rain and 30 mph north wind until just 50 seconds remained, when NU linemen Willie Griffin (84) and Lawrence Pete crunched OU quarterback Charles Thompson (6) on a fourth-down play, breaking both bones in Thompson's lower right leg.

"Jamelle has been making these quotes about us choking," said NU's Broderick Thomas, who had been silenced after the previous year's loss. "We just made sure we were going to play the fourth quarter the best we've played."

Nebraska's seniors had gone 1-3 against Oklahoma, but Thomas said they got even.

"OK, they won three games, but I think getting the last laugh was most important. Us seniors are going out in class. There's nothing they can say about it. They lost 'Their House.' We took their keys, and we're headed back to Lincoln." The victory gave 11-1 Nebraska its first outright Big Eight championship since 1983.

THOMPSON

PUZZLE PIECES THAT FIT TOGETHER

BY TOM ASH

They lined up side by side in the Big Eight Conference starting blocks. They would remain inextricably joined at the hip for the next 16 years.

One was a sprinter, the other built for the long haul. Both had interned for their head coaching jobs as good and loyal assistants, both were in their mid-30s, and both were eager that football season of 1973 when they became head coaches. There, the similarities mostly ended.

Tom Osborne was the ultimate Boy Scout. Didn't drink, smoke or cuss, kissed his mother good night and said his prayers. He would go the distance. Barry Switzer was the likable waif who tried it all, with a flair. He threw the spitballs from the back of the room and got marched to the principal's office. He burned rubber out of the blocks and waved back with a mischievous grin. Then he flamed out.

Switzer was a guard for a big school (Arkansas). Osborne was a quarterback for a small school (Hastings College).

Switzer was animated on the sideline. Osborne was stoic.

Switzer operated more as a CEO, delegating the details to his assistants. Osborne was hands-on, personally directing the intricacies of the offense.

Switzer never met a camera or microphone he didn't like. Osborne shied from the spotlight and found his solace in a darkened film room.

Switzer had a knack for luring difference-makers, as he called them, to his Oklahoma program. Osborne had the edge in X's and O's, with less talent at Nebraska.

Osborne lamented the fact that Switzer had "about 50 airplanes" at his disposal for recruiting while "we had two." But Switzer actually enjoyed schmoozing with the big oil boosters – his "Oilies," as he called them – who owned the planes, while Osborne reluctantly participated in the required social gatherings, with one eye on the exit.

Switzer eagerly courted the sportswriters who would publicize his program. Osborne merely tolerated them.

Switzer was a brash quote machine, as in: The Cornhuskers were "those impostors from the north, masquerading as the Big Red."

After a stunning upset by Arkansas in the Orange Bowl after the 1977 season, he said, "I guess you have to expect criticism when you get embarrassed every 58 games or so."

The key to one of his star running back's success, he said, was, "He's just faster than the guys chasing him."

On the academic problems of one of his players, he said, "It was like a heart transplant; we tried to implant college in him, but his head rejected it."

Osborne's quotes were typically analytical and often reflected his personal standards, such as:

- "I just think it's the right thing to do."
- "Alcohol abuse is the leading cause of death on college campuses."
- "The fans used to think Oklahoma was the enemy, but they actually made us better."

As he did with everything else, however, the introspective Osborne worked hard to improve his public utterances, and as he became more comfortable in the spotlight, his natural dry wit emerged. Like the time he endured the daily post-practice press routine with, "You'll have to forgive me. That wasn't too sharp a rundown, but this doesn't look like too sharp a group."

Osborne said his coaching philosophy was "to make an effort to win in a manner that reflects well on the university, that promotes personal development and has a positive effect on young people."

Switzer's philosophy: Win, and go party.

Switzer lived in a high-end house in Norman with a pool and a red Cadillac in the driveway. He said of his chosen lifestyle, "Why shouldn't I? You've got to take advantage of the benefits while you can in this business."

Osborne lived in a more modest three-bedroom home near Lincoln's Taylor Park that Nancy Osborne called "comfortable." He drove a Ford.

Both coaches raised three children, and both were, by all accounts, good fathers. Both also had younger brothers, Switzer's Donnie and Osborne's Jack.

After 18 football seasons together, Kay Switzer left Barry, although they remained good friends. Switzer later remarried. In his book, "Bootlegger's Boy," Switzer said, "I was too selfish and self-centered. When I became successful, many temptations entered my path."

Nancy Osborne's easy-going good humor was a perfect foil for Osborne's intensity and driven nature. They have been married 48 years at last count.

The upbringing of both of these legendary Big Eight rivals defined their personalities and character, and both bore emotional scars. Switzer's were much uglier.

He came home from the hospital as an infant to a houseboat in the swamp bottoms around Crossett, Ark., near the Louisiana border, as told in "Bootlegger's Boy." Soon, the Switzers upgraded to a shotgun house, built on stump logs, with no electricity or running water.

His father, Frank, ran the toll bridge over the Ouachita River until he figured out he could make a better living as a bootlegger of homemade whiskey and lending money to area blacks at high interest rates. He also enjoyed too much of his own product and was an incurable womanizer. He wouldn't let his boys go to the local Baptist church because it was full of pious hypocrites, Switzer said.

Frank was in and out of the family home and in and out of the local jailhouse before winding up in the state penitentiary when the state liquor authorities collared him.

His mother also turned to alcohol as the solution to her misery, Switzer said, and her struggles came to a tragic conclusion that would haunt him for the rest of his life. He was home from college the night she stumbled down to his room and asked for a good-night kiss. Switzer, as had brother Donnie, refused because he was repulsed by her condition.

She went upstairs and shot herself to death.

Years later, a psychologist told Switzer that he had come from a "totally dysfunctional environment," and it was a wonder he turned out as well as he did.

Osborne, meanwhile, was not without his own issues.

He didn't really know his father, Charles, until he was 10 years old because his father was off in the Army during World War II, and the youngster resented his dad's absence. The void was partially filled by his grandfather, for whom Tom was named, and his uncle Virgil, Osborne said in his book, "More Than Winning."

Grandpa Osborne was a cow puncher, a Presbyterian minister and a state senator. Tom admired him more from what he was told than what he remembered. His grandfather died when he was 5. Virgil took over and nurtured in his young ward a love for hunting and fishing.

When Charles Osborne returned from the war, he earned a living as a salesman and then managed an auto dealership when he wasn't immersing his boys in sports. Tom spent most of his remaining growing-up years trying to please his long-absent father. The Methodist church was an important element in his early development, but he didn't fully commit until he was in college.

But Osborne's adult demeanor was shaped as much as anything by an incident when he was 14 and playing Junior Legion baseball with players two and three years older. The talented youngster was gregarious and talkative. Too much so for some of his older teammates.

One of them tagged him with the nickname "Yak," and it stuck. Chastened, young Tom clammed up.

In "More Than Winning," Osborne said his quietness "served me well as an athlete." He became The World-Herald's athlete of the year as a senior at Hastings High. "The emotions, and sometimes hostilities,

I had pent up inside of me gave me tremendous drive and incentive to play well," he said.

But, he added, "At the same time, I developed some unhealthy emotional patterns in not really talking about my feelings, expressing neither joy nor anger." Thus, the stoicism on the sideline in later years.

The self-described "semi-loner" would spend the rest of his coaching career working on how NOT to suppress his emotions. Switzer, meanwhile, was working in the opposite direction.

Osborne and Switzer, the Big Eight's odd couple, started their celebrated race in that 1973 Nebraska-Oklahoma debut.

Switzer got off first and widened the lead to 5-0 before Osborne got out of the blocks with an upset over perhaps Switzer's best team in 1978. Switzer won the rematch in the Orange Bowl and eventually made it eight out of the first nine before Osborne hit his stride.

"Our people were not happy," Osborne recalled years later. "I knew at some point we were going to win. It was a little unfair, but that's the reality. To some degree, it became a one-game season for some folks."

The catch-up started with Nebraska's recruiting class of 1980. The roster contained an unusually high number of "keepers" that included quarterback Turner Gill, I-back Mike Rozier and wingback Irving Fryar. Switzer called them "The Triplets." Sportswriters referred to their exploits as the "Scoring Explosion."

Osborne, who had been flummoxed for years by the Sooner wishbone offense, swiped a page from Switzer's playbook and installed wishbone principles in a new option game to take advantage of his trio's speed and running skills. The Triplets went 3-0 against OU as Osborne closed the gap.

Switzer, however, answered with three more wins before Osborne closed their head-to-head dueling with a 7-3 victory in 1988. They were dead even at 4-4 over the final eight years, but Switzer held a 12-5 overall advantage in their historic matchups.

It ended for Switzer as it had begun, with his school under the NCAA microscope, ultimately leading to probation. Switzer had been an assistant to Chuck Fairbanks during a 1972 investigation over the alteration of Kerry Jackson's transcripts, but the penalty fell on his watch.

Switzer was forced to resign after the '88 season when five of his players were arrested on suspicion of felonies. Three were accused of rape (one was acquitted), one shot and wounded a teammate in a dorm, and quarterback Charles Thompson was imprisoned for selling cocaine to undercover FBI agents. Switzer left the proud Sooner program's reputation in shambles and heading for another sanction.

Without his old nemesis in the next lane, Osborne sailed into the 1990s, matched Switzer's three national championships and finished in a near-dead heat in winning percentage before he closed his career on his own terms after 25 years. Osborne's record over the final five years was a national record 60-3. He never won fewer than nine games in 25 seasons.

Their final career winning pace: Switzer .837; Osborne .836.

Voters in the National Football Foundation could not wait to induct Osborne into the College Football Hall of Fame. They waived the customary three-year waiting period and inducted him in December 1998.

Meanwhile, Switzer waited years for his work to be so recognized, paying the price for a reputation as a renegade among many of his peers. He had refused to attend the annual coaches conventions for years because, he said, he felt ostracized by his fellow coaches.

In 2002, his judges apparently felt that he had done enough penance, and he was finally admitted into the Hall of Fame for his record on the field.

Four years later, Osborne welcomed Switzer to Lincoln for a cocktail party. It was still not one of Tom's preferred activities, but Barry was in his element. Osborne was running for governor of Nebraska, and Switzer had offered to help his old rival with a fundraiser.

The two most successful football coaches of their time, side by side once again. What a formidable team.

Alas, this was not football.

Osborne-Switzer couldn't get the "W" in the 2006 election.

» **1989:** Quarterback Gerry Gdowski threw for four touchdowns, including one to Morgan Gregory (19), and ran for a fifth in leading the Huskers to a 42-25 win. It was NU's highest point total at home against Oklahoma since 1921. NU linebacker Chris Caliendo said thoughts of Sooner Magic never entered his mind. "Right from the opening kickoff, I knew we were going to win. I would have been really, really surprised if we'd lost." Coach Tom Osborne later expressed distaste for fans tearing down the goal posts at Memorial Stadium after the game. "I'm not too thrilled about that. I think that's probably a $4,000 to $5,000 tab for the university. I could see it if we had beaten Oklahoma only once in the last 30 years. But this is five of the last nine."

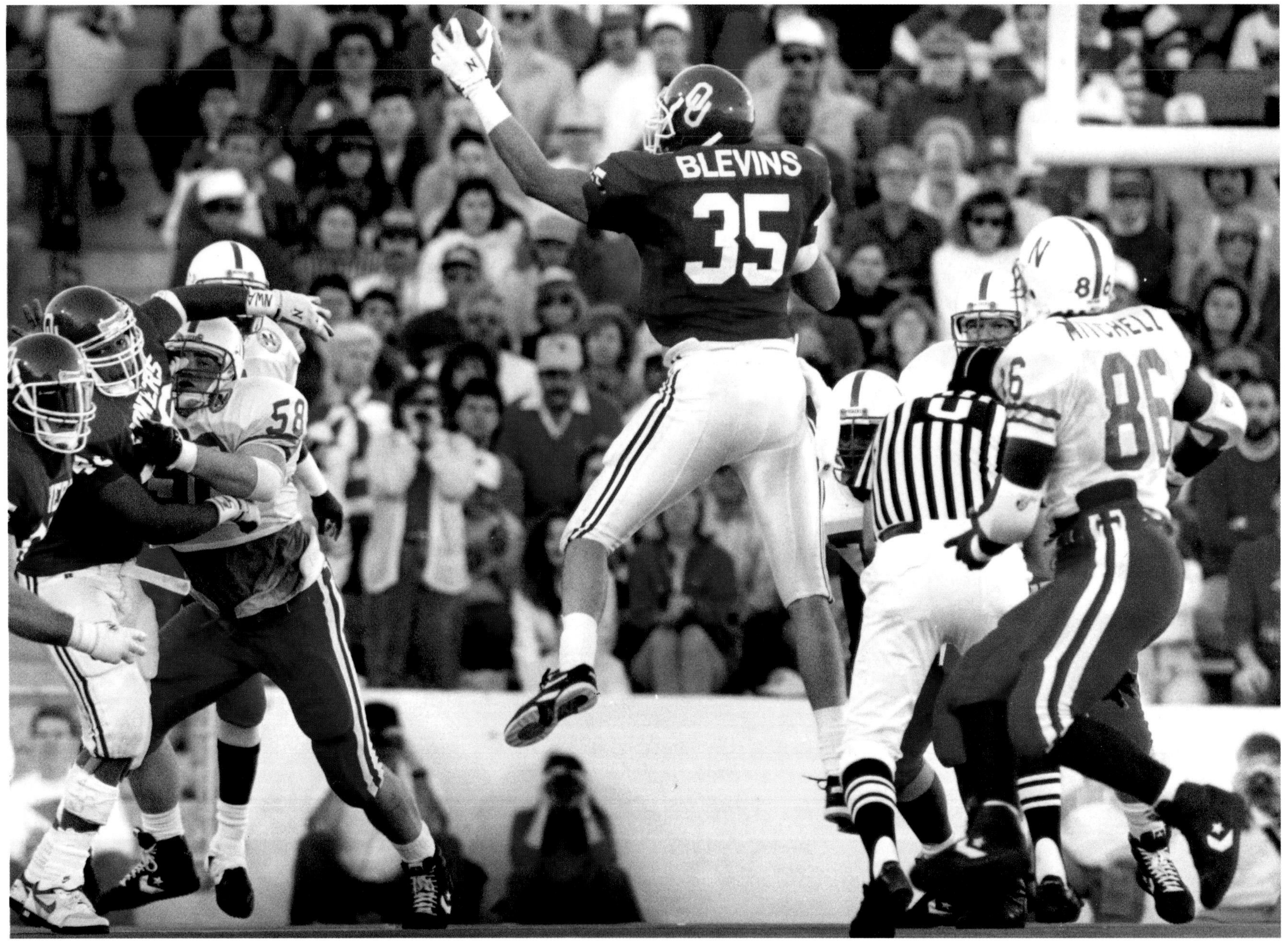

^ **1990:** The Huskers lost their quarterback in the first quarter, when Mickey Joseph suffered a 3-inch gash in the middle of his right shin when he crashed into a metal bench on the OU sideline after a 13-yard scramble. But the Huskers were still in the game in the third quarter when OU linebacker Frank Blevins (35) intercepted a pass intended for Husker tight end Johnny Mitchell (86). "That turnover just killed us," said coach Tom Osborne, who suffered his most lopsided loss, 45-10, in 18 years as a head coach. His biggest previous setback was by 31 points to the Sooners in 1977. "I am totally embarrassed. I thought we had a better football team than that."

« **1991:** Coach Tom Osborne called timeout with 3:08 left, trailing 14-13 and facing a fourth-and-1 at the OU 19. "He called the offense over and asked us what we wanted to do," NU quarterback Keithen McCant said. "We wanted to go for it. We weren't going to be denied." Freshman Calvin Jones (44) went 4 yards to the 15 for a first down. On the next play, Jones rambled in for the lead with 2:57 to play, and NU held on for a 19-14 win. The Memorial Stadium crowd, which hollered loudly through downpours, drizzle and light hail on a 32-degree day, tore down the goal posts for the fifth time after an OU game. Not all fans got good marks, though. Osborne stopped the game early in the third quarter to chew out "100 to 200 hammerheads" for throwing oranges. He used the referee's field microphone to suggest penalties against NU if the unsportsmanlike conduct continued, calling it "a lot of baloney."

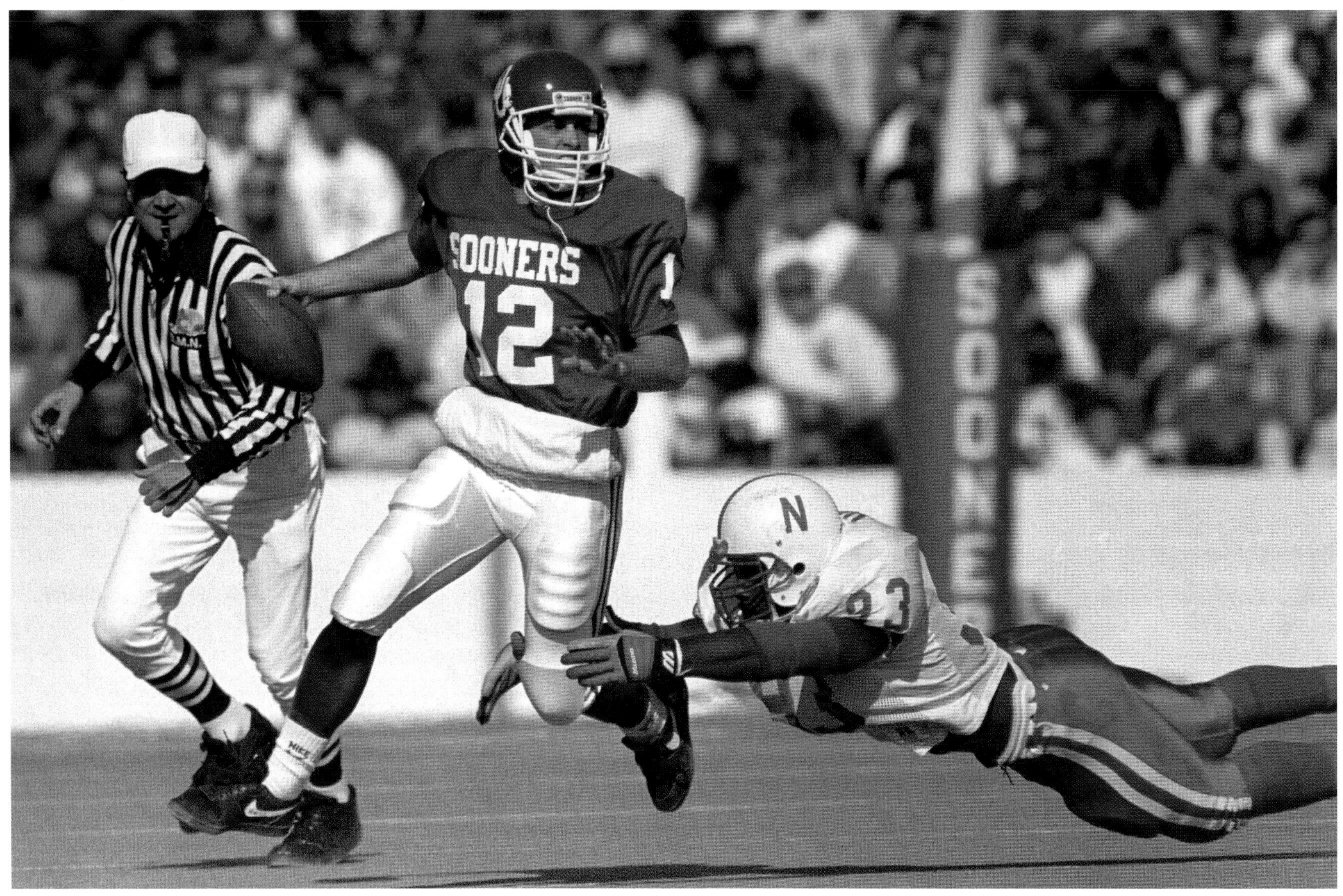

≈ **1992:** With the 12th-ranked Huskers trailing the unranked Sooners 9-7 in the second quarter at Owen Field, NU's Travis Hill (93) said thoughts turned to a painful loss suffered at Iowa State earlier in the season. "We told guys to remember the taste they had in their mouth after Iowa State," said the linebacker, who had eight tackles, including a sack of Sooner quarterback Cale Gundy (12) for a safety. "and then to remember the taste we had after beating Colorado and Kansas. It came down to asking, 'Which taste do we want?' We made up our minds real quick." The Huskers posted a tasty 33-9 victory.

⌃ **1993:** Nebraska rallied for a 21-7 win before another goal post-destroying crowd at Memorial Stadium. An interception set up a 2-yard touchdown run by quarterback Tommie Frazier that tied the score at 7-7 late in the first half. The Sooners lost control of the game when Nebraska scored twice in a 13-second span early in the fourth quarter. The kickoff temperature of 18 degrees combined with brisk west gusts for a wind chill of 7 below zero.

≈ **1994:** Osborne's No. 1-ranked Cornhuskers defeated Oklahoma 13-3 in Gary Gibbs' last game as Oklahoma's head coach. Quarterback Brook Berringer (18) – subbing for Tommie Frazier, who was out with a blood clot – ran for 48 yards and a touchdown and threw for 166 yards. There had been widespread speculation in Oklahoma newspapers that the Sooners might not play hard for Gibbs because some players were glad to see him leave. Tom Osborne pooh-poohed that idea. "If you're any kind of a person," he said, "you're going to play hard in that situation."

« **1995:** The Blackshirts were beaming after their performance in a 37-0 shutout of Oklahoma in the last Big Eight game ever played. After reading and hearing about the Huskers' powerhouse offense all season, they went out and soaked up the spotlight. "Before every series, we told each other that this is going to be up to us," said rush end Jared Tomich (93). "Finally, we have a game where we determine who's going to win instead of the offense just going out and running up the score." Oklahoma coach Howard Schnellenberger said, "We will have to improve a great deal in the years to come for us to begin to be a good football team and one that wins consistently." He left at the end of his first season, however.

» **1996:** The final statistics sheet didn't tell the real story about what Nebraska's defense accomplished in a 73-21 victory over Oklahoma, according to tackle Jason Peter (55). "When our first team is out there, we're the best defense in the country," said Peter, who had six tackles, including a sack, and tipped a ball that was intercepted. He and his Blackshirt teammates limited the Sooners to 89 yards on 44 plays in the first 45 minutes. Then came the fourth quarter, when the Huskers' lower-unit defensive players saw the bulk of their playing time. It was against them in the final 15 minutes that the Sooners scored all of their points, amassed 186 of their 275 total yards and recorded 10 of their 16 first downs. Repercussions, Peter said, would be forthcoming. "We'll get them at practice on Monday," he said, grinning.

« **1997:** The top-ranked Huskers gave Tom Osborne his 250th victory in a 69-7 triumph over the Sooners. Fullback Joel Makovicka (45) rumbled for three touchdowns and 101 yards to lead the offense.

A FITTING OPPONENT FOR THE 250TH VICTORY

The 1997 Huskers refused to let Oklahoma spoil another big moment for coach Tom Osborne, beating the team that had been the source of some of his biggest frustrations over the years for his 250th victory. "We didn't want to let coach Osborne down," Nebraska's Grant Wistrom (98) said after the 69-7 rout. "He'll be the first guy to downplay the significance of 250 wins and give credit to everyone else. We all know who got the program to this level, and we'd give our heart and soul to the man. That's why we went out there and played as hard as we could today." Wistrom almost single-handedly saw to it that the Sooners would have no chance to play spoiler. The All-American rush end put on one of his finest performances, finishing with 10 tackles, four of which produced losses of 23 yards. He recorded two sacks, forced three fumbles and recovered one. Nebraska conducted a brief postgame ceremony to commemorate the milestone, and the Huskers left the field as fireworks illuminated the early evening sky. "That was really unexpected," Osborne said. "It got to be quite a production out there." Said the coach's wife, Nancy: "This game used to be a nail-biter. It's sad what it's become."

» **2000:** Oklahoma's football resurgence under coach Bob Stoops built momentum, as the Sooners handed top-ranked Nebraska a 31-14 defeat in Norman. The Huskers had a 14-0 lead at the end of the first quarter, but OU quarterback Josh Heupel (14) led the Sooners to 31 straight points in about 18 minutes of the second and third quarters. Stoops said he showed a 5- to 7-minute highlight tape of past OU-NU games before team meetings the week before the game. "We educated them on the series, way back to its evolution," Stoops said. "And our guys appreciated that. They wanted to know about the history of it. Some of these things you take for granted that they know and understand, but they don't." Stoops got the reaction he had sought. "We wanted our guys to see how well Oklahoma had played against Nebraska all those years. Our guys have heard of 'Sooner Magic.' It's posted in our locker room. But a lot of them didn't really know where it came from. Of Switzer's 12 wins over Nebraska, eight came in the last few minutes of the game. Once our guys saw that and could relate to it, they started to identify with it. I definitely think it was a factor." The Sooner defense got the message as well, making NU quarterback Eric Crouch pay a heavy price for his 101 rushing yards and leaving center Dominic Raiola (54) deflated.

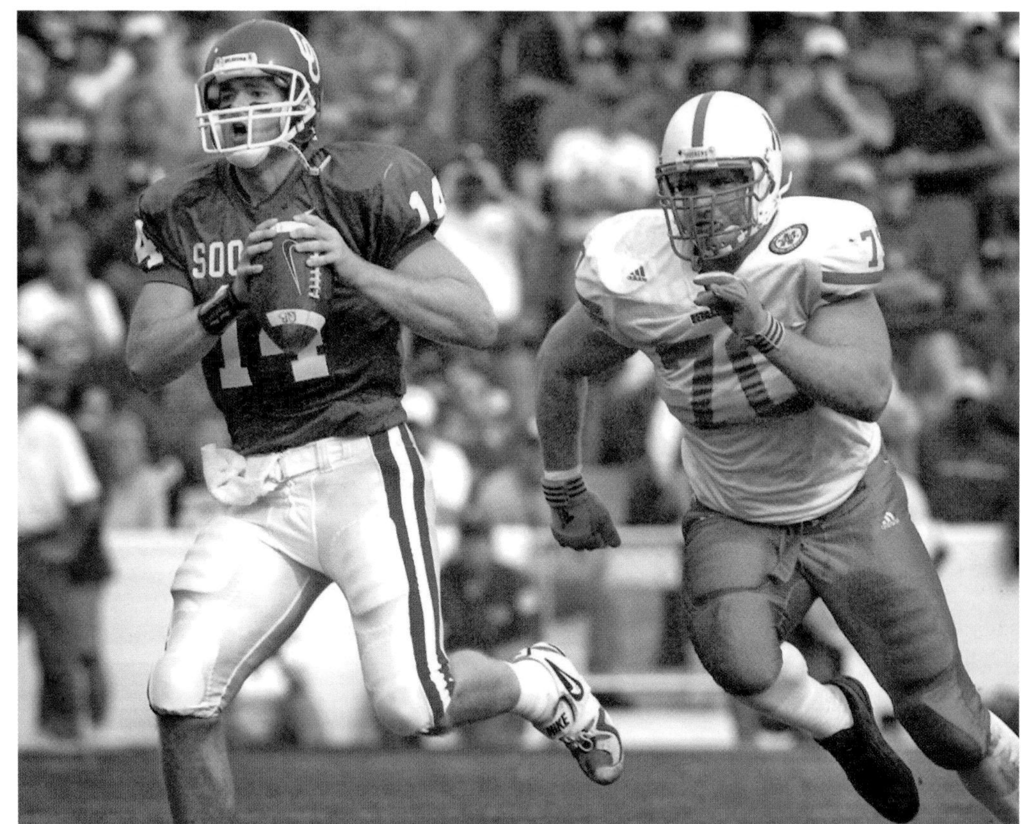

WILSON
NEBRASKA

« » **2001:** Victimized repeatedly in the past by Sooner Magic, Nebraska used some trickery of its own to make Oklahoma's 20-game winning streak disappear. The third-ranked Huskers sealed their 20-10 victory over No. 2 Oklahoma when quarterback Eric Crouch (7) caught a 63-yard touchdown pass with 6:17 to play. True freshman Mike Stuntz (16) fired the ball to Crouch off a reverse after taking a handoff from Thunder Collins, who had taken a handoff from Crouch. "They talk about all the trick plays that NU and OU have run through the years, and we even talked about it during meetings this week," Stuntz said. "They showed us some highlight tapes of the 'Fumbleroosky' and things like that. They kept showing some of those plays during the game (on HuskerVision). I thought to myself, 'What if this one shows up there years from now?'" While Nebraska coach Frank Solich saw his trick work, Bob Stoops had watched his similar play fail in the second quarter when OU quarterback Nate Hybl, who was wide open, slipped and couldn't make the catch. "In the end, on our reverse throwback, our guy fell down and we couldn't complete it," Stoops said. "There's more to it than that, but when I saw (Crouch) running down the sideline, I almost had to half chuckle to myself. Theirs worked and ours didn't."

61
83

⌃ » **2004:** Quarterback Jason White (18), who had won the Heisman Trophy the year before, torched the Huskers in OU's 30-3 victory in Norman. The Huskers crossed midfield just three times and needed a field goal on the last play to avoid being shut out for the first time since 1996. The game was one of the few in the series that generated hard feelings. Before the game, a Nebraska lineman collided with a member of OU's Ruf/Neks spirit squad and later faced criminal charges. The player was acquitted several months later. After the game, an Oklahoma newspaper reported, NU coach Bill Callahan yelled "(expletive) hillbillies!" toward the Sooner crowd as he left the field. There was some good will after the game, however. Bo Pelini, who had been fired 10 months before as Nebraska's defensive coordinator, had since taken a job as Stoops' co-defensive coordinator. NU linebacker Ira Cooper, who exchanged a long hug with Pelini after the game, said the Blackshirts were still close with their former coach.

« ≫ **2005:** Trickery made another appearance, as OU's Bob Stoops tried a fake field goal after the Huskers had blocked an earlier kick. "I just felt that the way they were rushing," Stoops said, "they were not regarding any fake whatsoever." Oklahoma converted a fourth-and-3 on the fake and scored on the next play for a 31-17 lead with 10:58 left. That stood as the deciding score in a 31-24 Sooner win in Lincoln. The day was a nightmare for Nebraska quarterback Zac Taylor (13), whose father had played for the Sooners. He was sacked nine times, threw an interception that was returned for a touchdown and overthrew a wide-open receiver on a play late in the game that could have given the Huskers a chance to tie or go ahead with a two-point conversion. Coach Bill Callahan's behavior again was called into question when he appeared to give a throat-slash gesture to an official after arguing for a holding call. "It is what it is, I guess," Callahan said when asked about it later.

» 2006 BIG 12 CHAMPIONSHIP GAME

An estimated 60,000 Husker fans came to Kansas City's Arrowhead Stadium for the matchup between the two rivals, but the air came out of the balloon early for Nebraska. The Huskers committed their first of five turnovers on the first play from scrimmage, setting up Oklahoma for a 21-7 win. Nebraska tried a reverse that failed on the opening kickoff and started from its 9-yard line. Quarterback Zac Taylor completed a short first-down pass to Maurice Purify (16), but the receiver fumbled and OU safety Reggie Smith returned the football to the 2-yard line. OU scored on the next play. Nebraska's trouble would build with a 66-yard Sooner touchdown pass in the first quarter, and it would peak with OU's 11-play, 99-yard drive in the third. That length-of-the-field accomplishment survived only because quarterback Paul Thompson (12), not known as a thrower, converted a third-and-10 play from the 1, throwing 35 yards to freshman tight end Jermaine Gresham.

« **2008:** The start of the game defied explanation, and afterward only coach Bo Pelini was around to offer one. The Huskers fell behind 28-0 in less than six minutes, trailed 35-0 after the first quarter and never recovered in a 62-28 beating in Norman. Pelini said afterward that his players wouldn't be available for questions. "It's disappointing, I mean, I can't tell you," Pelini said. "I'm embarrassed. I'm just not used to this. I take responsibility." He later said he silenced his team so it could move on as quickly as possible. "Reliving what happened wasn't going to do us any good," he said. "I wanted our players to move forward. That was really the single purpose behind it."

» 2009: THE FINAL REGULAR-SEASON CONFERENCE SHOWDOWN

"EVERYONE BELIEVES"

The Huskers scored first to take a 7-0 lead, then gutted out the next 43 minutes of play to capture a 10-3 victory in Lincoln. "It just shows the character of this defense, and everyone believes in the system and the coaches and believes in each other," said senior linebacker Phillip Dillard (52), who shared the joy with his position coach, Mike Ekeler. "It's not like a team, it's like brotherhood. We've got each other's back on offense and defense."

» 2009: THE FINAL REGULAR-SEASON CONFERENCE SHOWDOWN

AN EARLY BREAK

NU cornerback Prince Amukamara (21) intercepted a pass and returned it to the OU 1-yard line early in the second quarter, setting up the only touchdown of the game. "I would say the difference is (they got) the one turnover to set up their touchdown, and we didn't get a turnover," OU coach Bob Stoops said. "That's how close this game was."

SOONERS
44
93

« 2009: THE FINAL REGULAR-SEASON CONFERENCE SHOWDOWN

THE ONLY TOUCHDOWN

Quarterback Zac Lee threw a 1-yard play-action pass to sophomore tight end Ryan Hill (80) for a 7-0 lead in the second quarter. It was the game's only touchdown and Hill's only score of the year.

2009: THE FINAL REGULAR-SEASON CONFERENCE SHOWDOWN

THE PRESSURE

The Blackshirts weren't exactly impenetrable, but Ndamukong Suh (93) harassed OU quarterback Landry Jones (12) all night, forcing the redshirt freshman into throwing five interceptions. The Blackshirts never gave up the early lead, making plays at the right time to stall out OU. "It's a good win," Suh said. "It's one that's expected in my book. . . . For me, that is part of the expectations. That's what I came here to do."

2009: THE FINAL REGULAR-SEASON CONFERENCE SHOWDOWN

THIEF IN THE NIGHT

Senior Matt O'Hanlon (33) sealed the win by picking off his third pass of the game with 21 seconds left. "This game was about the battle of the defenses," O'Hanlon said. "I think we were up against their defense more than their offense." It was a night of redemption for O'Hanlon, who had been burned on a long pass in a loss to Virginia Tech earlier in the season.

» **2009: THE FINAL REGULAR-SEASON CONFERENCE SHOWDOWN**

THE FANS DID THEIR PART

The fans in Memorial Stadium got a well-deserved thanks from Huskers Roy Helu (10), Dontrayevous Robinson (27), Lazarri Middleton (2) and Marcus Mendoza (32) when the game was over. "When you walked in there, it was like somebody just turned on the electricity," said NU linebackers coach Mike Ekeler. "I mean, my hair was standing up. It was pretty awesome."

STILL HAVING NIGHTMARES ABOUT . . .

THOMAS LOTT

Quarterback

When was the first time you heard the word "swagger" used in connection with football? For many, it was in reference to Oklahoma in the 1970s, and nobody could swagger like Thomas Lott.

With a pirate's bandana sticking out of his helmet, Lott pushed all the right buttons in the Sooners' wishbone machine. His deceptive fakes, game-breaking keepers and perfectly timed pitches to running backs helped Oklahoma to three wins against the Huskers:

- 1976's 20-17 fourth-quarter comeback, the game that gave birth to the term "Sooner Magic."
- 1977's 38-7 blowout in which he ran for 143 yards and a touchdown.
- 1979's New Year's Day 31-24 Orange Bowl win, which washed away the Sooners' bad taste from Nebraska's upset victory in November.

Lott not only could walk the walk, he could also talk the talk.

"If you read the defense right and have the people to execute the offense, there is no way they can stop us," he said of the Huskers.

"The only thing that can stop us is us," he added, words that summed up Sooner swagger perfectly.

STEVE OWENS

Running back

Scored five touchdowns in a 47-0 Oklahoma throttling in 1968, the low point of the Bob Devaney era.

JACK MILDREN

Quarterback

Carried 31 times for 130 yards and two touchdowns and threw for two more in the Game of the Century.

THE SELMON BROTHERS

Defensive linemen

Stopped offenses cold in the '70s, with Lee Roy winning the Outland and Lombardi awards and Lucious and Dewey both named All-Americans.

BILLY SIMS

Running back

Rushed for 247 yards in 1979 against the Huskers – one year after he fumbled inside the 5-yard line to hand Nebraska a victory.

BUSTER RHYMES

Running back

Gave Nebraska another taste of Sooner Magic with his last-minute heroics in 1980.

JAMELLE HOLIEWAY

Quarterback

Started as a freshman and led the Sooners to two victories over Nebraska, but he was slowed by injuries his last two seasons.

KEITH JACKSON

TIGHT END

Reeled in a 41-yard reception on a third-and-12 with 9 seconds left in the game, setting up a field goal that gave OU a dramatic 20-17 win in 1986.

CHARLES THOMPSON

Quarterback

Took over for the injured Holieway in 1987 and led OU's offense to a dominating win in the Game of the Century II.

JOSH HEUPEL

Quarterback

Threw for 300 yards in 2000, leading a rally from a 14-point deficit to a 31-14 win on the way to the Sooners' national title.

Ralphie can reach a speed of up to 25 mph, so student handlers exercise her before the game to tire her out and slow her down.

COLORADO

NOT A SNOWBALL'S CHANCE OF MISSING EACH OTHER

BY MICHAEL KELLY | WORLD-HERALD STAFF WRITER

FEW KNOW HOW CLOSE Nebraska's most iconic figure may have come to taking another head coaching job – ironically, at Colorado. Ironic because of all the conference foes over the decades, Colorado probably was the most antagonistic to NU. Fans in Boulder hurled snowballs at the Husker band and bench. Ralphie the buffalo sometimes nearly ran people over on the field. Coaches circled the date of the Nebraska game on the calendar – and eventually won some big games. NU fans in Boulder often felt they had entered hostile territory.

Yes, it was Colorado that nearly lured Tom Osborne away. In December 1978, he visited CU and athletic director Eddie Crowder to talk about the possibility. Though Osborne's salary of $36,000 was one of the lowest in the Big Eight, friends told reporters that money wasn't a major factor. But six years after succeeding Bob Devaney as Husker honcho, Osborne was disappointed that he had not been able to rally the state. Fortunately for Nebraska and its fans, T.O. stayed – making several runs at national titles in the 1980s before winning national championships three times in the 1990s. He later returned as athletic director to help orchestrate a big move, Nebraska's departure for the Big Ten.

Long before the Big 12 Conference, Colorado joined the old Big Six, and Big Seven football began in 1948. The Buffs won some of those early games with NU, including in 1958 when future pros Boyd Dowler of Colorado and Pat Fischer of Nebraska leaped for the same crucial ball – and the 6-foot-5 CU receiver outreached NU's 5-9 defender. On a soggy field in 1961, now playing in the Big Eight, Nebraska didn't make a first down, complete a pass or score a point. Then came Devaney, and Nebraska ran off a streak that included turning a two-touchdown fourth-quarter deficit in 1966 into a two-point win. Eight NU turnovers led to a CU victory the next year.

Hospitality has been in short supply in Boulder.

After that, things began to snowball – and not in a good way. In a 1968 Husker victory at Boulder, CU students fired snowballs, including one with a rock inside that left a gash in the temple of a Lincoln woman. In '72, the "snowball bowl," 15 people were treated at a hospital for injuries and 34 were arrested. Crowder, the CU coach, had made an appeal for a cease-fire, but he himself got belted in the neck. "I would like our own people to act like sportsmen," he said afterward. "I was disappointed our own students did not use good judgment." Devaney angrily said the snowball-throwing had to stop. Ralphie, too, at times was a problem, and Devaney turned down CU's request to bring its live buffalo mascot to Lincoln in '71. In 1978, a Husker player had to dive at the last second to avoid being run over before the game. "It's kind of ridiculous to have that animal running around out there," Osborne said. "It would be very easy for someone to lose a player or two." CU coaches and players said they had been bad-mouthed by NU fans. The World-Herald reported that the Nebraska-Colorado series had "degenerated into an unhealthy state."

ROAD TRIP TO

BOULDER

University of Colorado

Founded: 1876

Enrollment: 30,000

Colors: Silver, gold and black

Conference history:
Began conference football schedule in 1948, as the Big Six became the Big Seven.

Stadium:
Folsom Field, capacity 53,613

History of "Buffaloes":
A newspaper contest in 1934 settled the matter. Before that, the teams had been referred to as "the Silver and Gold," along with Silver Helmets, Yellow Jackets, Hornets, Arapahoes, Big Horns, Grizzlies and Frontiersmen.

Distance from Memorial Stadium in Lincoln:
499 miles

Worth remembering:

Every eye in the stadium is on Ralphie when the 1,200-pound buffalo leads the team onto the field. While live animals have appeared off and on through the years, the current tradition began when a student's father donated a buffalo calf in 1966. The name originally was Ralph, although the reason is disputed, ranging from the sound of the beast snorting to the first name of the junior class president. It was changed to Ralphie when it was discovered that the calf was a female. For visiting Nebraskans, Folsom Field's traditions also include dodging snowballs and taking off their red hats after victories to thwart thieves.

Quote:

"There's that dadgummed buffalo. We told them they can run that buffalo around all they want to, but we're going to stay off the field."

– Nebraska coach Tom Osborne as Ralphie appeared on the screen during his narration of game highlights (1987)

Nebraska ran off 18 straight wins against CU, including 59-0 in Turner Gill's first start at quarterback, NU setting an NCAA record with 42 first downs. Bill McCartney arrived as CU head coach in 1982 and announced that Nebraska was the Colorado rival, with the schedule showing the game in red letters. The Huskers continued to dominate for a while, exploding for 48 points in the third quarter in 1983. Tom Rathman broke a 7-7 tie in '85 with an 84-yard run on the day he was honored by his hometown of Grand Island. But the Buffs were getting closer, and the Husker streak ended in Boulder in 1986 with a 20-10 upset of the third-ranked Cornhuskers at Folsom Field. With the band's "Glory, Glory Colorado" ringing in everyone's ears, McCartney said it was a game CU would always cherish. "I think we've got a rivalry now." He thanked CU fans, who stormed the field and tore down goal posts, and paid tribute to the 15,000 Husker fans, many of whom stood and applauded at the end for CU.

Colorado beat Nebraska again in 1989, Mac calling it "the greatest win I've ever been part of," as well as in CU's national-championship year of 1990, scoring all its points in the fourth quarter in Lincoln to win 27-12.

With snowballs splattering Folsom Field again the next year in 12-degree weather with a wind chill of 8-below, the teams met in a game that Osborne called the coldest he ever coached or played in. An NU field-goal attempt was blocked, and the game ended in a tie. John Reece's late interception locked up the '93 game for the Huskers. McCartney's plea for Colorado fans to treat Nebraskans with respect mostly worked. Osborne, meanwhile, apologized for the way some CU fans were treated the previous year in Lincoln. Still, 62 fans were ejected in Boulder for throwing snowballs. NU won some more close games, including a three-pointer in 1999 when Eric Crouch scored in overtime. Josh Brown kicked a game-winning field goal as time expired in 2000. But in 2001, the Husker wheels fell off in a 62-36 loss at Boulder that many later saw as the beginning of a Nebraska downturn. A day after NU coach Frank Solich received a Gatorade shower for a 2003 win over the Buffs, he was figuratively sent to the showers – fired. Bo Pelini coached the bowl game, but Bill Callahan was named head coach before the 2004 season. He lasted four years, including a 2-2 record against CU, before being fired by the new athletic director, Osborne. In Pelini's first year as head coach, Alex Henery kicked a school-record 57-yard field goal to put the Huskers ahead and Ndamukong Suh scored on a late interception.

Osborne had rallied the state anew. But the curious rivalry with Colorado ends not with snowballs splattering, teeth chattering, fullbacks battering or tradition mattering. Instead it's a scattering: Nebraska leaves the Big 12 for the Big Ten, and Colorado goes to the Pac-10. One heads east, the other west, as if turning their backs on each other for good.

A NEW ATTITUDE ABOUT ALTITUDE

The effects of Boulder's altitude (5,345 feet) have been debated ever since Nebraska started making the trip to Colorado. Coaches sometimes had their teams arrive earlier to adjust to the thin air in Boulder. Other times they tried arriving later with the idea that the altitude would be less of a psychological barrier. In 1968, a Lincoln welding supply company provided an oxygen tank to help out. While oxygen tanks are a common sight at games now, this one caused a stir. "The winning drive of the Huskers was helped by sniffs of oxygen each time they trotted off the field in the high, frosty altitude," The World-Herald's Tom Allan reported.

YESTERYEARS

» **1948:** Nebraska lost 19-6 at Boulder in its first game against new conference member Colorado. The Cornhuskers had won five of the first six games between the schools, the last of which was played in 1907. The Buffaloes finished fourth in their first season in the Big Seven, while the Huskers tied for fifth.

« **1950:** Nebraska's Bill Wingender reaches for a pass in the Huskers' 28-19 loss in Boulder. "Colorado had the better team today," coach Bill Glassford said, although NU had sophomore Bobby Reynolds, who ran for three touchdowns and 145 yards. The Buffs dominated the series in the '50s with six wins and a tie.

⌃ **1957:** Colorado's Howard Cook looks for room to run in the Buffs' 27-0 victory in Lincoln, Nebraska's eighth loss in nine games. "It appeared the Cornhuskers' sophomoric efforts to defend were more lack of savvy and tackling ability than any particular finesse on the part of the CU offense," The World-Herald noted. A crowd of 27,000 had dwindled to 12,000 by the end of the cold and dreary afternoon.

⌃ **1959:** Pat Fischer (40) is pushed out of bounds under the watchful eye of coach Bill Jennings. Nebraska won 14-12, ending a three-game losing streak to the Buffs. The university had to install new goal posts for the game because the previous set had been torn down after the 25-21 upset of Oklahoma two weeks earlier. The cost of the new goal posts: $170.

≈ **1960:** Colorado was on its way to a second-place finish in the Big Eight when it beat Nebraska 19-6 in Boulder. "There's something lacking, that's all there is to it," said end Don Purcell of the Huskers, who would end up tied for sixth with a 2-5 conference record.

≚ **1961:** The Buffs posted their fifth victory over NU in six games, winning 7-0 on a cold, muddy day in Lincoln. While the Huskers failed to make a first down and didn't complete a pass, Gregg McBride reported, "Nebraska faithful, most of whom stayed to the end, hoped for a miracle."

« **1962:** Trailing 6-0 at halftime, Nebraska put up 23 points in the third quarter on the way to a 31-6 victory. First-year coach Bob Devaney, at left with assistant John Melton, brought10,000 NU fans along on the trip to Boulder.

Smidt (N)

Symons (CU)

« **1963:** Maynard Smidt had a 6-yard touchdown run to help NU blast the Buffs 41-6. "It was just one man against another, and they just physically knocked our guys right back," said Eddie Crowder, Colorado's first-year coach.

^ **1964:** Nebraska won 21-3, holding the Buffs to two first downs and 51 total yards. The Huskers scored their first touchdown when quarterback Bob Churchich was chased out of the pocket and heaved the ball upfield. The ball went through the fingers of CU defensive back Hale Irwin (who later as a professional golfer won the U.S. Open three times) and into the hands of back Kent McCloughan (32), who raced into the end zone for a 53-yard score.

« **1965:** Larry Wachholtz (36) put on a show in the Huskers' 38-13 victory in Lincoln. The safety from North Platte intercepted a pass, returned three punts for a total of 111 yards, kicked five extra points and added a 28-yard field goal.

» **1966:** Nebraska's bench exploded after Pete Tatman scored with 53 seconds left in a 21-19 win. Devaney called the comeback, featuring two touchdowns in the last 11 minutes, the greatest since he had become coach of the Huskers. The fans also put on an epic battle in Boulder. "Countless fistfights and wrestling bouts broke out shortly after the game, with red-garbed Nebraska fans reacting to a siege of hat-snatching by youngsters and adults," Wally Provost reported. "So vicious were some of the brawls, Colorado's uniformed ushers refused to even try to part the battlers."

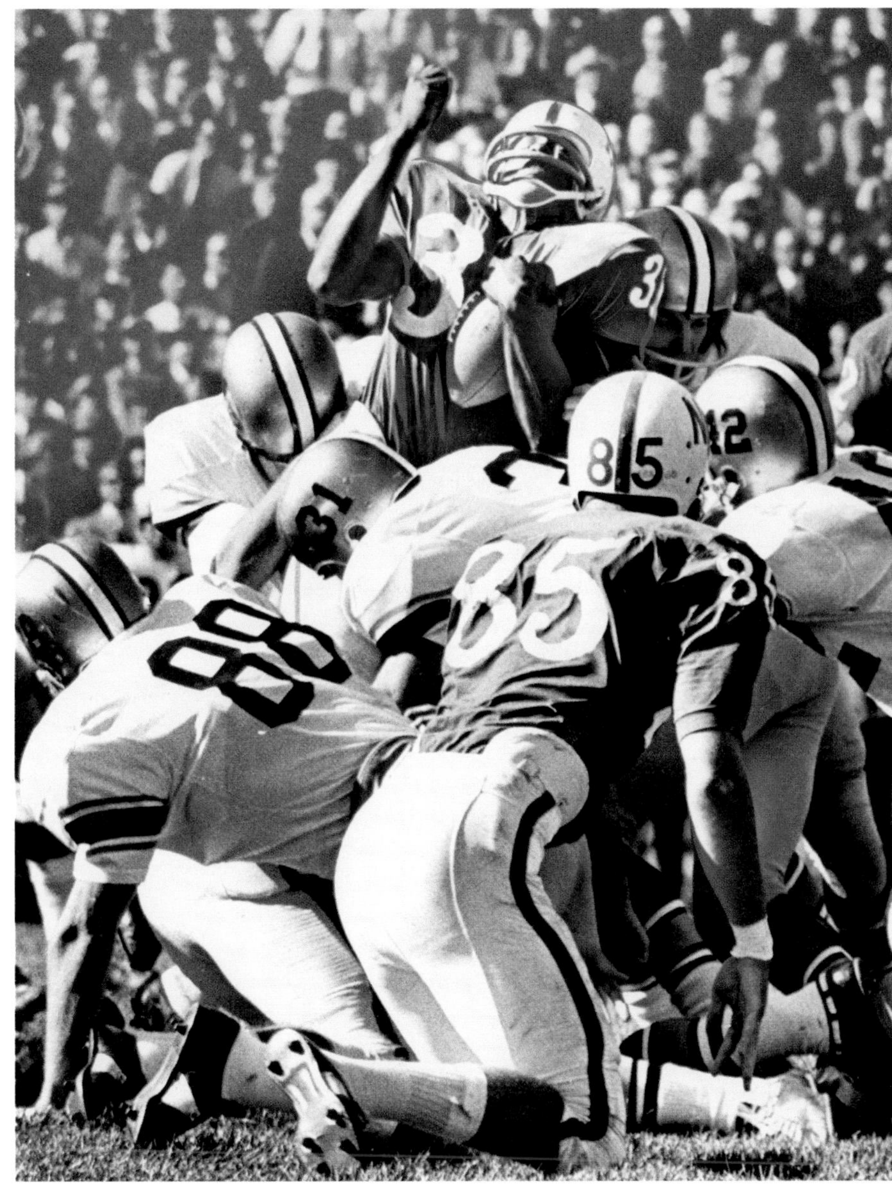

≈ **1967:** Unbeaten Colorado crunched sophomore running back Joe Orduna (31) and the Huskers 21-16, forcing four fumbles and intercepting four passes. The Huskers already were hearing from critics before the loss, but Wally Provost said those fans needed to accept that some of the other Big Eight members had improved. "If there are lollypop-lickers in Nebraska's fandom who can't figure that out, and who can't stand a bit of bad with a lot of good, they'd better hop off the bandwagon," he wrote.

« **1968:** Fullback Dick Davis (45) ran for 92 yards, "along with the body-racking blocking for which he has become known," The World-Herald reported on NU's 22-6 win. Colorado fans again reacted poorly to losing, pelting Nebraska players with snowballs throughout the fourth quarter.

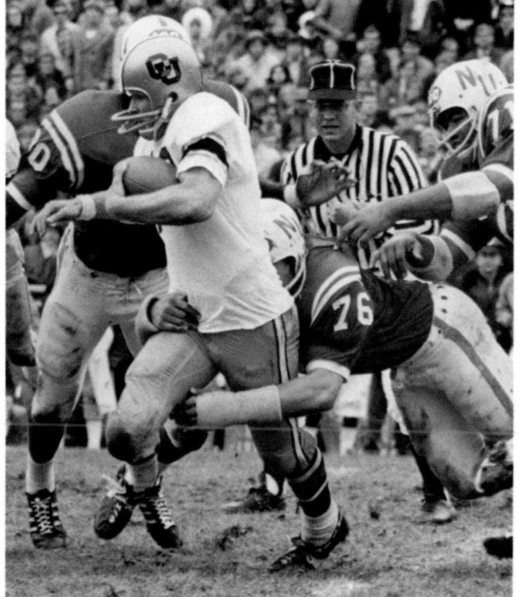

« **1969:** Dave Walline (76) and the Blackshirts shut down star CU quarterback Bobby Anderson in a 20-7 victory. Nebraska finished as co-Big Eight champion with Missouri at 6-1, while the Buffs were 5-2 in the conference.

» **1970:** The turning point in Nebraska's 29-13 victory, according to CU coach Eddie Crowder, was Husker Jeff Kinney's 79-yard kickoff return after the Buffs had pulled to within 15-13 in the fourth quarter. The Huskers scored the clinching touchdown a short time later. "The only mistake made on that return was a missed tackle," Crowder said. "But how can you tell? Perhaps it was more his ability as a great athlete."

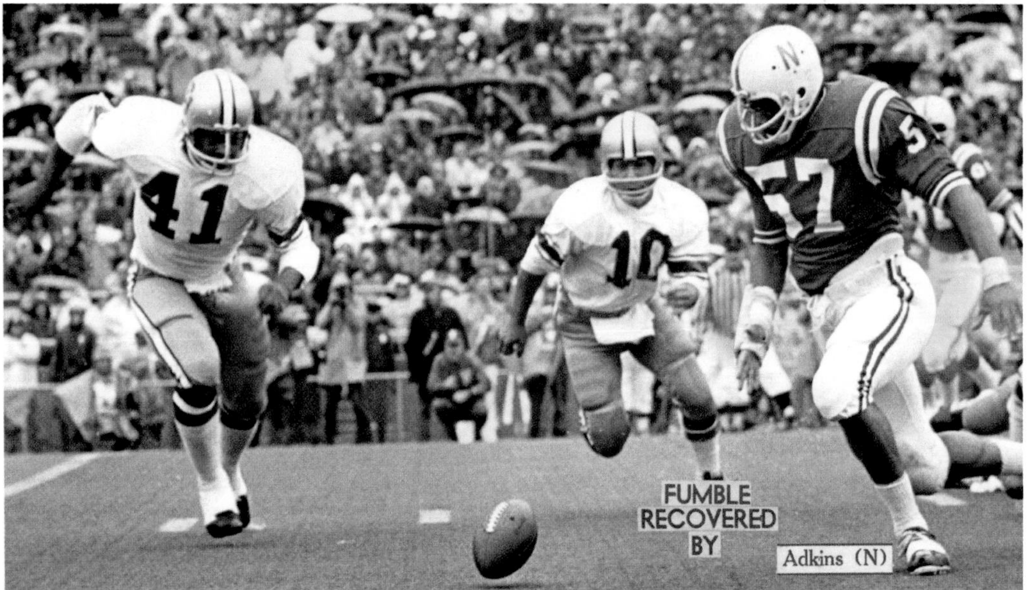

« **1971:** Top-ranked Nebraska won 31-7 against a Colorado team that would finish third in the nation. John Adkins (57) and the Blackshirts set up three of NU's touchdowns with fumble recoveries and held the Buffs to just 160 total yards and 11 first downs. Spirits were high for the game between Top 10 teams. A group of Colorado students gagged and bound one of their fraternity brothers to a stretcher and slipped him into a compartment on an Amtrak train headed from Denver to Omaha. A porter awakened the student when the train arrived at 3:30 Sunday morning, and the victim explained that he had upset his friends by cheering for the Huskers during the game. The student, whose father was a Nebraska graduate, flew back to Boulder.

« **1972:** The defense again led the way in the Huskers' 33-10 win, holding the Buffs to 85 yards passing (11 completions in 29 throws, plus an interception). The crowd in Boulder once again provided a sidelight to the game. "Something has to be done about throwing those snowballs out there," Bob Devaney said. "Eddie Crowder did everything he could to stop it, but it didn't do any good."

» **1973:** Nebraska assistant Rick Duval had previously been a Colorado aide and had the pleasure of coaching, in a 28-16 victory, several players he had failed to recruit to CU. "Our plans included John Dutton, and I thought we had him pretty well wrapped up, but (Husker assistant) John Melton got him," Duval said. Dutton (90), a defensive lineman, enjoyed a long career in the NFL with the Baltimore Colts and Dallas Cowboys. Duval also was pleased to be coaching for such supportive fans. "We always felt like the fans were worth 14 points to Nebraska. At Colorado, the fans are more interested in winning the snowball fights."

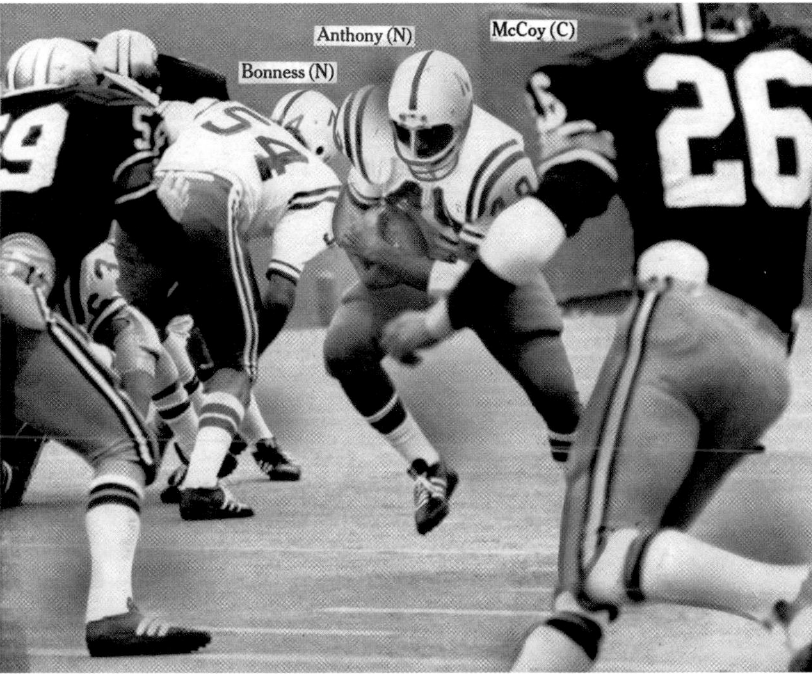

« 1974: PUNCHED OUT IN BOULDER

Colorado rookie head coach Bill Mallory showed up with a cast on his hand the week of the game.

"I was frustrated earlier this week, and I hit a door. I do some dumb things like that." He broke two knuckles on his punching hand. Then he lost his first go-round with the Huskers, 31-15.

Nebraska was cruising at 31-0 before coasting in, aided by 157 yards from freshman I-back Monte Anthony (49) of Bellevue. The Huskers' Osborne said of the finish: "We played like a bunch of grade school kids."

The next year, it was Osborne who applied the brakes in a 63-21 cakewalk. "Tom was a real gentleman about it," Mallory said. "He tried to hold the score down."

– Tom Ash

» **1975:** Dave Butterfield (34), a cornerback from Kersey, Colo., seemed to be at his best when he faced his home-state Buffaloes.

Butterfield, who turned down a Colorado scholarship offer to play at Nebraska, was named the Big Eight's defensive player of the week after NU demolished the Buffs 63-21.

That 1975 Colorado team was no slouch. It finished 9-3 and had six players taken in the NFL draft – three in the first round, and three in the third – before the first Husker, center Rik Bonness, was picked, also in the third round.

The next year, Butterfield was again honored as the Big Eight's defensive player of the week following NU's 24-12 victory at Colorado.

"Getting it two years in a row against them is more of a coincidence than anything else," Butterfield said.

– Larry Porter

» 1976: KEEPING IT INTERESTING

The game in Boulder, won by Nebraska 24-12, offered a number of interesting story lines.

Starting CU quarterback Jeff Knapple, from Boulder Fairview High, originally signed a letter of intent with Nebraska, then went to UCLA, then transferred to CU. He played valiantly in defeat.

Buff tailback Tony Reed, who was suspended the year before for shoplifting, was asked what he was doing to prepare for the Huskers. "Staying out of department stores," he responded.

The Buffs had a top-flight place-kicker named Pete Dadiotis, a walk-on from Greece who owned a Mexican restaurant in Denver with relatives. Loved to talk, too. Sportswriters were downhearted when he went out with a knee injury. His replacement? The president of the Boulder Civic Opera.

Mark Zetterberg, the replacement, was a walk-on from New York who majored in theater, drama and music. He already had a contract with the Seattle Civic Opera. He could kick, too.

Zetterberg nailed four field goals in the first half, and Nebraska was clinging to a 14-12 lead in the fourth quarter when the Buffs launched a 14-play drive to a first down at the Husker 5. Three plays and a yard later, Zetterberg was summoned for his easiest try of the afternoon.

The kick was blocked by Colorado native Butterfield.

After losing his first three games to Nebraska, Colorado coach Bill Mallory referred to the Buffs' nine-year losing streak and 14 losses to NU in 15 years. The Buffs "hadn't done much against Nebraska before I got here, and I haven't improved on it."

– Tom Ash

THE FIRST LADY COMES FIRST?

The 1976 Nebraska football team felt a bit deserted as it left the team hotel and began the bus journey to Colorado's Folsom Field for its game against the Buffaloes.

The Huskers had no police escort en route to the stadium.

The Boulder police gave their escort attention to Betty Ford, wife of President Gerald Ford, who attended the game.

"It was the first time in 10 or 15 years that we had no police escort," NU coach Tom Osborne said. "We spent 15 minutes at one intersection waiting for Betty Ford and her entourage to come by. I was beginning to doubt that we'd ever make it for the game."

A smiling Osborne said a visiting team would never be slighted in Lincoln.

"We have our priorities in order here," he said.

– Larry Porter

A TIME TO COME TOGETHER

BY LARRY PORTER

Colorado linebacker Tom Perry suffered a critical head injury during the Buffs' 1977 loss to Nebraska and had to undergo two surgeries.

The first was performed at Bryan Memorial Hospital in Lincoln shortly after the game. Perry then was transferred to the University of Nebraska Medical Center in Omaha.

CU coach **Bill Mallory** and one of his assistants were in the UNMC waiting room. So was Nebraska player George Andrews, a junior defensive end who had been one of the stars of the game.

Two years earlier, during Andrews' redshirt season, he had roomed with Rob Link, who was from Boulder. Link took Andrews home with him and introduced him to a few friends, and Debbie McCarthy was one of them.

Following the game in which Perry was injured, Andrews and McCarthy met again. She was a close friend of Perry's wife and had just learned that he was in critical condition in Omaha.

"She started crying and said she was going to drive to Omaha to be with Connie Perry," Andrews said.

McCarthy had never been to Omaha, so Andrews – an Omaha Burke graduate – volunteered to drive her there. When they arrived at the hospital, McCarthy went into an inner waiting room to comfort Connie Perry, and Andrews sat down in an outer waiting room with the two Colorado coaches. The three introduced themselves.

"I think Coach Mallory recognized my name, but I'm not sure," Andrews said. "We didn't mention one word about the game, though, which shows how concerned he really was."

Mallory told Andrews that Perry's second operation had taken five hours.

"The surgeon came out," Andrews said. "I heard him say Tom was in critical condition and that it would be 48 hours before they knew if he would make it."

Andrews stayed at the hospital until nearly 2 a.m. Then he called his parents and spent the night at home while McCarthy remained at the hospital with Connie Perry.

"They all thanked me for taking her," Andrews said.

Things turned out well. Perry recovered and became a college football coach after graduating.

1977: Colorado was threatening to add to a 15-3 lead in the second quarter when NU safety Larry Valasek intercepted a pass intended for Buff tight end Bob Niziolek at the Nebraska 16. The Husker offense woke up after that, grinding out 390 yards rushing, including 172 by I.M. Hipp, in a 33-15 win. Asked his opinion of CU's defense, Hipp responded, "They talk a lot. Instead of doing their job, they were out there saying, 'Hipp ain't going nowhere. Hipp ain't going to do anything.' It fired me up."

"I HATE 'EM MORE THAN DOG CRAP ON MY SHOES"

BY LARRY PORTER AND TOM ASH

Colorado hadn't yet circled in red its upcoming date with Nebraska. The Buffaloes had not yet named NU as the opponent they most wanted to defeat. That designation didn't come until 1982 when Bill McCartney took over as head coach. CU defensive tackle **Ruben Vaughan** was a few years ahead of the curve.

A sign in Nebraska assistant coach Cletus Fischer's office the week of the 1977 Colorado game read: "I hate Nebraska. I hate 'em more than dog crap on my shoes. I want their meat worse than anyone's in the country." The quote from the Rocky Mountain News was attributed to Vaughan, who said later that it was an off-the-cuff remark in a restaurant and wasn't meant for print. But that's how he felt anyway.

The chalkboard in the Nebraska locker room before the game contained the message: "Free Ruben sandwiches, Saturday, 1:30 p.m."

The Buffs led by 12 points late in the first half before wilting, 33-15.

While Vaughan never enjoyed a victory against NU during his career at Colorado, the Huskers were certainly aware of his presence.

Stan Waldemore, a senior offensive tackle from Belleville, N.J., who later played seven years with the New York Jets, successfully smacked helmets with Vaughan during the Huskers' 1977 victory.

In the locker room following the game, Waldemore's teammates began to chant: "Wally! Wally! Wally!" The chant grew to a roar as the Huskers praised their big lineman for the way he kept Vaughan under control. "That," Waldemore said later, "had to be the greatest thrill in my life. All my teammates – it was a great tribute. I will remember that all of my life. It was pretty emotional for a minute."

Vaughan was still in a talkative mood the following year as a senior. He was quick to tell sportswriters how much he reviled Nebraska prior to the Huskers' 52-14 triumph.

"He said a lot during the game, too," said offensive guard Steve Lindquist, who battled Vaughan for much of the game. "He talked probably more than anyone else we played."

"And that guy doesn't need to say a word," Lindquist continued, paying tribute to Vaughan's ability. "But he was doing all his talking when it was 14-3 (Colorado leading). When we tied it (at 14-14) and then in the second half, he didn't say a word. He was mum. That shows how much talking does for you."

After the game, Vaughan was on the receiving end of a long line of Husker handshakes and best wishes. "It was more heartache than anything else," Vaughan said of his four-year frustration. "But at least I got some respect from Nebraska. My freshman year, they almost spit on me and told me I was no good, but it wasn't that way today. Respect isn't as good as a win, but it's something."

Sportswriters never tired of hearing from Ruben. Three weeks later, they sought his views about who would win the annual conference title showdown – Oklahoma or Nebraska. Osborne took note of Vaughan's response while addressing the weekly Extra Point Club luncheon in Lincoln.

Fellow Big Eight coaches were being asked that same question, Osborne said, along with players of other conference schools and sportswriters in Nebraska and Oklahoma.

"But the only guy who impressed me with his answer was Ruben Vaughan," Osborne deadpanned. "He said Oklahoma would win because they had better athletes. He said Nebraska gets by on great coaching.

"Ol' Ruben is more of a philosopher and pundit than I thought he was."

» 1978: A SMILE OR A STOMACH CRAMP?

Tom Osborne was noted for his stoic demeanor during games, and he sometimes even fed the notion that he never smiled. For instance, student trainer Dave Regier couldn't wait to describe Osborne's reaction following a 42-yard touchdown pass from quarterback Tom Sorley to tight end Junior Miller (89) during NU's 52-14 victory at Colorado in 1978. "You should have seen (Osborne) after Junior Miller caught that touchdown pass," Regier said. "He was grinning from ear to ear."

Osborne was asked if he really had unleashed a wide smile. "I might have," he replied, back in his stoic mode. "Or it might have been a stomach cramp."

Emotions ran high in that game for CU's Mike Davis, a 6-foot-1, 205-pound defensive back. Some Husker fans questioned Davis' sanity after he took a swing at the 6-4, 222-pound Miller in the first quarter and drew a 15-yard penalty. "There was a misunderstanding," Miller said. "He thought I was holding, but I wasn't. So he took a swing at me."

Davis was also involved in a few other incidents, including one when he flipped Husker I-back I.M. Hipp out of bounds late in the third quarter. Plus, he was burned on Miller's touchdown catch.

"I think he's a highly emotional kid," Miller said of Davis. "He got pretty excited. But he had a nice attitude when I talked to him after the game."

– Larry Porter

« 1979: TOO MUCH FOR WORDS

Jarvis Redwine's No. 1 fan said she was speechless after her husband gouged Colorado for 206 yards rushing during a 38-10 conquest.

Frances Redwine, wearing a T-shirt that read, "Li'l Wine," still wore an astonished expression on her face nearly 1½ hours after the game. It proved to be the highest single-game rushing total in Redwine's two-year career at Nebraska. "It's amazing," Frances said. "I'm speechless. I always knew Jarvis was a good ballplayer, but I never thought he'd gain 200 yards."

Redwine (12) tried to prepare his wife for the intense scrutiny that goes with being an NU I-back when he transferred in 1978 from Oregon State, where he spent two seasons.

"Jarvis told me what to expect when we came to Nebraska," Frances said. "But at Oregon State there's not that many people, and the stadium is not that big. So I really couldn't imagine what it was like to see a crowd of this capacity, all wearing red."

As usual, Redwine gave credit to his blockers and to fullback Andra Franklin, in particular. "Franklin means to me what toast does to butter," Redwine said of his fullback. "He's so quiet. He never says much, but he's great to be around. It takes guts to go in there head-up on those defenders week in and week out. He means so much to not only me, but to all of our running backs."

– Larry Porter

THE JOB INTERVIEW IN BOULDER

BY LARRY PORTER

Tom Osborne won at least nine games in each of his 25 seasons as the Nebraska head football coach.

But that wasn't good enough for some fans – at least during the early years of Osborne's career. Oklahoma and Barry Switzer were the sandburs in Osborne's socks.

The flamboyant Switzer seemed to will his Sooners to improbable victory after improbable victory over the Huskers. Some NU fans believed that Osborne's even-keel demeanor would never produce a Big Eight championship – let alone a national championship.

Osborne's Huskers posted a 1-8 record against OU through their first nine meetings. By the late 1970s, the murmurs became loud enough for Colorado to hear.

Cletus Fischer, an offensive line coach, said Osborne gathered his assistant coaches together and told them that Colorado wanted to talk to him about taking the Buffaloes' head coaching job.

"He asked us if we would be willing to go out there with him," Fischer said. "To a man, we all said yes. I would have followed that man anywhere."

According to Fischer, Osborne went to Boulder and was shown around the campus and the city by an athletic department official. They drove past a country club, and the official told Osborne that he would be given a membership there.

"What about my assistant coaches?" Osborne asked, according to Fischer. "I want them to have memberships as well."

The official shook his head. No assistant coaches would ever be given country club memberships.

"Tom was this close to taking that job," Fischer said, holding his thumb and forefinger a quarter of an inch apart.

Osborne, of course, decided the grass really wasn't greener in Boulder and finally got it right against OU. His teams won 12 of their last 17 games, and he finished with a career record of 13-13 against the Sooners.

THE SECOND CHOICE

BY TOM ASH

Colorado Athletic Director Eddie Crowder turned to a fellow former Sooner, Chuck Fairbanks, as Buffalo coach after firing Bill Mallory in 1978. Mallory had produced four straight winning seasons – but he couldn't beat Nebraska and Oklahoma.

Mallory never had a warm relationship with Crowder, nor had he received the unconditional support of the school's big-money boosters. With Fairbanks, the big money got on board, at least initially, and his hiring drew attention nationally, in particular a Sports Illustrated article on his posh new office and lavish ways.

Meanwhile, Mallory was waiting for his next job and watching the CU program from a distance, while living off his $70,000 severance check and raising Morgan horses, pigs and chickens on his acreage east of Boulder.

"There's a little different feeling between Crowder and Fairbanks than there was between Crowder and me," Mallory said. "Chuck's program now is as good as Nebraska's and Oklahoma's. I don't know where they're getting the money, but they're sure spending it."

Mallory landed a job the next year at Northern Illinois, on his way to Indiana.

Fairbanks (at left) had won three Big Eight titles in six years at Oklahoma, enjoying 11-1 seasons his last two years. He left Oklahoma for the New England Patriots, just before the Sooners went on two years' probation for recruiting violations.

He continued his lightning-rod ways during a tumultuous NFL career, which included squabbles with the Patriots' owners and a lawsuit for breach of contract when he accepted Crowder's invitation to join him at CU. Colorado eventually bought out his New England contract.

Fairbanks lost his first CU game against Nebraska 38-10 for a 1-7 start. He hung it up in Boulder after three seasons and a 7-26 record to become coach of the New Jersey Generals of the USFL.

» 1980: A CALL FOR HELP

Roger Craig's first 100-yard game of his NU career came at Colorado during his sophomore season.

Craig hammered the Buffaloes for 176 yards after beginning the game as the No. 3 I-back. Senior Jarvis Redwine (12) limped to the sideline after bruising a thigh while crashing into the Colorado bench. Senior backup Craig Johnson left the game with a bruised shoulder.

"I was kind of scared," Craig said. "There was a lot of pressure on me. But the guys on the sideline kept talking to me and calmed me down."

The Huskers blasted Colorado 45-7, which helped make up for a burglary in which an estimated $300 worth of practice shirts and sweatsuits worn by coaches, managers and trainers were taken from their Folsom Field locker room.

– Larry Porter

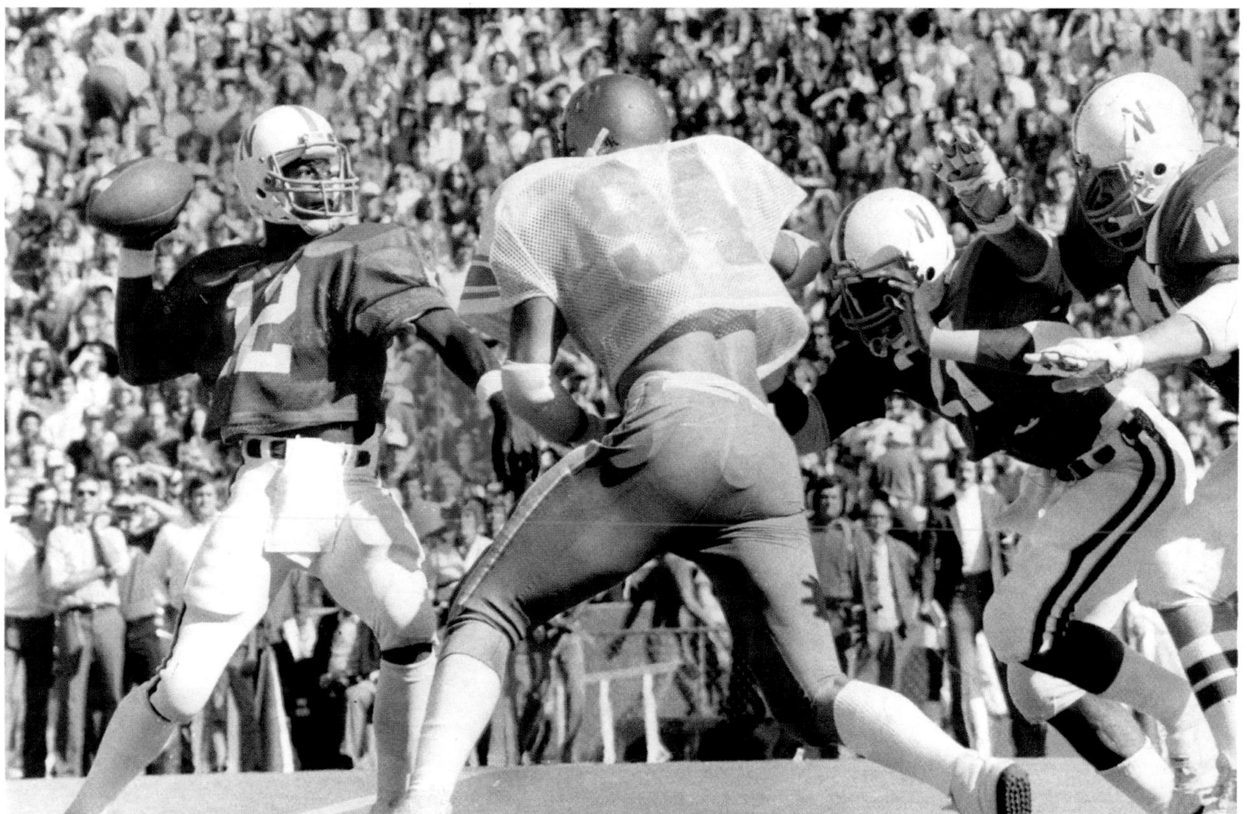

« 1981: INTRODUCING TWO LEGENDS

Nebraska needed a confidence boost in 1981 after going 2-2 to open the season with a schedule of difficult games against Iowa, Florida State, Penn State and Auburn.

It came on the day that two future Husker legends made their first career starts.

Nebraska trampled Colorado 59-0 as quarterback Turner Gill (12) and I-back Mike Rozier (30) made their starting debuts. Gill directed the offense to a then-NCAA record of 42 first downs and 719 yards in total offense and tied a then-school record with four touchdown passes.

I-back Roger Craig, who lost his starting job that day to Rozier, said he had never seen a quarterback like Gill.

"He's just turned the program around for us," Craig said. "He's something else."

Rozier rushed for 95 yards and two touchdowns on 11 carries.

The win over Colorado started a string of 27 straight Big Eight Conference wins for NU. Rozier went on to win the Heisman Trophy in 1983, and Gill finished fourth in the Heisman voting.

– Steve Sinclair

^ 1982: LAYING THE GROUNDWORK

The two years before Bill McCartney became football coach at Colorado, Nebraska defeated the Buffaloes by a combined score of 104-7. Colorado had lost 14 straight games to the Huskers. Not exactly what you would call a rivalry. McCartney changed that when he arrived in Boulder and found out the Buffaloes didn't have a rival. "We want one," he said at the time. "We choose Nebraska."

It turned out to be one of his best decisions, even though it's still debated in Nebraska if the rivalry is reciprocal. The Nebraska game became a red-letter day each year in Colorado. All games on the schedule in the Buffs' locker room were printed in black. The Nebraska game was highlighted in red. McCartney banned his staff and players from wearing red.

McCartney's first game against Nebraska was a 40-14 loss in 1982, but the Buffs made a statement. They trailed by only 20-14 entering the fourth quarter.

CU quarterback Randy Essington passed for 361 yards, the most ever by a Nebraska opponent at the time, although he completed only 24 of 51 attempts. Among his misses was a first-quarter toss to Kent Davis (7) with NU's Allen Lyday (18) and Bret Clark (10) defending.

It took four more years, but Colorado finally upset the then-third-ranked Huskers 20-10 in Boulder – ending a string of 18 straight NU wins over the Buffs since 1967.

The Buffaloes continued to make noise against their self-proclaimed rival by going 3-2-1 against the Huskers from 1986 through 1991. In 1990, they won their only national championship in a season that included a 27-12 win over NU, their first win in Lincoln in 23 years.

– Steve Sinclair

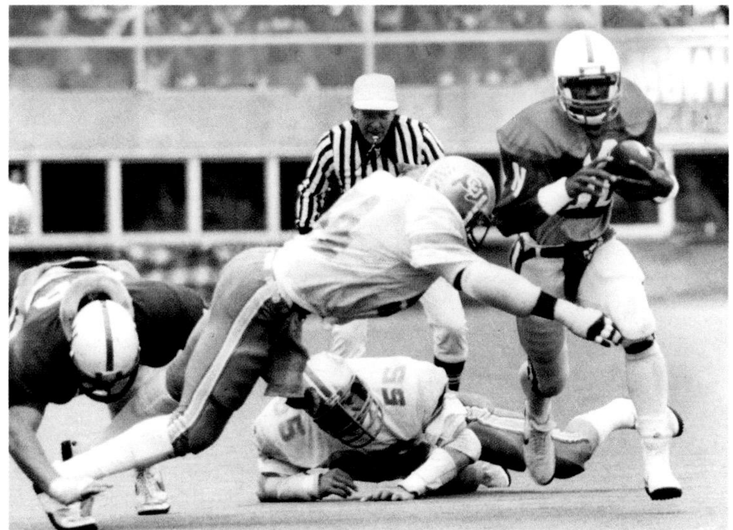

« 1983: BUFFS BLOWN UP

Nebraska promoted the 1983 football season with a poster of quarterback Turner Gill (12), I-back Mike Rozier (30) and wingback Irving Fryar under the words "The Scoring Explosion."

"They didn't make those posters for nothin,'" Fryar said after the Huskers provided a stunning example of their quick-strike scoring ability in a 69-19 victory over Colorado.

Nebraska exploded for 48 points in the third quarter against the Buffaloes, who were thinking upset after trailing the top-ranked Huskers 14-12 at halftime. The seven touchdowns came on 18 plays. The first four scores came in a possession time of 1 minute, 24 seconds.

"Every time our offense touched the ball," defensive back Mike McCashland said, "it was boom, boom, boom.

"I don't think I've ever seen anything like it."

The 48 points fell one shy of tying the NCAA record for points in a quarter, held by Davidson and Houston. A missed extra-point kick by Scott Livingston kept the Huskers from sharing the record.

Fryar and Rozier each scored two touchdowns, and Gill had one during the third quarter onslaught.

The '83 Huskers lived up to "The Scoring Explosion" expectations throughout their 12-0 regular season with 624 points, then an NCAA record. They averaged a whopping 52 points a game. Boom. Boom. Boom.

– Steve Sinclair

« **1984:** With Turner Gill gone, Nebraska alternated quarterbacks Craig Sundberg and Travis Turner. Turner, a walk-on from Scottsbluff, started the Huskers' 24-7 win over Colorado, but Sundberg replaced him in the second quarter after the fumble-plagued Huskers had trouble moving the ball. After NU trailed 7-3 at halftime, coach Tom Osborne used both quarterbacks in the third quarter.

Turner came in to direct the Huskers on a 79-yard scoring drive, scoring the go-ahead touchdown on a 1-yard run two plays into the fourth quarter. Turner scored again on a 3-yard run with 9:13 left and followed by completing three third-down passes on NU's final scoring drive, which ended with his 11-yard touchdown pass to tight end Brian Hiemer.

Turner said he didn't have any problems with NU's two-quarterback system. "I'm not trying to win the job from anybody," Turner said. "Craig plays well, and I want to see him play. Who starts doesn't really matter to me."

The Blackshirts held down the fort until the offense got going, limiting CU quarterback Steve Vogel (13) to 10-of-35 passing for just 84 yards.

– Steve Sinclair

» **1985: IT WAS HIS DAY**

Tom Rathman celebrated Tom Rathman Day in style by providing the biggest play in Nebraska's 17-7 win. Rathman (26), a senior fullback from Grand Island, gave his fans a thrill on the day his hometown saluted him: He broke a 7-7 tie with an 84-yard touchdown run in the final minute of the third quarter.

"I cut it clear back, jumped over a pile and outran everybody," Rathman said. "Well, I don't know if I outran them, but I got into the end zone before they tackled me."

Rathman finished with 115 yards on 11 carries. He also had a big game the next week when he rushed for 84 yards and two touchdowns in a 41-3 win at Kansas State.

Rathman, who later played for two Super Bowl winners with the San Francisco 49ers, posted his NU career-high rushing game later in 1985 when he ran for 159 yards on nine carries against Kansas. Rathman ended his senior season with an NU fullback rushing record of 881 yards, which still stands.

– Steve Sinclair

^ 1986: THE STREAK ENDS

Colorado linebacker Barry Remington (40) intercepted a pass intended for Nebraska's Rod Smith (88) with 3:14 to play, sealing the Buffs' 20-10 upset. By putting an end to NU's 18-game series winning streak, coach Bill McCartney answered the critics who said he made a mistake by choosing the Huskers as the Buffaloes' designated rival. "You achieve what you emphasize," McCartney said after the upset of the third-ranked Cornhuskers at Folsom Field. "It's my idea that whatever you do, whatever is your livelihood, you've got to find out who the pacesetter is and then go after him. That's how you've got to measure your program.". Colorado fans responded to a plea to wear gold to the game to counter the red of the estimated 15,000 visiting fans. NU fans stood and applauded Colorado players as they celebrated on their way to the locker room. "They have classy fans," CU linebacker Eric McCarty said, "but the red makes me sick."

« 1987: KEITH "ALL-UNIVERSE" JONES

Nebraska needed a quick recovery for its game against Colorado to end the regular season. The matchup came a week after the Huskers lost to Oklahoma in a matchup hyped as the Game of the Century II.

"A lot of us are having some questions about whether we're as good as we thought we were," Nebraska safety Jeff Tomjack said.

Nebraska responded just fine by pounding the Buffaloes 24-7 to finish the regular season with a 10-1 record. Senior I-back Keith "End Zone" Jones (6) led the Huskers with a career-high 248 yards on 26 carries, following the blocking of John McCormick (61) and his offensive line mates. Jones scored on runs of 50 and 44 yards, leading ESPN commentator Lee Corso to call him "all-universe" against the Buffaloes. "He hit the crease, and he was gone," said CU linebacker Mike Jones, who had 16 tackles.

Keith Jones, an Omaha Central graduate, finished his Husker career with 2,488 yards to rank No. 3 on NU's all-time rushing list.

– Steve Sinclair

» **1988:** Nebraska got lucky in a 7-0 victory. Midway through the second quarter, CU tailback J.J. Flannigan (2) squirted up the middle on a sprint draw, juked around an NU cornerback and ran free toward the goal line. But Flannigan fumbled the ball and had to stop to recover it at the NU 19. "The good Lord was looking over us on that one because he just flat dropped it," NU defensive coordinator Charlie McBride said. "That, as it ends up, was really the game. So we were very, very fortunate." A holding penalty and a 19-yard loss on a reverse pushed Colorado back to the NU 43 and forced a punt. The debate over whether the series was a rivalry continued. "I don't know what (Bill) McCartney is telling those guys," NU outside linebacker Broderick Thomas said. "But it's not good for the blood. Every year, they come around saying, 'It's our bowl game. We're going to try to beat Nebraska.' They hate us."

1989: "The significance of this win in my estimation knows no proportions," coach Bill McCartney said after the second-ranked Buffaloes defeated third-ranked Nebraska 27-21 behind quarterback Darian Hagan (3). "It's obviously the greatest win that I've ever been a part of – easily." The victory was the deciding blow in CU's march to the Big Eight championship and the Orange Bowl. It was the first Colorado team in 28 years to beat Nebraska and Oklahoma in the same year. "That's a big part of this," McCartney said. "To be able to compete with those two programs – that is our loftiest expectation, because those are two of the top five programs in the country every year." In a bit of irony on the final play of the game, Dave McCloughan, son of former Nebraska player Kent McCloughan, tipped away a pass in the end zone to preserve the victory.

» **1990:** For many Nebraska fans, the lasting memory of a 27-12 loss to Colorado was a ruling that NU quarterback Mickey Joseph (2) had stepped out of bounds on an apparent touchdown run. The score would have pushed the Huskers' lead to 12-0 in the third quarter on a rainy day, but the placing of the ball at the 9-yard line instead was followed by a missed field-goal attempt. The Buffs struggled for three quarters before running back Eric Bieniemy (1) got on track, scoring four times in the fourth period. For the Huskers, it was the first loss at home to the Buffs in 23 years. "There's a new boss in the Big Eight," yelled CU players as they left the field. Not really. The two teams tied for the Big Eight crown the next year, then Nebraska won the final four league titles before the conference dissolved into the Big 12.

"MUSIC TO HIS EYES"

As Nebraska seniors were introduced before the 1990 game with Colorado, an All-America defensive tackle didn't hear any cheers. Husker fans acknowledged Kenny Walker (57), who is deaf, not with a full-throated roar but with a gentle, moving tribute. They used the sign-language "deaf clap," raising their hands above their heads, spreading their fingers and rotating their wrists back and forth. Walker's interpreter, Mimi Mann, called the gesture "music to his eyes."

– Michael Kelly

⌃ **1991:** The game came down to the final play, a 41-yard field-goal attempt by Nebraska's Byron Bennett (13) for the win. While snowballs hurled from the CU student section splattered the field around the players, Bennett weathered three consecutive timeouts called by Colorado to shake his confidence. None of it mattered as the Buffs blocked the kick to leave the game tied 19-19. The temperature was 12 degrees and the wind chill was 8 below when the game started. "In terms of absolute temperature," coach Tom Osborne said, "it was the coldest I've ever coached or played in." Perhaps the fact that players from both teams endured such harsh weather was a factor in the respect they showed each other following the game, with plenty of handshakes and smiles.

≈ **1992:** Colorado, the No. 4 passing team in the country, completed only 12 of 34 attempts for 136 yards in NU's 52-7 rout on a misty Halloween in Lincoln. The loss ended Colorado's 25-game Big Eight unbeaten streak. "For this climate, you've still got to be able to jam it at people some," coach Tom Osborne said. "Colorado has committed itself to the pass, and it may turn out real well. But today it didn't." Buffs quarterback Koy Detmer (14) faced a heavy rush from Blackshirts Trev Alberts (34) and John Parrella (92), who had three sacks.

» **1993:** A diving interception by John Reece (6) with 1:21 left in the game iced Nebraska's 21-17 victory. NU quarterback Tommie Frazier, who gritted his teeth and played through a shoulder injury in the second half, said the Nebraska defense showed its colors by securing the win. "It's going to help us in the long run," Frazier said. "If we get down – with national championship title hopes on the line and the game's close – I'll guarantee you we'll pull it out." Coach Bill McCartney's plea to Colorado fans to treat Nebraskans with respect apparently worked, with a number of visiting fans saying they had no problems. "This is not what I expected," said one Husker fan.

CUNNINGHAM
8
18

« ≈ **1994:** Quarterback Brook Berringer (18) answered questions about whether he could direct the NU offense in the absence of Tommie Frazier, who was out with a blood clot. Berringer completed 12 of 17 passes for 142 yards and a touchdown in his fourth college start, a 24-7 victory in Lincoln. Tight end Eric Alford (88), who caught five passes, said he was surprised to see coach Tom Osborne call so many pass plays. "I was like, 'Is he sick or something?'" Alford said. "I guess not. T.O. knows what he's doing." Osborne had publicly pleaded with Husker fans to be loud but polite at the game. He got his wish, with Memorial Stadium roaring from start to finish in the battle between teams ranked second and third in the country.

≈ **1995:** Quarterback Tommie Frazier (15) was spectacular in second-ranked Nebraska's 44-21 win over No. 7 Colorado, completing 14 of 23 passes for a career-high 241 yards and leading the NU offense to a turnover-free and penalty-free performance. He also added a highlight-reel play in the second-quarter, taking a full-speed hit from a CU linebacker but staying on his feet long enough to dump a swing pass to I-back Ahman Green (30) for a 35-yard gain. "It was absolutely phenomenal," said outside linebacker coach Tony Samuel, who saw it from the press box. "That was as great a play as I've ever seen. It's unbelievable." Twenty minutes before kickoff, coach Rick Neuheisel had the Buffs take the field through the student section, then the team met at midfield as a man dressed as a Samoan warrior beat a drum and got the crowd chanting, "Wartime, Wartime." But the greatest warrior in the house wore red No. 15.

« **1996:** The feeling started during the bus ride to the game in Lincoln. "I started getting chills down my spine," said Husker rush end Grant Wistrom (98). "And we were still three miles from the stadium. I just knew it was going to be a special day." It ended up as a career day for Wistrom, who had 13 tackles – six for losses or no gains – in a 17-12 Husker victory. Defensive coordinator Charlie McBride said later that the team's film review was like watching a Wistrom highlight reel. "Even the players were saying, 'Boy, Grant had a great game,'" McBride said.

» **1997:** Quarterback Scott Frost (7) had 76 yards rushing and 92 yards passing in a 27-24 win to become the 12th player in NCAA Division I-A history to rush and pass for 1,000 yards in the same season. "I think what makes this special to me is the names on the list that I recognize," he said. "I watched some of those guys play, and they were great ballplayers." The Buffaloes completed their first losing season since 1984 and were kept from a bowl game for the first time in a decade.

« **1998:** NU rush end Mike Rucker (84), a preseason All-America candidate, entered the final game of the season with no sacks. He sacked Colorado quarterback Mike Moschetti (4) twice as part of a six-tackle day in a 16-14 victory, and both times Moschetti fumbled. "It felt really good to get that monkey off my back," Rucker said. "I've been disappointed with a lot of things, but to go out at Memorial Stadium with a win, I don't care about anything else right now." The victory in coach Frank Solich's first year extended the Huskers' NCAA record of consecutive nine-win years to 30.

» 1999: HUSKER PRAYERS ANSWERED

Quarterback Eric Crouch's (7) touchdown in overtime ended what might have been the greatest game in the series, a 33-30 Nebraska win. Trailing by 24 points, Colorado mounted a comeback that tied the game, then saw kicker Jeremy Aldrich miss a game-winning field goal on the final play of regulation. "There is a God!" a Nebraska fan shouted, raising her arms and looking to the sky after the kick sailed wide right. "And He's a Husker!" Aldrich came back to kick a 33-yarder on Colorado's overtime possession, but Crouch sealed the victory by sneaking over from the 1-yard line, sending linemen Dominic Raiola (54) and Jon Rutherford (66) into delirium. "I don't know if you can call this luck or fate," Crouch said. "All I know is that we tried our hardest there at the end and got it done."

66
54
18
52

« 2000: ANOTHER MIRACLE FINISH

Was Nebraska's 34-32 win in Lincoln even better than the previous year's miracle? The Huskers entered the fourth quarter with a lead, but Colorado scored with a little more than 14 minutes left to go ahead 24-21. Nebraska tied it up with 9:22 left on a field goal by Josh Brown (26), then went ahead 31-24 with 5:20 remaining on a 26-yard run by Eric Crouch. But that lead also failed to hold. Colorado drove 68 yards in 11 plays, then passed for two points on the conversion with 47 seconds left to take a 32-31 lead. The Buffaloes' revenge for the previous year's heartbreak? Not so fast. Colorado's attempt at a squib kickoff backfired when the ball was returned to the NU 41-yard line. From there, the Huskers got the ball to the CU 29 with 10 seconds remaining. At that point, Brown would have faced a 46-yard attempt. But Crouch connected with receiver Bobby Newcombe (12) at the 12-yard line with five seconds left. Brown kicked it through and was carried away on the shoulders of his teammates. "I can die a happy man right now," said Brown, who had missed a key kick in a 29-28 loss earlier in the season at Kansas State. "Bobby's catch took a lot of pressure off of Josh," Crouch said.

^ 2001: BUTCHERED IN BOULDER

A 62-36 loss in Boulder was one of the most painful in Nebraska history, leaving Huskers John Garrison (52) and Erwin Swiney (16) in shock at the end. Colorado coach Gary Barnett had a simple explanation. "We just blocked them and broke tackles," Barnett said. "We felt like no one had really come out and lined up and run right at them all year. That was what we were going to do. That's sort of our strength." The Buffs scored their first touchdown less than three minutes into the game, and by the time the Huskers looked up at the scoreboard early in the second quarter, it was Colorado 35, Nebraska 3. "They gashed us," Craig Bohl, Nebraska's defensive coordinator, said of the Buffs' 380 rushing yards. "This is obviously one of the worst days that we've had." Overlooked amid the disastrous afternoon was that the Huskers had rallied to within 42-30 late in the third quarter behind the outstanding play of Eric Crouch, who rushed for 162 yards and passed for 198. But the Buffs were able to get things going again in the fourth quarter, putting the game away with three touchdowns in a little over three minutes. "This is pretty much a nightmare for us," Crouch said.

» **2002:** Colorado's 28-13 victory in Lincoln ensured that Nebraska would not have a nine-win season for the first time in 34 years. Brian Calhoun (2), a fourth-string I-back who said he knew little about the rivalry, ran for 137 yards on 20 carries to lead the Buffs. Cornhusker fans in the northwest portion of Memorial Stadium showered the winners with warm applause as they left the field. "The significance is it's a great tribute to the University of Nebraska and their fans, and what a difficult place to play this is," CU coach Gary Barnett said afterward. "We put a lot of emphasis on playing Nebraska, and it's all out of respect because of what they've done, what they have accomplished. I hope they take that as a compliment because it's meant that way."

« **2003:** A 31-22 win in Boulder earned Nebraska its ninth win for the 34th time in 35 seasons and erased some of the sting still left over from the 62-36 nightmare two years earlier. But most of all, players said, it was for their embattled coach. "When I walked into the locker room, I told Frank Solich I loved him," said NU linebacker T.J. Hollowell (2), who came up with a game-saving interception in the fourth quarter. "He's been there for us, and I'm happy to get a win for him." Solich was fired the next day.

» **2004:** Colorado's 26-20 win in Lincoln ensured Nebraska's first losing season since 1961 and its first season since 1968 without a bowl game. "Sometimes you need to start over again in order to really appreciate what happened in the past," said Husker sophomore quarterback Joe Dailey (12).

» **2005:** NU's 30-3 win as a 17-point underdog represented the largest Husker upset in at least 20 years. Junior quarterback Zac Taylor (13) played a big part by throwing for 255 first-half yards on the way to 392 for the game. Colorado fans littered Folsom Field with trash in the second half, delaying the game for seven to eight minutes and leading to the removal of two entire sections of students.

« **2006:** NU coach Bill Callahan dug deep into his bag of tricks in a 37-14 win, calling no fewer than seven "special plays," as the Huskers referred to their gimmickry. The starting strong safety ran for a first down. The backup quarterback threw a touchdown pass – to a defensive end. The starting QB drew a pass interference call. The place-kicker deposited a punt at the 1-yard line. The first hint of what was to come occurred late in the first half when, out of a field-goal formation, backup quarterback Joe Ganz hit defensive end Barry Turner (99) with a 29-yard touchdown pass.

≈ **2007:** Bill Callahan coached his final NU game, a 65-51 loss in Boulder that sealed a second losing season out of four for the coach. "They've been great years," Callahan said after the game, although he had not yet been officially informed of a decision on his fate. "I have no regrets being here at Nebraska."

2008: DID THAT REALLY HAPPEN?

BY RICH KAIPUST

Nebraska coach Bo Pelini was asking Alex Henery (90) if he could kick a field goal that would be 9 yards longer than any he had made before as a Husker. The sophomore looked Pelini in the eye and said yes.

Up in the Memorial Stadium press box, where objectivity and impartiality sit separate from the fans below, the majority of news media members seemed to be saying, "No way he makes this." Some even stood as the NU field-goal unit trotted out.

Henery then put a 57-yard field goal through the uprights with 1:43 left, giving Nebraska a 33-31 lead on Colorado in what would eventually be a 40-31 victory. The Huskers would finish the 2008 regular season at 8-4 instead of 7-5, and head for the Gator Bowl on New Year's Day.

The reaction in the press box was about as loud as it gets, not in celebration but amazement and appreciation of what the soft-spoken, modestly built kicker from Omaha Burke had just done. To be sure, it was one of the most memorable kicks in Nebraska football history.

And also the longest.

"Normally, his range is right around 52," Pelini said after the game. "He kind of looked at me and said, 'I made it in warmups. I've been hitting it good.' I said, 'OK, let's go.' "

What did Henery honestly think? "I'll admit I was a little iffy on the yardage," he said.

Pelini had to be as much relieved as excited about the kick. Earlier in the game, the first-year coach had called for a fake field goal with Nebraska leading 24-17, only to watch a Colorado defender swipe an overhead pitch from holder Jake Wesch – intended for Henery – and return it for a touchdown.

⌃ **2009:** Nebraska sealed its 28-20 victory in Boulder by pounding the Buffaloes in the fourth quarter with a bullish, downhill-style ground attack. Leading 21-14 with 13:35 left in the game, Nebraska got the ball on its 20-yard line and drove 80 yards while eating up 6:52 on the clock. Thirteen of the 15 plays were rushes, with freshman running back Rex Burkhead (22) churning out 61 yards in 10 carries on the drive. Burkhead finished it off with a 7-yard run to seal the victory. "I thought that was a statement drive for us, and that won us the football game," Bo Pelini said.

STILL HAVING NIGHTMARES ABOUT . . .

DARIAN HAGAN

Quarterback

Darian Hagan said he was warned about the game plan that former Nebraska defensive coordinator Charlie McBride had waiting for him in 1989. Gary Barnett, then the Buffs' offensive coordinator, said the Huskers were going to take away the pitch and make the CU quarterback keep the football as much as possible.

"They were right," Hagan said. "And I was sore after that game, too."

Hagan carried 25 times for 86 yards in the Buffs' 27-21 win in Boulder. The sophomore did find a way around NU's strategy once, though, freezing NU safety Reggie Cooper on a fake pitch, turning upfield and then dumping off the ball to J.J. Flannigan on what turned into a 70-yard touchdown play.

It was the start of a three-year stretch in which Hagan led Colorado to a 2-0-1 record against the Huskers. Overall, he was 28-5-2 as a starter with a 20-0-1 mark in Big Eight play.

"What I remember most about those games was the intensity level," Hagan said of NU-CU. "Those guys wanted to beat us, and we wanted to beat them. We were out to make a point that Colorado football was for real and we took those games really, really seriously. It's fun when you look back at how intense the coaches got for it."

Hagan, now an assistant coach at Colorado, is referred to as "arguably the best all-around athlete in the history of the CU football program" in his bio on the school's website.

Nebraskans might not argue, recalling the explosiveness and charisma that made Hagan very much like some of the Oklahoma quarterbacks that gave the Huskers fits through the 1970s and '80s. Hagan and tailback Eric Bieniemy fueled a 27-point fourth quarter as CU rallied for a 27-12 win in Lincoln in 1990, then Hagan ran for two touchdowns and threw for 140 yards in the 19-19 tie in 1991.

Thickening the plot was the fact that Hagan at one point had told former NU assistant George Darlington that he was coming to Lincoln. Darlington was even at Hagan's high school in Los Angeles when CU coach Bill McCartney and his staff made their final push, all showing up in black blazers. "I thought it was the FBI," Hagan said.

But Hagan said he always respected Nebraska and made it a point to find coach Tom Osborne before or after games. "It was always special to go out and shake his hand," Hagan said.

– Rich Kaipust

MICKEY PRUITT

Safety

Was a three-time All-Big Eight selection and led the Colorado defense that held NU to 123 rushing yards and 10 points in the 1986 upset.

ERIC BIENIEMY

Running back

Fumbled five times in the first three quarters of the 1990 game but came back to score four fourth-quarter touchdowns as Colorado rallied for its 27-12 win.

GREG THOMAS

Safety

Leaped and blocked Byron Bennett's attempt at a 41-yard field goal, with a barrage of snowballs flying, on the last play of a 19-19 tie in 1991.

CHRIS BROWN

Running back

Ran for 198 yards and six TDs as Colorado tore through the Nebraska defense in a 62-36 rout in 2001.

DICK ANDERSON

Defensive back

Intercepted a second-quarter pass and lateraled to Mike Veeder for a touchdown in 1967 that aided the fourth-ranked Buffs' 21-16 win in Lincoln.

Boone Pickens Stadium provided a hospitable setting for the Huskers in their 2010 game in Stillwater.

OKLAHOMA STATE

COWBOYS' STARS RARELY SHONE IN VICTORIES

BY MICHAEL KELLY | WORLD-HERALD STAFF WRITER

STILLWATER RUNS DEEP with affection for its Cowboys in "Orange Country," as Oklahoma State University calls its fandom. A college town, Stillwater is friendly but loud on game days, never more so than in 2002, when the football team ended an 0-35-1 stretch against Nebraska with a 24-21 win. "For all those people that played on the past teams that Nebraska beat," said All-America receiver Rashaun Woods, "this is a good feeling for them also." Though the Pokes couldn't beat the Huskers for a long time, it's not as though OSU lacked star power. Heisman Trophy winner Barry Sanders, Thurman Thomas, Hart Lee Dykes, Leslie O'Neal, Terry Miller and others dealt NU fits at times, but couldn't get a W. In recent years, though, the university and its athletic department have benefited from a superstar alum whose love of the school has fit OSU's needs to a T – Boone Pickens, the oilman-entrepreneur whose $165 million donation is the largest ever given to a university athletic department. Players make their traditional walk down Hester Avenue two hours before game time to the renovated stadium, now called Boone Pickens Stadium.

But for all those years against Nebraska, it was mighty slim pickin's. The former Oklahoma A&M had become Oklahoma State University in 1957 and joined the Big Eight Conference in 1960, winning the first two meetings with Nebraska. But from the time Bob Devaney arrived as NU coach in 1962, things went the Huskers' way. The 1964 win included an 89-yard kickoff return by Frankie Solich. OSU, led by future pro Walt Garrison, put a scare into Nebraska the next year before losing by four. The Huskers won by a point in 1968 on a touchdown pass with 57 seconds left. By contrast, in a 65-31 win in 1970, Nebraska "used nearly every mode of transportation to the end zone." The only non-loss for the Cowboys during the streak came in 1973, a 17-17 tie. With fourth and a foot for the Huskers, OSU stopped them on a goal-line stand. The next three games were close, including a four-point NU win in '76 with the help of a school-record 30 tackles (14 unassisted) by

The crowd at Boone Pickens Stadium is close to the action, as Nebraska receiver Maurice Purify discovered in 2006.

ROAD TRIP TO
STILLWATER
Oklahoma State University

Founded: 1890, as Oklahoma Agricultural and Mechanical College, changed to current name in 1957

Enrollment: 33,000

Colors: Orange and black

Conference history: Began conference football schedule in 1960, as the Big Seven became the Big Eight.

Stadium: Boone Pickens Stadium, capacity 60,218

History of "Cowboys": Oklahoma A&M sports teams at first were referred to as the Agriculturists or Aggies. A U.S. deputy marshal who served in the Old West, Frank "Pistol Pete" Eaton, headed a Stillwater parade in the 1920s, and the image of the tough old cowboy became a cartoon drawing that caught on.

Distance from Memorial Stadium in Lincoln: 391 miles

Worth remembering:
The stands at Boone Pickens Stadium put the fans close to the action, so visiting teams get an earful on the sidelines or when they run out of bounds. After singing the alma mater, Oklahoma State players will celebrate a victory by jumping into the student section with a "Lewis Field Leap," which began under the stadium's previous name. How big is donor Boone Pickens at OSU? His biography appeared in last year's football media guide 20 pages before coach Mike Gundy's.

Quote:
"Tough. They've played us tough up here and down there. They'll be in the game all the way to the end. They won't lay down on you."

– NU defensive tackle Mike Fultz, asked to describe Oklahoma State (1976)

T. Boone Pickens donated $165 million to Oklahoma State athletics.

linebacker Clete Pillen. Nebraska employed what defensive coordinator Monte Kiffin called a "bend-but-don't-break" defense. "It's nerve-wracking," he said, "but it will win for you more often than gambling on defense."

Among those playing for the Pokes in 1980 was a senior and future college head coach – Nebraska years later tried to hire him – named Houston Nutt. He had auburn hair, and his brother Dick had red hair. Houston said that when both played on the OSU basketball team and his brother went to the foul line, NU students sang: "It's Howdy Doody time."

NU won a few by big scores, but the 1983 Huskers – who Sports Illustrated said might be the best college team ever – hung on at Stillwater to win 14-10 on a Bret Clark interception in the end zone on the final play. Jimmy Johnson, the OSU coach, said the Cowboys could have won if they had two more minutes. Okie State wore its spurs the next year in Lincoln, too, but was saddled with a 17-3 loss in part because of a punt return for a touchdown by an experienced rodeo cowboy, Shane Swanson of Hershey, Neb. He was sprung on a block by unheralded cornerback Dave Burke, who played the game of his life – a diving interception in the end zone, seven tackles (six unassisted), a fumble recovery, two key pass breakups and a partially blocked field-goal attempt.

In 1985, OSU was ranked fifth in the nation and Nebraska ninth, but the Huskers won again. Both were ranked nationally in '87 (NU second, OSU 12th) when the teams bumped into each other at the movies the night before the game and exchanged harsh words. Coach Tom Osborne didn't witness what happened, saying the movies he watches on Friday night are game films, and that he thought the incident was blown out of proportion. NU's Broderick Thomas said OSU's Thurman Thomas taunted Nebraska by saying it would take all 11 defenders at once to stop him. Collectively, at least, they did – holding him to 7 yards on nine carries.

Nebraska won big the next few years, including a 55-0 victory in 1992. Posting his 200th coaching victory at Stillwater in '93, Osborne was congratulated by a surprise visitor, Barry Switzer. "Just go for 300, coach," said the former Oklahoma head coach. Because of the top two quarterbacks' health problems, third-stringer Matt Turman of Wahoo, Neb., came on to guide NU to a 1994 win, center Aaron Graham saying afterward: "It brought tears to my eyes to see him come into the game. I thought of all the things he has gone through to get to that point." In 1995, Ahman Green, another in a long line of Omaha Central running backs at NU, ran 18 yards on his first carry for Nebraska. With the move to the Big 12 Conference, the teams didn't meet in '96 and '97, and played the '98 game at Arrowhead Stadium in Kansas City, Mo.

Then came 2002, the end of the streak, the toppling of the goal posts. But Nebraska won again the next year, inspired by more than 800 Husker lettermen trotting onto the field as part of a Husker Nation Reunion – led by Osborne, the former coach and by then a congressman. NU linebacker Barrett Ruud came up with the winning touchdown, a 15-yard fumble recovery. His dad, Tom Ruud, who played in the 1970s, heard the stadium rock to the sound of "Ruuuuuuud!" The Cowboys won again in 2006 and '07, the old streak a thing of the past. Their home field, formerly Lewis Stadium and now named for Boone Pickens, oddly lines up not in a standard north-south direction but in an east-west direction. That field alignment came about in 1913, OSU says, "to avoid the prevailing strong winds." Now the winds of change have prevailed, and Nebraska has aligned itself with the Big Ten Conference – an entirely new direction.

BATTLE OF THE BANDS

In the late '70s, Big Eight football coaches voted to ban school bands from sitting directly behind the players' benches. Oklahoma State coach Jim Stanley had complained that the band noise at Nebraska was terribly rude and distracting. Nebraska assistant coach John Melton, representing the Huskers at the conference meetings, informed Stanley that it was the OSU band that was parked behind his bench. The coaches thought it was a good idea anyway and voted unanimously to move all bands.

– Tom Ash

Cornhuskers Mike Green (34), Joe Buda (52) and Dan Delaney (67) had to tune out fans, cheerleaders and a glaring Pistol Pete during a trip to Stillwater in 1968.

≫ **1960:** Oklahoma State upended the Cornhuskers 7-6 in the first Big Eight meeting of the two schools. The game was played before a crowd of 24,000, the "smallest Lincoln turnout in years," The World-Herald's Gregg McBride reported.

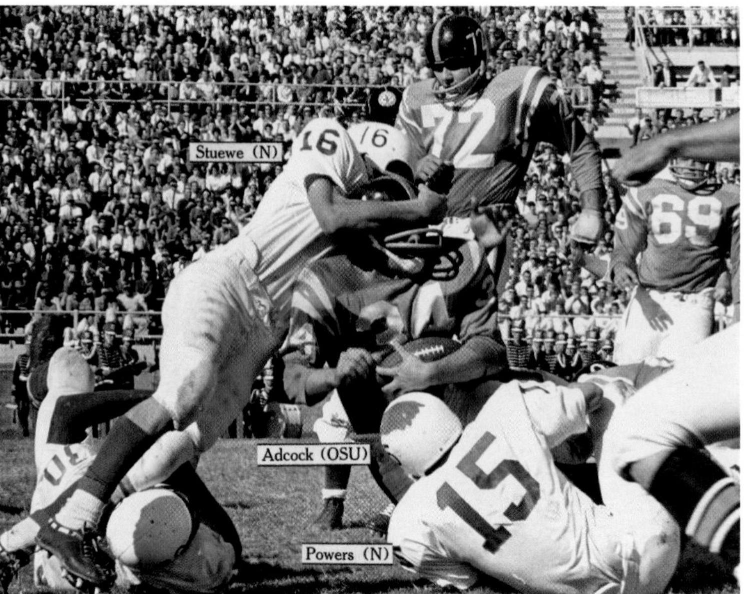

« **1961:** Bob Adcock fought his way past NU's Dennis Stuewe (16) and Warren Powers (15) to cross the goal line and send Oklahoma State on its way to a 14-6 win. A fumble recovery on Nebraska's 1 helped set up the score. The schools ended up tied in the conference standings that year with 2-5 records. Powers later became a Husker assistant coach and Missouri head coach.

» **1962:** Nebraska scored twice in the first quarter and held on for a 14-0 victory on a soggy Memorial Stadium field sprinkled with sawdust and fanned by a helicopter up to an hour before game time. The victory pushed the Huskers' record to 8-1 under first-year coach Bob Devaney, bringing pleasure to members of the 1920, '21 and '22 teams that were honored at the game. "It's great to see this old place buzzing again," said Link Lyman, a former lineman and an assistant coach with the Huskers' 1941 Rose Bowl team. "Yes sir, Nebraska fans are getting their reward this year for their never-failing support through the bad years."

« **1963:** All-America offensive lineman Bob Brown (64) also played linebacker, as NU held off the 1-7 Cowboys 20-16 in Stillwater. Nebraska, which had left three injured starters at home, had a long injury list after the game. "I'm darned glad it's over. If we had to play a little longer, it might have been a long ride home," Bob Devaney said.

« **1964:** NU ran its record to 9-0 with a 27-14 win. Frank Solich's second-quarter kickoff return put the Huskers ahead for good. "As blocks were thrown and bodies fell, slick Frank turned on the afterburners," The World-Herald's Wally Provost reported.

» **1965:** Frank Solich (seated) passed out the oranges in the locker room after Nebraska rallied for a 21-17 win that secured the Orange Bowl for the Huskers. It was another rugged game between the two schools, with OSU fullback Walt Garrison being pulled down on the NU 5-yard line as time expired. "I always worry about Oklahoma State," said Nebraska co-captain Mike Kennedy. "I've got more respect for them than any other team in the league. But one thing about our club, these guys never quit."

1966: The Huskers beat OSU 21-6 on a chilly November afternoon in Lincoln to wrap up their fourth straight Big Eight championship. The 15-point margin was the largest of the schools' first 10 conference games.

≚ **1967:** Middle guard Wayne Meylan (66) totaled 13 tackles, nine unassisted, and made life miserable for OSU quarterback Ronnie Johnson (12) in a 9-0 shutout. "I sure did feel that Nebraska rush," Johnson said. "It was there that Meylan played real good." OSU coach Phil Cutchin, sitting in the stands after the game and puffing on a cigarette, summed up the Cowboys' efforts: "Gentlemen, it is my opinion that the game of football is blocking and tackling. That's the name of the game. My present impression is that we failed to do this very well today."

» **1969:** Husker quarterback Jerry Tagge (14) ran for 20 yards and a touchdown and threw for 174 yards in Nebraska's 13-3 victory in Lincoln. "I'll tell you one thing," first-year OSU coach Floyd Gass said, "Nebraska has the greatest fans in the world. They are more courteous and gracious than a lot of people. They don't throw things at you or get on like . . . well, I don't want to point out anybody, but it is getting to be a problem and something has to be done about it some places."

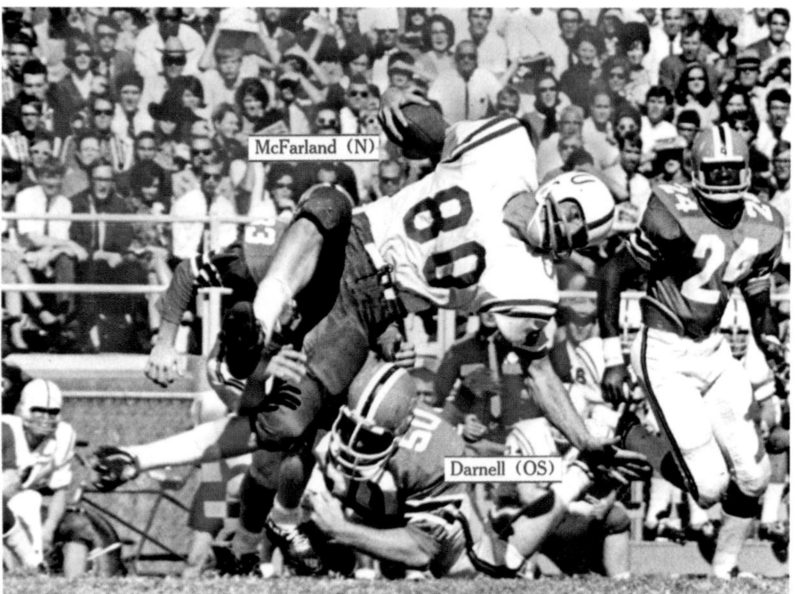

≙ **1968:** The winning 21-20 margin was the result of OSU's decision to go for two when it scored with seven minutes left. The run failed, and Nebraska tied it up on a 5-yard pass reception by Jim McFarland (80) with 57 seconds left in the homecoming game in Stillwater. The extra-point kick sent the OSU fans home grumbling.

« **1970:** The series had its first blowout, with the Huskers blasting OSU 65-31. Seven players scored touchdowns for Nebraska, which scored its most points in a game since 1922. Husker reserves were pleased to get some action after coach Bob Devaney cleared the bench. "We practice all week," said third-team defensive end Bill Pogge, an Omaha Holy Name grad. "I guess I spend three or four hours a week just holding dummies. We're all happy to get in."

« **1971:** NU tight end Jerry List (85) scored on a 42-yard pass to help the Huskers to a 41-13 win in Stillwater, but Oklahoma State claimed a moral victory. The Pokes scored two late touchdowns, the first given up by the Blackshirts in a conference game. Oklahoma State President Robert B. Kamm dashed into the locker room afterward and shouted, "We were the first to score on them in Big Eight play!" The home crowd, undaunted by the score, taunted the Huskers at the end with shouts of "Nebraska is No. 2," in reference to the buildup for NU's coming game with Oklahoma.

« **1972:** The Husker offensive line opened huge holes for fullback Bill Olds (44), as NU ran for 228 yards in a 34-0 victory. But as usual, the Cowboys provided tough hitting. "It's the worst beating I've taken for a while," wingback Johnny Rodgers said. "I took a lot of shots. They were hitting." Middle guard Rich Glover agreed. "The last couple of plays I was in, someone put their hand in my eye. But that's part of it."

» **1973:** First-year Nebraska coach Tom Osborne became better acquainted with the art of second-guessing after a 17-17 tie in Stillwater. Osborne chose to go for a touchdown instead of a field goal from inside the 1-yard line with 2:23 left in the game and NU was stopped a foot short. "We figure we can make fourth and a foot 70 to 80 percent of the time," he said. "Sure, some people will criticize the decision, but we can't start listening to the people. We have to go with what the percentages are." Leonard Thompson's TD dive had put the Cowboys up 17-10 in the third quarter.

» **1974:** Nebraska defensive coordinator Monte Kiffin, left, and assistant Rick Duval were in a mood to celebrate after OSU fumbled on the NU 1 with 3 minutes left, preserving a 7-3 Husker victory. "We had Nebraska on the ropes all day and didn't kill them," said Cowboys coach Jim Stanley. "We should have beat them. It seemed like they were waiting and saying, 'Go ahead and finish us off.' "

1975: OSU, trailing by 8, got the ball down to the NU 2-yard line with 49 seconds left. Then Nebraska's defense became confused by the scheme called by defensive coordinator Monte Kiffin. "I'm on the sideline signaling for a tiger defense, and we've got our goal-line people in the game," Kiffin said. But the Blackshirts improvised and stopped Cowboy back Terry Miller one yard short to preserve the 28-20 victory in Stillwater.

1977: WHEN GIRDLES WERE IN STYLE

Terry Miller (43) was the Heisman Trophy runner-up in 1977. He was also ahead of his time in the underwear department.

Long before it became common practice for athletes in several sports, Miller drew attention, and some derision, for wearing a panty girdle – Playtex, XL – to prevent muscle pulls in his massive thighs. He started a trend when two other leading Big Eight rushers, Dexter Green of Iowa State and Mack Green of Kansas State, also adopted the practice.

Before the showdown with Miller and OSU in 1977, Nebraska's premier running back I.M. Hipp was asked if he wore such a garment. Laughing, Hipp said, "No, no girdle for me!"

Miller won the head-to-head matchup with Hipp, who was held to 71 yards, the first time in six weeks that he failed to gain 100 yards. Miller reached 100 for the 16th straight game, finishing with 116, but the Huskers prevailed in Stillwater, 31-14.

"Won the battle?" Miller said later. "I know only that we lost the war."

– Tom Ash

« 1976: A 30-TACKLE GAME

Battered and bruised after a 14-10 Husker win, Clete Pillen (61) looked as though he would have to be scraped off the floor before he could shower.

"This has to be the worst I've ever felt," the senior linebacker and co-captain said after logging 14 unassisted tackles and 16 assists during the game.

Those 30 tackles stand as the Blackshirts' single-game record. But they surpassed Pillen's own record by just three tackles. He logged 27 tackles against Oklahoma as a junior and was named the national defensive player of the week.

"I don't know how those backs can carry 30 times and get hit from every side," the weary Pillen said.

"Now I have to shower and dress. That will be more work than playing the game."

Nebraska coach Tom Osborne praised Pillen's play against the Cowboys, calling it the game's most significant defensive performance.

"Without Clete playing the type of game he did, we probably would have lost the game," Osborne said. "He made tackles all over the field. He has great instincts for the ball. He probably gave us the finest individual defensive performance of the season."

– Larry Porter

THE JIMMY JOHNSON ERA

BY TOM ASH

Jimmy Johnson (at right) finally got his head coaching job at Oklahoma State after kicking around the league as an assistant at Iowa State, Oklahoma and OSU with nomadic stints at Louisiana Tech, Wichita State, Arkansas and Pittsburgh.

Among the things he learned along the way was how to make noise. In his first season, 1979, he talked incessantly about developing a "class" program. He made the athletic dorm off-limits to his players after 9 a.m. to encourage them to go to class. The result, he said, was raising the grade point average for about 15 of his key players from 1.5 to 3.0.

He established the "Orange Room," a locker room with special privileges "for players who have demonstrated that they are contributors." About 35 players were admitted that season. They had their names inscribed on wood-grain lockers, and they had hair dryers, massage nozzles in the showers and fresh laundry in their lockers. The noncontributors had more spartan digs and had to stand in line for clean laundry.

After getting whipped at home, 36-0, by Nebraska that year, Johnson said, "They were just an awesome football team. Junior Miller was the best tight end I've ever seen. He just smothered our little cornerbacks. I felt like a man hanging on a cliff, and someone was standing on my fingers."

But Johnson's confidence never wavered. He came out before the next season and said, "Mark it down. We're fixin' to knock their (opponents') damn eyes out."

Johnson lasted five years at OSU before taking his 29-25-3 record to Miami, where he won a national championship, before moving on to the Dallas Cowboys, the Miami Dolphins and the television studio.

1978: Lawrence Cole blocked an Oklahoma State punt to set up the go-ahead touchdown in a 22-14 win in Lincoln. The Cowboys came into the game with a losing record, but Nebraska once again got more than it wanted. "We like to have the reputation as being the most physical team in the Big Eight, and I guess we are," said NU monster back Jim Pillen. "But today we met a team about as physical as we are."

1979: BREAKING THE WINGBACK BARRIER

Johnny Rodgers is the quintessential Nebraska wingback who capped his outstanding career by winning the Heisman Trophy in 1972.

Yet it wasn't until the 1979 season that a Husker wingback rushed for more than 100 yards in a game. Against Oklahoma State, Kenny Brown did what Johnny the Jet never did – break the 100-yard rushing barrier. Brown collected 111 yards on just eight carries in a 36-0 victory.

Until that memorable October afternoon in Stillwater, Brown had not distinguished himself as a ball carrier. He had gained only 29 yards in just eight carries prior to mangling the OSU defense.

Brown said the Cowboy defenders had players other than himself on their minds.

"They were keying on our I-backs," Brown said. "They were overplaying a lot. They were following our I-backs everywhere. So we hit them with misdirection."

As a result, Brown finished as the leading rusher in a game in which the Huskers galloped for 433 yards on the ground and amassed 596 yards in total offense.

The success of the wingbacks extended beyond Brown. Tim McCrady picked up 29 yards on three carries, and Anthony "Slick" Steels scored the first touchdown of his Husker career on a 5-yarder around right end late in the fourth quarter.

"I always thought my first touchdown would be on a pass," said Steels, a sophomore. "But all the blocks were there. It was wide open. I thought, 'Finally, a touchdown.' It means a lot. I just hope I get some more."

– Larry Porter

» **1980:** Nebraska blasted OSU 48-7 in Lincoln, out-yarding the Pokes by 560 to 143. The passing combination on the Huskers' first touchdown had a ring to it: Quarterback Jeff Quinn hit tight end Jeff Finn (87) for the score.

» **1981:** Nebraska gained 546 yards in a 54-7 rout of an OSU team that came into the game ranked No. 2 nationally in total defense. Cowboys coach Jimmy Johnson said before the game that NU quarterback Turner Gill (12) "will be the best quarterback they've ever had at Nebraska," and he hadn't changed his mind afterward. "He certainly is an outstanding player with tremendous ability," Johnson said. Gill left the game with sore ribs after throwing a touchdown pass in the third quarter.

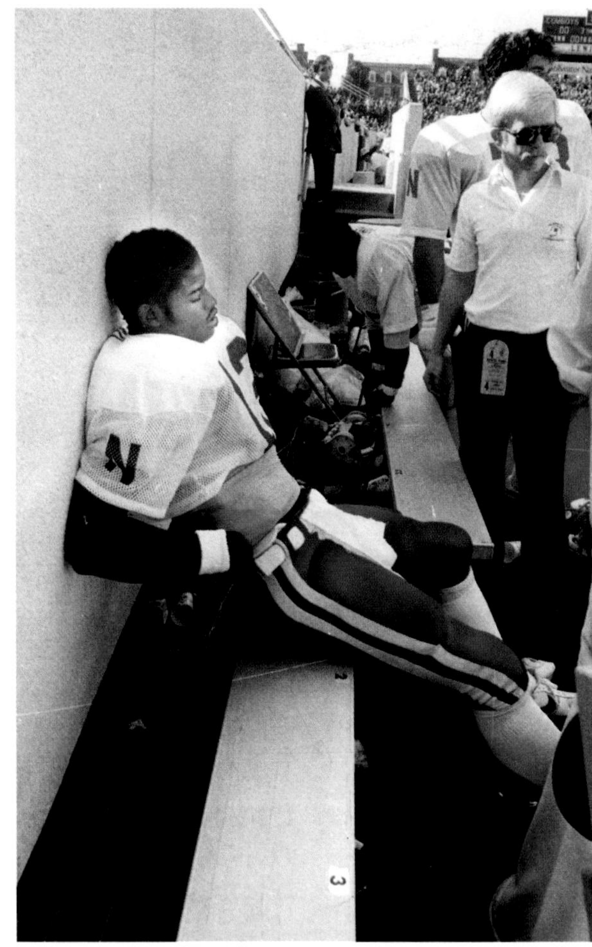

1982: AND THE WINNER IS . . .

The game was hyped as a showdown between two of the nation's top running backs – NU's Mike Rozier (30) and OSU's Ernest Anderson. It ended as a record-breaking one-man show with Rozier, the No. 5 rusher in the country, running 33 times for 251 yards, then a career best, and four touchdowns. Anderson, who ended up as the nation's leading rusher that year, was held to 68 yards on 15 carries. Nebraska won the game, 48-10.

The 251 yards boosted Rozier's season total to 1,379 yards as he broke Bobby Reynolds' single-season record of 1,342, which had been on the books for 32 years. Rozier's single-game total also ranked third best in school history at the time behind Rick Berns' 255 and I.M. Hipp's 254.

Rozier, typically, downplayed his effort and praised his teammates. "I've got a great offensive line in front of me," Rozier said. "I think we could beat some pro teams right now."

– Steve Sinclair

« 1983: CLOSE CALL FOR SI's "BEST TEAM EVER"

Sports Illustrated put Nebraska on the highest pedestal five games into the 1983 season when it declared the Cornhuskers the greatest college football team ever.

Oklahoma State almost knocked the Huskers off that lofty perch a few days after the national sports magazine published the story under the headline "Staking a Claim to Best Ever."

Nebraska needed an interception by safety Bret Clark in the end zone on the final play of the game to hold off the Cowboys 14-10.

Before playing OSU, the top-ranked Huskers were averaging an astonishing 57.8 points a game and had outscored their opponents 289-56.

Nebraska overpowered Syracuse 63-7 in its final tune-up for Big Eight play. "The significance," SI's Douglas S. Looney wrote after the Syracuse game, "was that the win provided more evidence that the Huskers are – pause, please, for drum roll – the greatest college football team in history."

But the Huskers left Stillwater thankful to escape with a win.

"All of those magazines and you sportswriters can save that 'greatest ever' stuff until after the season is over," NU linebacker Mark Daum said. "I think people can forget all this hoopla they have been reading about Nebraska being the best team ever."

OSU used a blitzing defense similar to one Missouri used on quarterback Turner Gill (12) in a 6-0 loss to the Huskers in 1981. By unofficial count, the Cowboys blitzed two defenders or more 10 times in the first half and 12 times in the second.

Oklahoma State coach Jimmy Johnson, who went on to win a national championship with the University of Miami and two Super Bowls with the Dallas Cowboys, said after the game he didn't want to hear any talk about moral victories.

"I don't think that there's anybody in this room or in that locker room who doesn't feel that if we'd had another couple of minutes on the clock, we'd have beaten them," Johnson said.

– Steve Sinclair

⌃ 1984: A DAY FOR THE DEFENSE

Nebraska and Oklahoma State battled into the middle of the fourth quarter in a 3-3 defensive struggle. Then senior Husker wingback Shane Swanson changed the game with a 49-yard punt return for a touchdown with 8:51 left that led to a 17-3 victory. "We had been kind of frustrated on offense," Swanson said, "and something needed to be done."

Swanson took Cary Cooper's 39-yard punt up the middle, then cut to his right. With only Cooper to beat, he faked to the inside, Cooper slipped to the turf and Swanson sprinted down the sideline. NU iced the win with Travis Turner's 64-yard touchdown pass to freshman Jason Gamble in the final two minutes.

– Steve Sinclair

» 1985: HUSKERS WERE UNDERDOGS

Fifth-ranked Oklahoma State, 4-0, was the higher-ranked team for its showdown in Stillwater with No. 9 Nebraska, which was 3-1.

But Nebraska downed the Cowboys 34-24 for its 23rd victory over OSU in 24 years.

Sophomore McCathorn Clayton directed a big-play Nebraska offense a few days after he was described in a Tulsa newspaper as a quarterback who runs like a deer and throws like a deer.

Clayton completed 8 of 16 passes for 161 yards, including a 38-yard touchdown to split end Robb Schnitzler.

"I heard somebody said he passes like a deer," said Nebraska I-back Doug DuBose, who contributed 139 yards rushing. "When I heard that, I said they were going to be surprised. He's a young guy, but he showed he's the key to our offense."

Oklahoma State rallied from a 20-3 deficit to pull within 20-17 after three quarters. Quarterback Ronnie Williams led the Cowboys with school records of 27 completions and 363 passing yards.

But it was linebacker Marc Munford's fourth-quarter interception of a Williams pass that proved decisive. As NU defenders Brad Smith and Chris Spachman chased Williams toward his own end zone, he tried to dump a pass to Thurman Thomas. Munford (41) picked it off at the OSU 10 and returned it to the 7. Three plays later, fullback Tom Rathman scored and NU led 27-17 with just 13 minutes to go.

– Steve Sinclair

1986: Rod Smith (88) helped ignite Nebraska's 30-10 victory with a 63-yard punt return for a touchdown in the first quarter. Coach Tom Osborne had said that Memorial Stadium sometimes was like a tomb, but the fans showed some life at this game. "They were really enthusiastic tonight," Osborne said. "I was afraid nobody would show up." If Husker fans ever had an excuse not to show up, it was for the televised game against a 28-point underdog after it had rained all day.

NOW SHOWING: UNFORGIVEN

Oklahoma State running back Thurman Thomas bumped into the Huskers as the teams were leaving a Stillwater theater complex the night before the 1987 game. "Thurman walked by," NU defensive end Broderick Thomas said, "and right in front of our whole defense said, 'You guys won't be able to stop me one-on-one. It will take all 11 of you.'" Nebraska's defenders weren't amused. "That really pumped the defense up," tackle Neil Smith said after the 35-0 Husker win. "We couldn't settle the fellas down until we got back to the hotel. But we got together and saved that frustration so we could use it on the field instead." Coach Tom Osborne downplayed the theater incident afterward saying, "I think that if we'd gone to a different movie, we'd have played the same ballgame." Osborne said he used to accompany players to pregame movies. "But I feel like I can spend my time better working X's and O's and looking at films," he said.

1987: A SLIGHT MISCALCULATION

Barry Sanders (21) went on to win the Heisman Trophy in 1988 for Oklahoma State and followed with a Pro Football Hall of Fame career with the Detroit Lions.

But in 1987, Sanders was the Cowboys' No. 2 tailback behind Thurman Thomas and an electrifying return specialist with high hopes of ending OSU's long victory drought against Nebraska.

"We're not playing Mike Rozier, Dave Rimington, Johnny Rodgers, Turner Gill," Sanders said. "I've been watching Nebraska all my life, and they're more beatable than they've ever been."

Sanders miscalculated.

The second-ranked Huskers blanked 12th-ranked Oklahoma State 35-0 in Stillwater to extend their unbeaten streak against the Cowboys to 26 games.

The Huskers also backed up a pregame prediction by defensive end Broderick Thomas that they would stop Thurman Thomas, who had been the nation's leading rusher with a 140-yard-per-game average.

"He's going to need wings and be able to fly if wants to gain yards against us," Broderick Thomas said, "because we're not going to let him run against us."

Nebraska held Thurman Thomas to a career-low 7 yards on nine carries. Sanders gained 60 yards on seven carries.

– Steve Sinclair

« **1988:** Coach Tom Osborne said Nebraska's 63-42 win in Lincoln was beyond his comprehension. "I don't even know quite how to approach it," he said after witnessing a combined 1,117 total yards and 105 points. Nebraska scored on its first, fourth, ninth and 12th plays on its way to a 42-0 lead less than 19 minutes into the game. Though the Cowboys never really got close to breaking their long winless streak against NU, they never were completely out of the game, either. The Cowboys failed to score on their first six possessions, then posted touchdowns on six of the final seven. Future Heisman Trophy winner Barry Sanders gained 189 yards on 35 carries and scored four touchdowns. NU I-back Ken Clark (32), meanwhile, ran for 256 yards and three touchdowns.

« **1989:** The Blackshirts, embarrassed by their performance against OSU the previous year, held the Pokes to just 42 yards rushing on 33 carries in a 48-23 win.

« **1990:** Leodis Flowers (23) ran for 138 yards and a touchdown in NU's 31-3 victory. Gerald Hudson joined the list of great Oklahoma State running backs who were shut down by the Blackshirts. Hudson came into the game as the nation's fourth-leading rusher but gained just 47 yards and was stopped behind or at the line seven times.

^ **1991:** The Huskers handled OSU 49-15 in the conference opener in Stillwater, as I-back Derek Brown ran for three touchdowns. Still, Cowboy coach Pat Jones said the Huskers were not as good as past teams. "I don't think it's vintage Nebraska," Jones said. "I don't mean that derogatorily speaking. I've seen them when I thought they were better."

« **1992:** The Blackshirts allowed only three snaps in NU territory and did not give up any pass completions in Nebraska's 55-0 bombing of OSU. Starting quarterback Mike Grant (1) and freshman backup Tommie Frazier each threw two touchdown passes.

« **1993:** The Huskers were supposed to cruise past the 18-point underdog Cowboys while allowing coach Tom Osborne to reach 200 victories. Instead, they fell behind by 10 points in the second quarter before pulling out a 27-13 victory. "That wasn't a thing of great beauty," Osborne said. Cornerback Barron Miles blocked a punt and recovered it in the end zone with 14:09 left in the game to give the Huskers their first lead.

≈ **1994:** Nebraska's Darin Erstad (6) kicked his first collegiate field goal in a 32-3 win, but that would not be his lasting memory of the game. Instead, Erstad can look back at his catch of Jon Vedral's desperation pass on a bungled extra-point try. "It was like a dream," said Erstad, who also played baseball for the Huskers and went on to a 14-year career in the major leagues. "You talk to your friends about scoring a touchdown. . . . Well, this was close enough. And it happened right in front of where my buddies sit." Erstad's 2-point catch came on what was supposed to be a typical extra point, but holder Vedral mishandled the snap, then scrambled backward under pressure. Erstad alertly flared out into the left flat, and as Vedral was being tackled, he unloaded a perfect spiral, which Erstad caught in stride in the end zone. "I'm not incapable of catching a football," Erstad said. "It wasn't a fluke thing."

« **1995:** Asked earlier how he envisioned his first carry as a Nebraska I-back, Ahman Green (30) said he just hoped he wouldn't be so nervous that he fumbled. His time came late in the third quarter of NU's 64-21 rout, and he held onto the ball for an 18-yard gain. After the game, the freshman out of Omaha Central wore a relieved look on his face. "Doing that was one of the dreams of my life," Green said. "For a freshman or any first-year guy, it's a great feeling to get that first carry out of the way."

⌃ **1998:** The Cowboys held Nebraska to 73 rushing yards, its fewest since being held to 70 by Oklahoma in 1975, but still fell short in a 24-17 loss at Arrowhead Stadium in Kansas City. The winning points came on a 73-yard punt return by Joe Walker (25) in the fourth quarter. Cowboys coach Bob Simmons deflected talk that moving the OSU home game from Stillwater to Kansas City might have hurt the Cowboys' upset hopes. Nebraska had about twice as many fans as OSU in the crowd of 79,555. "We played well enough to win," Simmons said. "Who's to say the same thing would have happened in Stillwater?"

⌃ **1999:** The talk around Stillwater all week was that this would finally be the year that OSU defeated Nebraska for the first time since 1961. It was all just talk. A year's worth of confidence gained by almost beating the Huskers in 1998 quickly fizzled in the Cowboys' 38-14 loss in Lincoln. Eric Crouch (7) scored just 5 minutes into the game and by halftime it was 31-0.

⌃ » 2002: THE STREAK ENDS

Rashaun Woods (82) had 134 yards receiving and a touchdown in OSU's 24-21 victory, but the Cowboys said the win wasn't just for themselves. Oklahoma State hadn't beaten Nebraska since defeating the Bill Jennings-coached Huskers 14-6 in Stillwater in 1961. Many of the players celebrated with the fans, who stormed Lewis Field and made fast work of tearing down the goal posts. Coach Les Miles had downplayed the fact that OSU was 0-35-1 in the previous 36 games in the series, emphasizing that the Cowboys were playing against the 2002 Huskers, not against the previous Nebraska squads and the tradition they helped to foster. But once the Cowboys were in the locker room, Miles addressed the importance of their accomplishment. "It was a wonderful feeling with great emotions all around," defensive lineman Greg Richmond said. "Coach Miles told us that we hadn't beaten them in 41 years. It was just sweet."

« **2003:** Bo Pelini, hired as the defensive coordinator in the offseason to help the Huskers shake a dismal 7-7 year, uncharacteristically cracked a smile on the sidelines as the clock ran down and Nebraska had its first win over a ranked opponent since October 2001. Nebraska held OSU to 183 yards of total offense in a 17-7 win in the season opener in Lincoln. "Everybody knows the Blackshirts are back," said NU cornerback Fabian Washington. "It shows the system Coach Pelini put in is a great system, and when 11 guys run to the ball, it's going to work." The day started with nostalgia, with more than 800 alums trotting on the field as part of a Husker Nation Reunion. "I came out seeing all those guys going nuts," said NU linebacker Barrett Ruud (38), who scored the winning touchdown on a 15-yard fumble recovery in the third quarter. "I loved it."

» **2006:** Nebraska controlled the tempo with its ground game early, with I-back Brandon Jackson (32) finishing the first quarter with 11 carries for 99 yards. But as OSU came back from a 16-0 second-quarter deficit, the Huskers began to pass more, and the Cowboys were able to pull away for a 41-29 win in Stillwater.

⌃ **2007:** The Cowboys started the scoring on their first possession at Memorial Stadium and led 38-0 by halftime. By the time Oklahoma State had wrapped up its 45-14 victory, many of the Husker fans were gone. "It's too much to watch," said one fan who left at halftime. "I've never seen anything like it." Athletic Director Steve Pederson was fired two days after the game and later replaced by Tom Osborne.

STILL HAVING NIGHTMARES ABOUT . . .

WALT GARRISON »

Fullback

Garrison was a Cowboy through and through.

The Denton, Texas, native also spent time in professional rodeo, played for the Dallas Cowboys and became a TV pitchman for smokeless tobacco, advising viewers to "put just a pinch between your cheek and gum."

And if any man ever resembled a bucking bronco, it was Garrison on a November afternoon in Stillwater in 1965.

The ultimate Cowboy ran for 121 yards and got loose on the game's final play, rumbling 18 yards before finally being dragged down at NU's 5-yard line as time expired in a 21-17 Husker victory.

Garrison lay on the ground with his face in his hands as his teammates stood over him, saying they wished they had blocked better on the play.

Nebraska's players then pulled him to his feet, shook his hand and patted him on the helmet. Finally, NU assistant George Kelly and head coach Bob Devaney stopped to whisper words of encouragement.

Garrison left the field in tears.

CLEVELAND VANN

Linebacker

Scored a TD on an interception return during the 17-17 tie in 1973.

TERRY MILLER

Running back

Ran for 100 yards in two games and scored three touchdowns in another. He finished second to Earl Campbell in 1977 Heisman Trophy balloting.

LESLIE O'NEAL

Defensive tackle

Recorded 21 tackles (10 solo), forced a fumble and recovered another in a 14-10 loss in 1983, had 20 tackles in a 17-3 loss in 1984 and 14 tackles in a 34-24 loss in 1985.

BARRY SANDERS

Running back

Totaled 189 yards and four TDs on 35 carries in a 63-42 loss to NU in 1988, his Heisman season.

RASHAUN WOODS

Wide receiver

Caught 11 passes for 134 yards in his team's 24-21 win over NU in 2002.

DANTRELL SAVAGE

Running back

Tallied 117 rushing yards in a 2006 win and amassed 212 more during the blowout one year later.

Texas coach Mack Brown and his Longhorns again hooked the Huskers in 2010 at Memorial Stadium.

TEXAS

HUSKERS USUALLY GOT THE WORST OF IT WHEN THEY HOOKED UP

BY MICHAEL KELLY | WORLD-HERALD STAFF WRITER

EVERYTHING IS BIGGER in Texas, the expression goes, and that has included Husker heartbreaks. None hurt more than the 2009 conference championship game in Arlington, after time had expired with NU ahead. A video replay showed that on the apparent final play, a Texas pass had landed out of bounds with one second left. The clock was reset to 0:01, which allowed Texas to zero in on the goal posts and kick a game-winning field goal.

The Huskers had played so well, especially on defense. Led by All-America lineman Ndamukong Suh, the Associated Press national college football player of the year, the Blackshirts stifled the Texas attack throughout the game. On one memorable play, Suh tossed UT quarterback Colt McCoy like he was a rag doll. Late in the fourth quarter, Nebraska took a 12-10 lead on an Alex Henery field goal, and the NU defense needed to shut down the 'Horns one last time. But a rare Nebraska kickoff out of bounds gave Texas the ball at its 40. A pass completion and a 15-yard "horse-collar" penalty against NU gave Texas a first down at NU's 26-yard line. After two plays went nowhere, UT tried once more, with six seconds left. McCoy rolled out to the right, looking for a receiver with the seconds ticking down. Feeling Suh's breath and finding no one open, McCoy heaved the ball out of bounds – and the clock read 0:00.

Huskers poured onto the field in celebration. But officials took another look, and the replay showed that Texas should have one more second. It proved to be the longest in Husker history. In a powerful drama, the teams lined up, the ball was snapped and the kick soared ... just inside the left upright, a 46-yard field goal that gave the 'Horns a 13-12 victory. Thus ended a magnificent game. Even though the defeat disappointed the Cornhuskers and their fans, and as much as coaches hate talking about moral victories, there was nevertheless a moral to this story: The Huskers, who had endured an uncharacteristic slump through much of the decade, were back.

The Longhorns celebrated a win in Austin in 1999 but lost in the Big 12 title game.

The Longhorns won nine out of 10 games against Nebraska after the creation of the Big 12, including 37-27 in the league's first championship game, in 1996 in St. Louis. So close were most of the games that Husker fans felt as though there must be a jinx, or perhaps a series of Texas hexes. Losses came by four, four, three, two and three points before the one-point loss in 2009. In 1998, the 'Horns ended the Huskers' 47-game home winning streak by scoring with less than three minutes to play. Many Husker fans, in a postgame tradition, applauded the 'Horns off the field. But some went further, which UT coach Mack Brown has cited in lauding Nebraska fans: They saluted UT running back Ricky Williams with shouts of "Heisman! Heisman!" The next year in Austin, NU again lost by four – after a fourth-quarter Husker fumble on the Texas 2-yard line. But the teams met again that year in the Big 12 title game, and this time the Huskers won 22-6 behind quarterback Eric Crouch's two touchdowns and the Blackshirts' seven sacks of Major Applewhite. In 2002, a Texas interception at

ROAD TRIP TO

AUSTIN

University of Texas

Founded: 1883

Enrollment: 48,000

Colors:
Burnt orange and white

Conference history:
Founding member of the Southwest Conference in 1914, began Big 12 play in 1996

Stadium:
Darrell K. Royal-Texas Memorial Stadium, capacity: 100,119

History of "Longhorns":
The cattle were a key chapter in Texas history, the breed that was driven on the trail during the 19th century. Newspapers began referring to Texas teams as Longhorns about 1900, and the name caught on.

Distance from Memorial Stadium in Lincoln:
799 miles

Worth remembering:
"The Eyes of Texas," sung to the tune of "I've Been Working on the Railroad," is played before and after games. The "Hook 'em Horns" hand sign is among the most easily identifiable symbols of college football, and Bevo the live longhorn is among the best-known live mascots. "Burnt orange," which also is identified only with Texas, was chosen as the school's color because the original orange of its jerseys would fade as the season wore on. Opponents began calling the team the "yellow bellies," and Texas coach Clyde Littlefield had enough, ordering a darker shade of orange in 1928.

Quote:
"We've said it all along: We feel like we can line up against any college football team in the country and have great success against them. We don't consider Texas any different, that's why we're at Nebraska."

– Nebraska defensive coordinator Carl Pelini (2009)

the end of the game preserved a three-point win in Lincoln. The next year, Texas won easily in Austin behind Vince Young. In 2006 in Lincoln, Nebraska led by a point late in the game but fumbled, setting up a 22-yard game-winning field goal with 23 seconds left. In '07, NU led by 14 points in the second half before falling to the 'Horns by three. Because Nebraska and Texas were in different divisions of the Big 12, they didn't meet annually. The one-point loss in '09 came in the conference championship game.

The 'Horns visited Lincoln in a much-anticipated rematch on Oct. 16, 2010. The Huskers and their fans relished a second chance. No more Texas hexes, it was hoped, and no more drama in the final seconds. But the Longhorns shut down Nebraska's running game, and the Huskers dropped the ball – several of them when receivers ran wide open – as UT won 20-13. Nebraska's only touchdown came near the end of the game, a Husker-record 95-yard return of a pooched punt by Eric Hagg.

Long before the Big 12, the schools first met in football in 1933, and they share a heritage through a legendary coach of old – Dana X. Bible – who played a part in the national prominence of both football programs. Dana Xenophon Bible coached Nebraska from 1929 through 1936, and Texas from 1937 through 1946. Before Nebraska played Texas in Austin in 1960, he walked the UT campus and fondly recalled his days in Lincoln, saying that "you can't beat the Nebraska stadium for beauty." Bible won six conference championships in his eight years at NU, and three in his 10 years at UT. He felt such strong allegiance to both universities, he said, that he hoped the game that week ended in a tie. Little chance of that, though, with the Longhorns ranked No. 4 nationally under coach Darrell Royal. The Huskers, coached by Bill Jennings, were unranked. But NU's Pat Fischer, a native of St. Edward, Neb., who graduated from Omaha Westside High, led the Huskers to a 14-13 upset victory. Fischer, who later played 17 years in the NFL and helped lead the Washington Redskins to a Super Bowl, quarterbacked the Huskers, played cornerback on defense and returned a punt 76 yards. The NU offensive backfield, by the way, consisted of Fischer, who is white, and three blacks – Bernie Clay, Clay White and Thunder Thornton – while Texas was all-white. The Longhorns' 1969 squad was the last all-white college football team to win a national championship.

Pat Fischer (40) moved from halfback to quarterback for his senior year and led the Huskers to a 14-13 victory over Texas in Austin in 1960.

Texas played a role in another part of Husker history, NU's first national championship. The Longhorns were voted No. 1 in the final coaches' poll, which in 1970 was still taken before the bowl games. But the Associated Press writers' poll waited. Going in to the New Year's Day games, the Huskers were ranked third behind Texas and Ohio State – and both lost. After beating LSU that night in the Orange Bowl, the Nebraska Cornhuskers earned their first national championship. In the Cotton Bowl after the 1973 season, Osborne's first as head coach, Nebraska defeated Texas 19-3. That was the last game between the schools until the Big 12 began in 1996. The 2010 contest in Lincoln marked the final regularly scheduled conference game between Nebraska and Texas. Even though Nebraska would leave the Big 12 after only 15 years, its departure actually meant leaving behind affiliations of more than a century – the Big 12, Big Eight, Big Seven, Big Six and Missouri Valley conferences. Before officially joining the Big Ten on July 1, 2011, the Huskers played one more season against some longtime Big Red rivals – and then said farewell to a conference. But who knows what the future holds? As UT athletic director DeLoss Dodds said of the Huskers: "We'll see 'em again sometime."

REMAINING A FORCE IN THE LOCKER ROOM

Prior to the 1999 Big 12 championship game against Texas, the Cornhuskers listened in the locker room to a videotaped message from former Husker defensive end Grant Wistrom. The players and coaches were still buzzing about the power of the message for days after NU's 22-6 victory. Wistrom, who had moved on to the NFL, later related what he had said: "There's a lot of pride that comes from wearing the Nebraska colors and playing for that program. But you have no idea what it means while you're there. Once it's gone, it's gone. I told them that it was just ridiculous to have people put Texas on the same level with us because they'd beat us the last three times."

BIG RED AND THE RED RIVER SHOOTOUT

Darrell Royal
Texas

Tom Osborne
Nebraska

Barry Switzer
Oklahoma

A telephone call from Texas coach Darrell Royal to Nebraska coach Tom Osborne drew some attention in the days leading up to NU's 1976 collision with Oklahoma.

Osborne acknowledged that Royal had called and asked if Osborne would send some film of Oklahoma games in which the Sooners could be detected using "clothesline" tackling methods against Nebraska.

Osborne said the long-standing feud between Royal and Sooner coach Barry Switzer had apparently erupted again and that the Texas coach was gathering a collection of such tackling incidents involving OU players.

"I sent him some film," Osborne said, explaining that he had questioned "a couple of incidents" in OU games.

However, he stressed that he was not joining the feud. "That's entirely between them," Osborne said. "I respect Coach Royal, and I respect Coach Switzer. I like them both. But I just wish they'd stop all this wrangling in public. In fact, I told both of them that. It's unfortunate they have to do it. But apparently it's a difficult thing for them to iron out."

Osborne said the latest chapter in the feud apparently stemmed from an incident in which a Texas player was injured and an Oklahoma player was ejected from the game.

"We haven't had any problem with Oklahoma," Osborne said. "Those things happen. I'm sure we could be made to look bad if someone wanted to take film clips from all of our games."

– Larry Porter

NO HOME-FIELD ADVANTAGE FOR NU

The Texas Longhorn flag waved in victory again in 2010 at Memorial Stadium. The series has been especially disappointing to Nebraska when playing at home, with the Longhorns taking the last five meetings in Lincoln between the two schools. The only Cornhusker victory at home was in the first game, 26-0 in 1933.

» 1996 BIG 12 CHAMPIONSHIP GAME: BACKING UP HIS WORDS

James Brown's Texas teammates wondered if their quarterback had lost his mind.

Days before the three-touchdown-underdog Longhorns were to meet No. 3 Nebraska in the first Big 12 championship game, Brown (5) had predicted a Texas victory. Or at least that's how some observers interpreted his comments.

Brown insists he never pulled a Joe Namath, who gained fame before Super Bowl III for predicting the New York Jets would beat the Baltimore Colts.

"I knew we could win this game," Brown said. "But I didn't make any predictions. That's not smart football."

Brown said someone asked him early in the week how it felt to be a 21-point underdog.

"All I said is that they might lose by 21 points," Brown said. "I said that, and I didn't back down from that."

Brown backed his words with plenty of action, passing for a career-high 353 yards in a 37-27 upset that knocked the Huskers out of the national championship chase. He completed 19 passes, the most important coming on a fourth-and-inches play from the Texas 28-yard line.

He hooked up with tight end Derek Lewis for a 61-yard gain. On the next play, Priest Holmes bolted 11 yards for his third touchdown of the game to seal the Longhorns' shocker.

Lewis said his initial reaction in hearing about Brown's supposed prediction of victory was surprise.

"I thought, 'Whoa, James, there's no need to get these Nebraska boys any more riled up than they already are,'" Lewis said. "But then after hearing what James had to say about the whole thing, I knew he was only saying what we all felt."

– Steven Pivovar

« **1998:** Nebraska's home winning streak ended at 47 games when Texas scored with 2:47 remaining to win 20-16 at Memorial Stadium. Blackshirt Mike Brown (21) logged 19 tackles in helping slow Texas running back Ricky Williams (34), but Longhorn redshirt freshman quarterback Major Applewhite passed for 269 yards and threw a touchdown pass for the game-winning points.

« **1999:** While I-back Correll Buckhalter (36) scored a touchdown in a 24-20 loss in Austin, the play he might most remember would be a fumble near the Texas goal line in the fourth quarter. Nebraska dropped the ball five times in the game, losing three of them.

« 1999 BIG 12 CHAMPIONSHIP GAME: NO DOUBT THIS TIME

Nebraska avenged its only loss of the season with a 22-6 dismantling of Texas at the Alamodome in San Antonio, with Julius Jackson (left) and his teammates sacking quarterback Major Applewhite (11) seven times. Nebraska got two touchdown runs from quarterback Eric Crouch and a pair of field goals in building a 22-0 lead after the first three quarters.

A LOSS FOR NU FANS

BY STEVEN PIVOVAR | WORLD-HERALD STAFF WRITER

Greatest fans in the world? You would have had trouble convincing Chris Simms (2) of that after he led Texas to a 27-24 victory in 2002 that snapped Nebraska's 26-game home winning streak.

Simms threw for 419 yards, setting several school records in the victory. As Simms made his way back to the locker room after the game, he was the target of a verbal assault from the fans who lined the route. Some of the taunts directed his way would have made a longshoreman blush.

To his credit, Simms never acknowledged the boorish behavior, nor did he show any emotion when asked about it after the game. Instead, he stayed classy and enjoyed a moment he shared with former teammate Major Applewhite, who in 1998 had helped Texas snap the Huskers' 47-game home winning streak.

"This is the most special thing I can say about my football career right now," Simms said. "For our school to come into a place like Nebraska, where football is everything and there's such great tradition, and be the only school to give them their only two losses in 75 games is just unbelievable."

^ **2002:** Nathan Vasher's interception of Jammal Lord's pass to Mark LeFlore (27) preserved the Longhorns' 27-24 win at Memorial Stadium. "I feel badly for our players," said NU coach Frank Solich, who chose to take one shot at a touchdown with 10 seconds left, rather than play it safe with a field-goal attempt that could have sent the game into overtime. "I thought they played their hearts out. They put themselves in position to win the game." Weighing in the decision were problems on two earlier field-goal attempts by Nebraska and the Blackshirts' inability to stop Longhorn receiver Roy Williams, who had caught 13 passes for 161 yards. The interception overshadowed a great performance by Lord, who ran for 234 yards and passed for 98.

« **2003:** Texas quarterback Vince Young (10) torched the Blackshirts for 163 rushing yards and a touchdown in a 31-7 win. "Sometimes those quarterback plays, they're tough to stop," NU linebacker Barrett Ruud (38) said. "But that's mostly just being disciplined."

« **2006:** Nebraska was trying to run out the clock on a one-point lead when Texas defensive back Aaron Ross' hit on NU receiver Terrence Nunn (83) caused a fumble that gave No. 2 Texas one last chance to avoid the upset. The Longhorns' 22-yard field goal with 23 seconds left produced a 22-20 win in Lincoln.

« **2007:** Nebraska led 17-3 in the third quarter before the Longhorn running game got on track with Jamaal Charles (25), who scored three times in the final 12:23.

2009 BIG 12 CHAMPIONSHIP GAME: A NIGHT FOR THE DEFENSES

The title game at Cowboys Stadium in Arlington, Texas, was a defensive battle for the ages, with the Huskers gaining just 106 yards and the Longhorns only 202. Nebraska's Ndamukong Suh (93) led an NU defense that sacked Longhorn quarterback Colt McCoy (12) nine times and intercepted three of his passes.

⌃ 2009 BIG 12 CHAMPIONSHIP GAME: THE HUSKERS PULL AHEAD

DeJon Gomes (7) intercepted a pass intended for Dan Buckner (4) in the fourth quarter, and the Huskers put together a drive to the Longhorn 26. Alex Henery (90) nailed a 42-yard field goal to give Nebraska a 12-10 lead with 1:44 remaining in the game.

» 2009 BIG 12 CHAMPIONSHIP GAME: ONE SECOND WAS THE DIFFERENCE

Texas got a break when Nebraska's kickoff after the go-ahead field goal went out of bounds, and the penalty gave the Longhorns the ball on their 40-yard line. Quarterback Colt McCoy led a drive into Nebraska territory but, under pressure from Ndamukong Suh, threw the ball away as the clock wound down. The Huskers stormed the field in the belief they had won, but an official review determined that one second remained. Hunter Lawrence (15) then kicked a 46-yard field goal as time expired. The 13-12 Texas win will be remembered as one of the best and most controversial finishes in the history of the conference championship game.

TEXAS
32
5
38
33

The Huskers huddle before the opening kickoff against Texas Tech at Jones AT&T Stadium in Lubbock in 2008.

TEXAS TECH

A 60-POINT LOSS LEFT A LASTING STAIN ON NEBRASKA

BY MICHAEL KELLY | WORLD-HERALD STAFF WRITER

FANS OF COLLEGE FOOTBALL love far more than the football – they are drawn to the trivia, the trombones and the traditions. Texas Tech University features many of the latter, including "The Masked Rider," who dons a cape, rides a black quarter horse and leads the Red Raider football team onto the field while fans form the "guns up" hand signal to symbolize their intent to shoot down the opponent. Texas Tech describes The Masked Rider as a "mysterious and striking symbol" of the school's spirit and pride. The marching band, known as "The Goin' Band from Raiderland," gets the crowd going, too. All very fun and cool.

What happened to the Nebraska Cornhuskers in Lubbock, Texas, on the night of Oct. 9, 2004, was also mysterious, a kind of twilight zone of a football nightmare. With many proud traditions of its own, Nebraska was shot down like never before or since – Texas Tech delivered the worst defeat in the history of the Husker program, 70-10. Nebraska had defeated Texas Tech all seven times the schools previously met, starting with the 1976 Astro-Bluebonnet Bowl, and including the first four as members of the Big 12 Conference. But Tech won the last four over Nebraska, twice beating teams coached by Bill Callahan and twice over teams coached by Bo Pelini. That 2004 embarrassment, though, was Callahan's. Texas Tech scored seven touchdowns in one stretch of just over 12 minutes, helped by five consecutive NU turnovers. Because of the miscues deep in Nebraska territory, the huge point total can't be blamed totally on the defense. Still, the defenders gave up 523 yards from scrimmage. And in retrospect, it was even clearer that NU had a big problem in how the players were coached – the talent was there. Of the players on the Husker defense that night, 12 later spent time on National Football League rosters.

Texas Tech's Gabe Hall celebrates a 34-31 win over the Cornhuskers with a "guns up" for the crowd at Memorial Stadium in 2005.

The year after the blowout, unranked Nebraska lost to Texas Tech in Lincoln by three. In 2008, under Pelini, the Huskers came from behind to force overtime, but lost. "We're not about moral victories," Pelini said. "Nebraska never will be as long as I'm head coach. If we start being about moral victories, you need to get a new coach." That's the moral of that story. But the morale-crushing 60-point loss by a Nebraska team was downright sinful.

ROAD TRIP TO

LUBBOCK

Texas Tech University

Founded: 1923

Enrollment: 30,000

Colors:
Scarlet and black

Conference history:
Joined Southwest Conference in 1958, began Big 12 play in 1996

Stadium:
Jones AT&T Stadium, capacity 60,454

History of "Red Raiders":
Originally called the Matadors because of the Spanish architectural influence on campus, the name changed after a sportswriter in 1936 referred to "the Red Raiders from Texas Tech, terror of the Southwest." It caught on, and the change became official.

Distance from Memorial Stadium in Lincoln:
714 miles

Worth remembering:
Red Raider fans love to give the "guns up" gesture when things are going well. The hand sign actually has been around since 1972 but really wasn't that noticeable until the team started scoring a lot more after coach Mike Leach arrived.

Quote:
"The interesting thing is that football is the only sport where you quit playing when you get a lead. In basketball you don't quit shooting when you're ahead. In golf you don't quit playing. . . . But in football, somehow magically, you're supposed to quit playing when you're ahead. I don't subscribe to that, and the truth of the matter is Nebraska never has either."

– Texas Tech coach Mike Leach responding to questions about his 70-10 rout of Nebraska (2004)

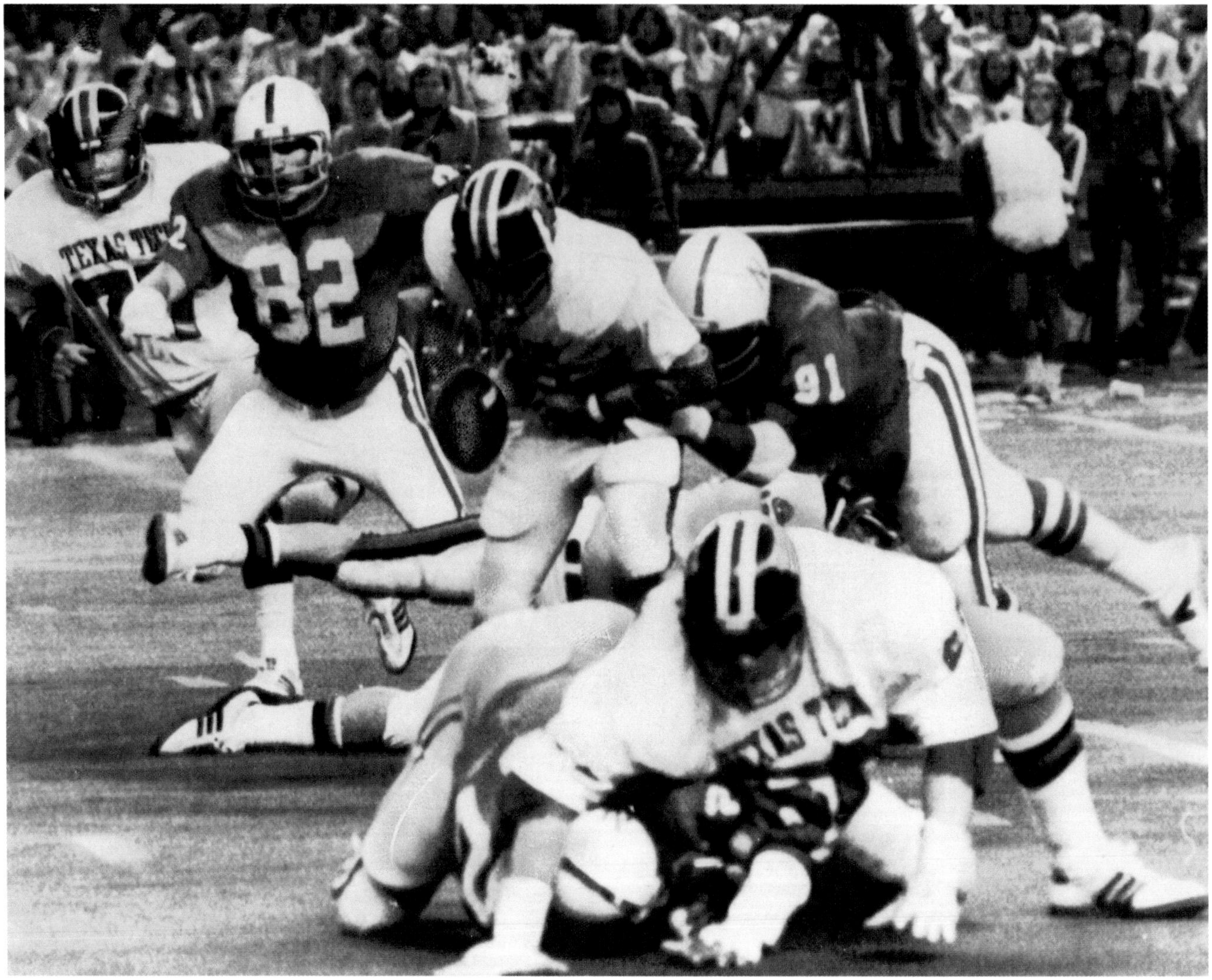

OSBORNE'S BIGGEST GAME?

The most important game in Tom Osborne's coaching career might have been the 27-24 nonconference victory over ninth-ranked Texas Tech in the 1976 Astro-Bluebonnet Bowl in Houston. After the game, Osborne said, a member of the NU Board of Regents told him "it was no secret that we had to win that game." The implication was that Osborne would have been fired if Texas Tech had won. Instead, the victory capped a 9-3-1 season for Nebraska. "That regent is a good friend of mine," Osborne said prior to the 1980 season. "He may have been overstating something, but I don't think he was blowing smoke. Maybe things would have been different around here if we had lost that game."

– Larry Porter

PLEASED TO MEET YOU!

Nebraska might have gotten a little spoiled after its first Big 12 meeting with Mike Leach in 2000. The Huskers were an established juggernaut, and Texas Tech was still getting acquainted with the quirks of its new coach. The result wasn't pretty. Dominic Raiola (54) and quarterback Eric Crouch (7) led Nebraska to a 56-3 pounding of the Red Raiders in Lubbock, the worst loss in Tech history. But Leach would get his revenge. Oh, did he ever.

– Jon Nyatawa

IT WAS THE WORST SINCE . . .

If you wanted to break it down, Texas Tech scored seven touchdowns in 722 seconds during a 49-point second-half explosion when it blistered Nebraska 70-10 in 2004. In the west Texas flatlands where there's not a mountain to be found, it was an avalanche like no other experienced by the Huskers.

As the Red Raiders went from 21-10 to 42-10 to 70-10 with amazing ease, even those well-versed in Nebraska football history were scrambling in the Jones AT&T Stadium press box.

Sitting just left of The World-Herald crew was Mike Babcock, who had covered Husker football in some capacity for all or parts of four decades. Because of the tight deadline for the night game in Lubbock, we scrambled to research numbers that would fit perhaps the two most important sentences in the game story for our Sunday paper.

"It was the most points scored on a Nebraska team since . . . "

"It was the worst loss by the Huskers since . . . "

Because the avalanche kept coming from Mike Leach and his Red Raiders, the numbers had to be updated as Texas Tech scored with 4:16, 2:24 and 2:03 left in the third quarter, then with 11:16, 9:36, 9:05 and 7:14 remaining in the fourth.

A lot of the damage came from 523 total yards by Texas Tech, including 436 passing and five TDs by Sonny Cumbie (15). But the Red Raiders were helped by seven NU turnovers, including several deep in Husker territory.

The answers to the above sentences? Well, the Texas Tech point total that October night easily set a record for any Husker opponent (until Kansas scored 76 on the Huskers three years later). And the 60-point margin of victory was the largest ever against Nebraska.

– Rich Kaipust

LAST-SECOND CHANGE OF FORTUNES

Cody Hodges started one game in Memorial Stadium, and he'll remember it for the rest of his life.

Hodges led the Red Raiders to a thrilling 34-31 victory in 2005, completing a 10-yard touchdown pass to Joel Filani (8) on fourth down with 12 seconds left to stun Nebraska.

But it was the game's final moments that made the win so sweet for Hodges and so gut-wrenching for Husker fans.

Texas Tech surged to a 21-0 lead by the second quarter, though NU battled back and took its first lead in the fourth. But on the game's final drive, the magic happened.

Nebraska defensive tackle Le Kevin Smith intercepted a Hodges pass. The game would have been over if Smith had just fallen to the ground. Instead, Smith headed up field and promptly fumbled. Texas Tech recovered and Hodges got a second chance.

On a fourth-down play, the Husker pass rush got to Hodges quickly. He was backpedaling, running out of time.

"We practiced that scramble drill every day for five years," Hodges said later. "I knew that if I went left, (Filani) was going to continue that slant route. I just threw it to a spot, where he was supposed to be." And, of course, Filani was there.

An understudy until his senior year, Hodges said that last-second TD pass sticks out as one of his career highlights.

"I just remember walking on the field to warm up and fans are telling me, 'Good luck,' and patting me on the back. Strange," he said. "When we won, they clapped, out of respect. Just going to Lincoln, there's that aura there that the Cornhusker fans have. It was special to be a part of."

– Jon Nyatawa

Nebraskans have made themselves right at home in Floyd Casey Stadium in Waco, probably no more so than at the 2009 game.

BAYLOR

A NEIGHBORLY HOST FOR THE VISITING HUSKERS

BY MICHAEL KELLY | WORLD-HERALD STAFF WRITER

BAYLOR UNIVERSITY, on the Brazos River in Waco, is the only private university in the Big 12. Although an excellent institution of higher learning, it is not an institution of higher scoring. So Nebraska usually had its way with the Bears on the football field, the only loss coming in Lincoln in 1956 – and none since NU began playing Baylor in conference games. After a number of blowouts, though, Baylor lost its last three games to Nebraska by an average of only 10 points. Chartered by the Republic of Texas in 1845 through the efforts of Baptist pioneers, Baylor is the oldest continually operating university in Texas. In recent years, it has led the Big 12 in graduation-success rate. Its president is Ken Starr, formerly a U.S. solicitor general and special prosecutor.

The school and the surrounding community work hard at welcoming visitors. In 1997, NU ticket manager John Anderson was surprised after a visit in Lincoln by members of the Waco chamber of commerce who encouraged a Big Red migration. "It was the first time I've ever experienced something like that," Anderson said. "I was quite impressed. They gave an entire presentation about Waco, just to me in my office. They had bumper stickers, pencils, everything you could imagine, all with a Waco theme. They really want us down there." Husker fans don't need much encouragement to migrate, and they often brought their sea of red to Floyd Casey Stadium. It wasn't hard to get tickets. In 2009, the North Texas Nebraskans group hosted 102 soldiers, all with Nebraska ties, from Fort Hood in Killeen, Texas, an hour away. They enjoyed a pregame tailgate party and were provided camouflage-style shirts, each with a red N.

In a 1990 nonconference game in Lincoln, the Bears played the Huskers tough, losing 13-0. BU coach Grant Teaff, who had won six Southwest Conference coach-of-the-year awards and once was named national coach of the year, was so moved by the reaction of Nebraska fans that he wrote a letter to The World-Herald. In 28 years as a head coach, he said, he had sensed "every level of

The Baylor Line, made up of freshmen, traditionally storms through the gates before the game and forms lines through which the players emerge onto the field.

sportsmanship or lack of it," but not once had experienced what he and his team felt in Lincoln – a "tumultuous roar" and a standing ovation for the Bears. It's a long tradition at Memorial Stadium for Husker fans to applaud the opponent off the field, win or lose, but Teaff was touched by the shouts of praise that left his players with a feeling he said they would never forget. "Saturday night was what college athletics are all about – two great universities with two excellent teams playing their hearts out before fans who really appreciate the way the game of football should be played," he wrote. "There is another way to spell Nebraska. You simply spell it CLASS."

He didn't leave it at that. Though Nebraska dropped one spot to ninth in the national coaches' poll after that somewhat narrow win over the underdog Bears, the Huskers surprisingly received one first-place vote. A Baylor spokesman, when asked, confirmed that it was cast by the coach of the Baylor Bears – Grant Teaff.

ROAD TRIP TO

WACO

Baylor University

Founded: 1845

Enrollment: 14,600

Colors:
Green and gold

Conference history:
Founding member of the Southwest Conference in 1914, began Big 12 play in 1996

Stadium:
Floyd Casey Stadium, capacity 50,000

History of "Bears":
A student vote in 1914 established the name. The tradition of having a live bear in the stadium began in 1917, when an Army unit stationed nearby brought a beast named "Ted" to the Texas A&M game. When the unit departed, it left the bear in the hands of the athletic department.

Distance from Memorial Stadium in Lincoln:
694 miles

Worth remembering:
Waco isn't the most desirable location for a vacation, and it isn't the easiest to get to, but it had one thing going for it as a destination for Nebraskans: Plenty of good seats available. Until the 2010 season, Baylor football teams were mostly bottom feeders in the Big 12, so there has been no bandwagon for Bears fans to jump aboard. Husker visitors generally were treated well when they made the long trip to Waco.

Quote:
"Football has got to be your priority. I'm not sure everybody on campus feels that way right now. I'll probably get in trouble for saying that, but that's the way it is."

– Baylor coach Guy Morriss (2004)

LINEMAN NO MATCH FOR SECRET SERVICE

Elaborate security measures were taken by Secret Service agents who locked down Memorial Stadium in advance of a visit by former President Gerald Ford, who wanted to drop by and say hello to Nebraska's 1977 football team.

Steve Glenn, a junior offensive lineman, managed to inadvertently touch off some locker room drama.

Glenn and some friends went trapshooting that Thursday morning. Afterward, he stashed his shotgun in his locker, took some loose shells from his pocket and placed them on the top shelf. That afternoon, Glenn joined his teammates for a 1½-hour practice as the Huskers continued to prepare for Baylor.

Practice ended at 4:30 p.m. Players showered, dressed and waited until Ford arrived in the locker room at 5:15.

"I got there a little late," Glenn said. "I walked in and thought, 'Wow! Here is the President.' I smiled and waved, then went over to my locker and opened the door. Those shotgun shells rolled off the top shelf and scattered on the floor.

"Those Secret Service agents were aghast. Out came all those guns. I was 6-foot-4 and weighed 262 pounds, but they could have been linebackers because they had me up against the wall and spread-eagled in two seconds."

Glenn said he was detained for more than two hours while the agents verified his claim that he had been trapshooting that morning.

"This was serious," Glenn said. "More guns were flashed around than I had ever seen before. It was quite a deal."

– Larry Porter

TOUGH DAY ON THE PLAY-BY-PLAY

Baylor's punts in a 1977 nonconference game, won by the Huskers 31-10, included opposing players with oddly similar names: Nebraska's Randy Rick and Baylor's Ricky Rand. NU's Rick, a defensive end playing special teams, made a huge early play, blocking a punt by Baylor. The ball trickled into the end zone, where lineman Larry Young fell on it for the Huskers' first touchdown. Rick said he sought out Rand after the game. "I told him it probably wouldn't be a big deal with him, but I had to talk to him about his name," Rick said. "He thought it was kind of funny, too."

– Larry Porter

TOMMIE BACK IN LINCOLN

Former Nebraska quarterback Tommie Frazier was reunited with coach Frank Solich and Husker fans in a 2000 game at Memorial Stadium. Frazier, the Baylor running backs coach, wasn't able to provide much helpful information on his former team. NU defeated the Bears 59-0.

NO NU CONFERENCE LOSSES TO THE BEARS

Nebraska's first Big 12 game against Baylor, a 49-0 blowout in Lincoln in 1996, was a sign of things to come. The scores of the next five games were similar, 49-21 in 1997, 59-0 in 2000, 48-7 in 2001 and 59-27 in 2004. The Bears finally made a game of it in 2005, falling 23-14 in Waco, and gave the Huskers tough battles in their final two meetings. But the series concluded with NU winning all eight conference matchups.

» A SIGN OF HOPE

Nebraska got its glimpse of Robert Griffin (10) in 2008, and you can bet the coaching staff would have preferred not to have experienced that again. One game against a dynamic playmaker will do that to you. Griffin, an explosive speedster at the quarterback spot, nearly led his team to a monumental win in Memorial Stadium in 2008. And given the fragility of Nebraska's program at the time, a loss to Baylor likely would have launched Husker fans into a panic. Griffin was lethal in that game, running for 121 yards and throwing for 134. Baylor led for nearly three quarters as a result. Nebraska ended up winning 32-20, but it was no cakewalk. NU simply began executing its defense down the stretch to gain the upper hand, according to Husker linebacker Cody Glenn. "Really, just trying to contain him is playing smart, playing disciplined and not trying to play outside yourself," Glenn said. "Because if you do, he's a great athlete, he's got a lot of speed and one mistake and he's probably going to take it for 80."

Griffin never got a do-over against Nebraska. He tore his ACL early in 2009, keeping him out of Nebraska's 20-10 win in Waco, and Baylor was off NU's schedule in the 2010 regular season. NU fans were sure to enjoy watching him perform – against someone else.

– Jon Nyatawa

Games at College Station feature one of college football's greatest traditions: kissing your date when the Aggies score.

TEXAS A&M

THE GAMES DIDN'T ALWAYS LIVE UP TO THE TRADITIONS

BY MICHAEL KELLY | WORLD-HERALD STAFF WRITER

THE NEBRASKA-TEXAS A&M RIVALRY wasn't as storied as others, but it offered interesting connections. The first is a historical footnote: Before Nebraska hired Bob Devaney as head coach in 1962 and watched him usher in the modern era of Big Red, NU offered the job to . . . Hank Foldberg. Maybe you don't know the name. He turned down Nebraska to accept the position at Texas A&M. In three years there, he posted a record of 6-23-1. Devaney, who said he got the Husker job despite spilling soup on himself at the home of Chancellor Clifford Hardin, built NU into a national powerhouse and was inducted into the National College Football Hall of Fame. Tradition-rich A&M has done well for itself over the decades. It eclipsed Texas to take first place in the 2009-10 all-sport composite standings in the Big 12 – under Athletic Director Bill Byrne, a former A.D. at Nebraska. What if Foldberg had accepted the Nebraska coaching job before it was offered to Devaney? What if Byrne, who oversaw $100 million in improvements in and near Memorial Stadium in 11 years, hadn't left NU in 2002? Would the football downturn that began during his final year, a 7-7 record, have lasted as long as it did? Who can say for sure?

The Huskers and Aggies became conference-mates in 1996 and have played some close games, including a 28-21 A&M win at College Station in 1998. The Huskers eked out one-touchdown and one-point wins there in 2002 and 2006, respectively, and the Aggies won handily in Lincoln in '07. The games at Kyle Field are loud, especially with A&M's always-standing "12th Man" student body and its Corps of Cadets, the largest uniformed student group outside of the U.S. military service academies. Students and other fans kiss their dates when Texas A&M scores, and lots of smooching smacks of the kiss of death to opponents. The teams' very nicknames speak of the nation's breadbasket – the Aggies and the Cornhuskers. But in 1988, Nebraska and Texas A&M traveled to East Rutherford, N.J., across the Hudson River from New York City, to open the season in the nationally televised Kickoff

Games at Kyle Field provide a unique experience for visitors.

ROAD TRIP TO

COLLEGE STATION

Texas A&M University

Founded: 1876

Enrollment: 48,700

Colors: Maroon and white

Conference history:
Founding member of the Southwest Conference in 1914, began Big 12 play in 1996

Stadium:
Kyle Field, capacity 83,002

History of "Aggies":
Originally the Agricultural and Mechanical College of Texas, A&M teams took on the "Aggies" name frequently given to ag schools.

Distance from Memorial Stadium in Lincoln:
804 miles

Worth remembering:
If you're looking for college football tradition, you've come to the right place. "The 12th Man" began when a student came down from the stands in 1922 to help a shorthanded Aggie team. When the game ended, the student was the only player left standing on the sidelines. The gesture has come to be associated with fans' enthusiasm. Student yell leaders keep the crowd alive, even during a dull game, with their cheers. The Aggies' live mascot is "Reveille," a collie that is addressed as "Miss Rev, ma'am." If the Aggies' defense ever returns to past glory, expect to hear about "the Wrecking Crew," the A&M equivalent of the Blackshirts.

» **Quote:**
"I've laid awake in bed for 23 years, thinking about a game like this."

– Nebraska quarterback Zac Taylor (13) after throwing a touchdown pass with 21 seconds left to beat Texas A&M at Kyle Field (2006)

Nebraska quarterback Zac Taylor and coach Bill Callahan celebrated a come-from-behind win in 2006.

Classic. It was live from New York on a Saturday night, both teams ranked in the nation's Top 10. Nebraska trailed at halftime, but a hard tackle by NU's Leroy Etienne on the kickoff opening the second half seemed to change the momentum, and the Huskers won 23-14. The teams didn't play each other again until 1997, Nebraska winning 54-15 in the Big 12 title game on the way to a national championship.

Tom Osborne stepped down as head coach after that season, anointing longtime assistant Frank Solich as his successor. Solich did well before that 7-7 year in 2002, and a year later Athletic Director Steve Pederson replaced him with former National Football League coach Bill Callahan. After a four-year Big 12 record of 15-17, including a 36-14 loss to Texas A&M in Lincoln in 2007, Callahan was dismissed by Osborne, who had replaced the fired Pederson in midseason. Osborne then hired Bo Pelini as head coach and helped orchestrate Nebraska's monumental move from the Big 12 to the Big Ten, which takes effect in 2011. Aggie fans, meanwhile, became excited about a possible move to the Southeastern Conference. But A&M decided to stay with the Big 12, and Byrne was criticized by those who wished for a conference identity separate from the University of Texas. "If anyone feels that a shadow is cast by our friends in the state capital," Byrne said, "the way to remedy that is to beat them on the fields of play along with all of our other opponents."

Texas A&M is the home of the presidential library of George H.W. Bush, 41st president of the United States. His name is known worldwide, and Bob Devaney's is widely known to fans of college football. Hank Foldberg? He is a good man whose name is a Nebraska football footnote.

ONE FOR THE ROAD

Longtime Nebraska offensive line coach Milt Tenopir said he was especially proud of his players after a 38-31 comeback win in College Station in 2002. The Huskers, who took a 5-3 record into the game, had lost their previous five road games and fallen behind by 17 points midway through the third quarter. But with Tenopir's big linemen paving the way, NU scored 24 straight points to end the game. "The reason I was most proud of them was because they've taken a lot of flak this year," Tenopir said. "These kids have been slapped in the face a lot of times."

Asked to compare his feelings to the pride he felt after another game, Tenopir could only come up with one: the Huskers' 1984 Orange Bowl loss to Miami.

^ 1997 BIG 12 CHAMPIONSHIP GAME: NO CONTEST FROM THE START

Nebraska scored on all seven of its first-half possessions in a 54-15 romp at the Alamodome in San Antonio. Texas A&M, meanwhile, was held to two first downs and 83 yards in the first 30 minutes, 63 of them on one second-quarter pass play. Scott Frost (7) led the Huskers by passing for 201 yards and rushing for 79 in a performance that came a week after he had learned that he had been picked to the coaches' all-Big 12 third team.

» A LESSON LEARNED

Dat Nguyen (9) was on the field for the Big 12 title game blowout in 1997. Nguyen had nine tackles and a forced fumble in that 54-15 beatdown. And less than one year later, he and his teammates got their revenge.

Texas A&M upset Nebraska, ranked No. 2 at the time, surviving a late rally to earn a 28-21 victory in 1998 in College Station that snapped the Huskers' 19-game winning streak. It might as well have been a championship for the Aggies.

"Everyone says we can't win the big game," Nguyen told The World-Herald after the win. "All week we heard people say how we choke in the big games. The sky is the limit for us now."

Truth is, skeptics had a right to be critical heading into the showdown. Texas A&M hadn't beaten a top 10 team in the 1990s and had never upset a squad ranked as high as No. 2. Nebraska, fresh off its third national title in four years, had won its last 40 regular-season conference games. Plus, the Huskers had demolished A&M in the league title game a year earlier.

But behind a Nguyen-led defense, which executed flawlessly for three quarters, Texas A&M pulled off the stunner. Nguyen, the eventual Lombardi and Bednarik Award winner, had eight tackles, leading the charge.

Nebraska ran 42 plays in the first three quarters and gained 117 yards. The Huskers had managed just one run longer than 7 yards and trailed 28-7 in the fourth.

NU did mount a comeback, capping 76-yard and 66-yard drives with touchdowns. But its final possession ended with an interception.

The College Station-style celebration began immediately. Nguyen was right in the middle of it, like he always was, crying with his teammates.

The win helped propel the Aggies to an 11-3 season, a Big 12 championship and an appearance in the Sugar Bowl.

Nguyen, who started all 51 games of his college career, ended his time at A&M as the school's all-time tackle leader. He went on to play seven seasons in the NFL for the Dallas Cowboys and has returned to College Station to coach the Aggie linebackers.

– Jon Nyatawa

« **THROW IT, PLEASE**

The Aggies probably were happy to see Nebraska switch to a passing offense in the 2004 season. Up to that point, Nebraska's running quarterbacks had given Texas A&M fits. Eric Crouch ran for 137 yards and a touchdown in a 37-0 win in 1999. Jammal Lord (10) burned the Aggies twice, for 159 yards in a 38-31 win in 2002 and 109 yards and two touchdowns in a 48-12 blowout in 2003.

» THE COMEBACK

After taking over on their 25-yard line with 1:57 on the clock in the 2006 game, the Huskers moved 75 yards to win 28-27 and clinch their first Big 12 North championship since 1999. The last of quarterback Zac Taylor's five final-drive completions was a 9-yard touchdown pass to Maurice Purify (16), who set his feet, leaped high and pulled down the curtain on Texas A&M with 21 seconds left.

ˆ CHANGE WAS IN THE AIR

A&M outscored the Huskers 20-0 after halftime in a third straight ugly NU loss in 2007, and coach Bill Callahan's days appeared to be numbered. New interim Athletic Director Tom Osborne was cheered when he made an appearance on the sideline, but fans started to leave Memorial Stadium after the third quarter. The Aggies coasted home to a 36-14 victory.

The Nebraska band marches toward Memorial Stadium before the 2010 Missouri game.

ONE LAST TIME

THE CORNHUSKERS' FINAL MARCH THROUGH THE BIG 12

BY RICH KAIPUST | WORLD-HERALD STAFF WRITER

NEBRASKA WON 10 regular-season games, made it to the last Big 12 championship game and had a chance to leave the league on top.

It was almost too good to be true. Even had a fairy-tale element to it when you threw in the fact that the Huskers were playing Oklahoma one last time with a conference title on the line.

The Sooners, however, did as they had done many times before, beating Nebraska 23-20 in the last Big 12 championship game at Cowboys Stadium in Arlington, Texas.

Still, Nebraska improved its regular-season win total for the third straight year under head coach Bo Pelini. It won at Washington, Kansas State, Oklahoma State and Iowa State, and gave itself the inside track to the Big 12 North title by beating Missouri in Lincoln.

The Huskers at one point even reached No. 5 in the Associated Press poll, their best ranking since the 2001 season.

The losses were narrow – by seven points to Texas and three to Texas A&M before a field goal separated NU and Oklahoma in the Big 12 final. The Huskers also beat all of their old Big Eight rivals but OU in their last trip through the league before heading to the Big Ten.

"I'm proud of our football team and how hard they've worked," Pelini said on the eve of the Big 12 championship game. "You know, it's not easy. This is a great conference. There's a lot of tremendous competition."

Coach Bo Pelini leads the Huskers onto the field against Iowa State in Ames.

PLAYMAKERS

Quarterback Taylor Martinez (3) ran for 241 yards and four touchdowns, and Lavonte David (4) led the Blackshirts in slowing star KSU back Daniel Thomas (8). The fans in Manhattan were feisty at the beginning of the game, ready to make Nebraska pay for its decision to move to the Big Ten, but Martinez quickly quieted them.

SEASON SNAPSHOT

Nebraska got off to a fast start in its Big 12 schedule with a Thursday night road win against a Big 12 North contender.

RIVALRY FOOTNOTE

The Huskers' victory followed the series' pattern: NU took the last six games against the Wildcats.

PLAYMAKERS

Longhorns sophomore quarterback Garrett Gilbert (7) surprised the Blackshirts with his running ability in taking his team to an early lead. Nebraska was sadly lacking in offensive stars, with three potential scoring passes dropped. Perhaps the most painful one was by Rex Burkhead (22) near the Texas goal line in the second quarter.

SEASON SNAPSHOT

Facing a tough road game the following week at Oklahoma State, NU was in danger of digging itself a deep hole early in the conference season.

RIVALRY FOOTNOTE

Once again, the Longhorns delivered a crushing defeat for Husker fans, who for 10 months had hoped to avenge the loss in the 2009 Big 12 title game.

PLAYMAKERS

Niles Paul (24), who had been heckled about his dropped passes in the Texas game, returned a kickoff 100 yards for a touchdown and caught eight passes for 123 yards. It's no surprise when kicker Alex Henery (90) comes up big on special teams, but this time it was on a 27-yard run on a fake punt.

SEASON SNAPSHOT

The Huskers got their championship hopes back on track in a wild game in which the two teams combined for 1,035 total yards.

RIVALRY FOOTNOTE

The Cowboys again were unable to ride their stars – running back Kendall Hunter, receiver Justin Blackmon and quarterback Brandon Weeden – to victory.

PLAYMAKERS

Roy Helu (10) ran for a school-record 307 yards – topping Calvin Jones' mark of 294 set in 1991 against Kansas – and scored three touchdowns on long runs. It was the Huskers' first victory over a top 10 team (Missouri was No. 7) since the 2001 Oklahoma game.

SEASON SNAPSHOT

The win gave Nebraska the upper hand in the race for the Big 12 North title.

RIVALRY FOOTNOTE

The Nebraska-Missouri game once again featured head-knocking play. The Blackshirts rattled Tiger quarterback Blaine Gabbert (11), with hard hits coming out of a new defensive look. Lineman D.J. Jones (73) celebrated with the Victory Bell, which will remain in Lincoln for a long time.

PLAYMAKERS

The game came down to one play, with Eric Hagg (28) leaping to intercept a fluttering pass that would have given the Cyclones a two-point conversion and the win in overtime. Rex Burkhead (22) ran for 129 yards and two touchdowns, including the game-winner on a 19-yard dash in overtime, while quarterback Cody Green (17) kept the offense on track in the absence of the injured Taylor Martinez and Zac Lee.

SEASON SNAPSHOT

The shaky victory, combined with Missouri's loss to Texas Tech that night, put Nebraska in the driver's seat in the Big 12 North.

RIVALRY FOOTNOTE

It was a sunny day in Ames, but the weather was anything but pleasant. The wind gusted to more than 25 mph, and only one touchdown in regulation was scored by the team heading into the wind.

PLAYMAKERS

The Blackshirts stole the show, holding Kansas to just 87 yards of offense. Jayhawk quarterback Quinn Mecham, who had engineered a 35-point comeback win the previous weekend against Colorado, completed just 3 of 13 passes for 15 yards and was sacked six times. "I'm very impressed," NU defensive tackle Jared Crick (94) said of the defense's performance. Crick had two sacks among his nine tackles.

SEASON SNAPSHOT

Quarterback Taylor Martinez and cornerback Alfonzo Dennard (15) returned after missing the Iowa State game with injuries. Martinez was hampered by his injured ankle but still ran for 71 yards. Dennard, who had been out with a concussion, got his fourth interception of the season in the third quarter.

RIVALRY FOOTNOTE

NU won its 21st straight over Kansas in Lincoln to close out the conference series. While the score wasn't as lopsided as in some previous games, many Husker fans probably preferred not to pile up points on a team coached by NU legend Turner Gill (top right).

PLAYMAKERS

In a game dominated by the defenses, Texas A&M running back Cyrus Gray (32) stood out with his 137 yards rushing. For Nebraska, Lavonte David (4) logged 14 tackles, including a sack. But the key stat in the game was Nebraska's 16 penalties for 145 yards. The Aggies were flagged just twice for 10 yards.

SEASON SNAPSHOT

Nebraska had a chance to wrap up the Big 12 North title with a victory or a Missouri loss to Iowa State, but neither occurred on the next-to-last weekend of the regular season. Quarterback Taylor Martinez (3) reinjured his right ankle in the first quarter, and coach Bo Pelini spent much of the game in meltdown mode over officials' calls. The Huskers were forced to regroup as they prepared for Colorado.

RIVALRY FOOTNOTE

The final battle between the two tradition-rich football programs had the ingredients of a November classic: Both teams were still in the hunt for Big 12 division titles and playing before a national television audience and record crowd in College Station. But Husker fans will be left instead with the memory of yellow flags on the ground and their coach snarling on the sidelines.

PLAYMAKERS

Sophomore Rex Burkhead (22) did everything he could to make senior day a success at Memorial Stadium. He ran for 101 yards and a touchdown and threw two scoring passes, one for 26 yards to Brandon Kinnie (84) and another for 4 yards to Kyler Reed (25) on a broken play. "Nothing Rex Burkhead does surprises me," coach Bo Pelini said. On defense, senior DeJon Gomes (7) led the way with a third-quarter interception and a fumble recovery that he returned 19 yards in the fourth quarter.

SEASON SNAPSHOT

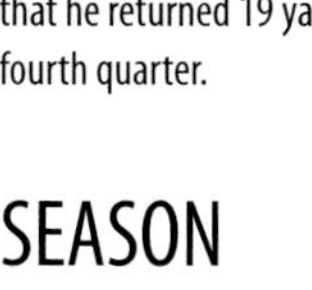

The Huskers wrapped up the Big 12 North title with the victory and learned two days later that they would face Oklahoma in the conference championship game. After a grinding march through the Big 12 – both teams lost two games – the two old rivals once again settled the league title at season's end.

RIVALRY FOOTNOTE

The Nebraska-Colorado series has featured some wild finishes over the years, but the two schools' final conference showdown ended quietly. The Huskers – CU's designated rival – for the fifth time provided a season-ending loss that kept the Buffs from qualifying for a bowl game.

OKLAHOMA 23 NEBRASKA 20

THE IMPERFECT ENDING

BY RICH KAIPUST | WORLD-HERALD STAFF WRITER

Nebraska could have found a better way to say goodbye to the Big 12.

It could have taken its 17-0 lead, put its cleats on Oklahoma's throat and run off to the Big Ten with a big old smirk on its face.

It could have, even with its lead trimmed to 20-17, squeezed something – anything – out of eight second-half offensive possessions at Cowboys Stadium.

And it could have simply given Alex Henery one more chance to work his kicking magic instead of fumbling the football and taking sacks at some of the worst possible times.

The Huskers instead walked away with heads hung, losing 23-20 to the Sooners in a Big 12 championship game in Arlington, Texas, that they might remember for all the wrong reasons.

"We just did too many things out there to overcome and beat a good football team," NU coach Bo Pelini said.

There's nothing Taylor Martinez (3) or Bo Pelini can do as the clock winds down at Cowboys Stadium.

Oklahoma's Travis Lewis jumps in front of Rex Burkhead to grab an interception in the end zone in the second quarter. Nebraska led 17-7 at the time and was within field goal range.

NU PLAYMAKERS

The Huskers scored first, with Roy Helu (10) dashing 66 yards for a touchdown. Later in the first quarter, Alex Henery (90) delivered his longest field goal of the season – a 53-yarder. Courtney Osborne (12) intercepted a pass and returned it 33 yards to the OU 12 to set up a touchdown that gave Nebraska a 17-0 lead with 12:14 left in the first half.

SEASON SNAPSHOTS

Nebraska's 2010 Big 12 Conference games, as seen through the pages of the Omaha World-Herald.

POSTGAME

Taylor Martinez sets Nebraska's single-game quarterback rushing record with 241 yards

Blackshirts are stingy against Kansas State star Daniel Thomas: 63 yards on 22 carries

UNTOUCHED

Martinez's Magic leaves Little Apple feeling rotten

NEBRASKA **48**
KANSAS STATE **13**

POSTGAME

TEXAS TAKEOVER: The Longhorns maintain a mastery of Nebraska with a fast start and stingy defense

ZONED OUT: Huskers' zone read is stuffed, dropped passes haunt NU receivers, and Taylor Martinez is benched

Opportunity dropped

Did Huskers' passion work in reverse?

Maybe it's a good thing this series is over

TEXAS **20**
NEBRASKA **13**

POSTGAME

A GIANT LEAP

It's an important day in quarterback's wonder year

T-Magic takes to air, brings Pokes down to earth

NEBRASKA **51**
OKLAHOMA STATE **41**

POSTGAME

RUNNING START

Bo bags a big one, keeps Huskers in the hunt for more

Helu's record day lifts NU past Mizzou, ending home slump

NEBRASKA **31**
MISSOURI **17**

OU PLAYMAKERS

Travis Lewis (28) led an Oklahoma defense that made the game a nightmare for NU quarterback Taylor Martinez (3). Lewis intercepted a Martinez pass in the first half and also recovered two fumbles, accounting for three of the four Nebraska turnovers. Quarterback Landry Jones (12), who had five interceptions against NU in 2009, threw for 342 yards against the Blackshirts in the championship game.

POSTGAME

NU's tough road win, Mizzou's loss put Huskers alone atop North standings

Burkhead-led Wildcat, Cassidy's pick six help Nebraska survive without Martinez

MAN OF STEAL

Escaping Ames with a win requires both pluck and luck

Hagg bags an overtime win with heads-up play on fake

NEBRASKA **31**
IOWA STATE **30**
(OT)

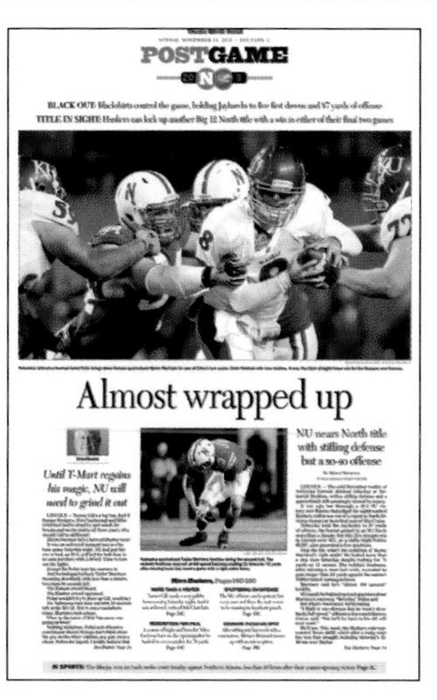

POSTGAME

Almost wrapped up

NU nears North title with stifling defense but a so-so offense

Until T-Mart regains his magic, NU will need to grind it out

NEBRASKA **20**
KANSAS **3**

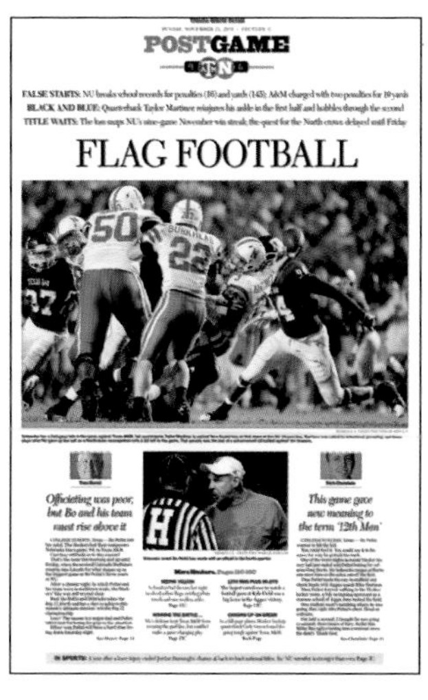

POSTGAME

FLAG FOOTBALL

Officiating was poor, but Bo and his team must rise above it

This game gave new meaning to the term '12th Man'

TEXAS A&M **9**
NEBRASKA **6**

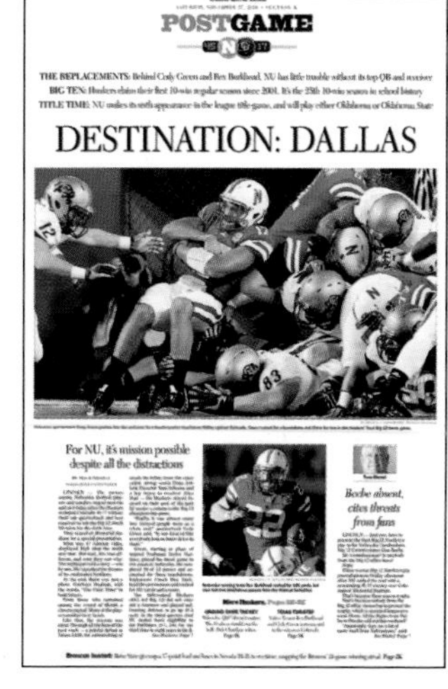

POSTGAME

DESTINATION: DALLAS

For NU, it's mission possible despite all the distractions

Bo, be absent, cites threats from fans

NEBRASKA **45**
COLORADO **17**

BIG 12 POSTGAME

PARTING SHOT

No fingers to point this time; Huskers have selves to blame

Nebraska gives the Sooners one too many chances

OKLAHOMA **23**
NEBRASKA **20**

RIVALRY FOOTNOTE

The Sooners once again spoiled Nebraska's dreams at the end of the conference season, and time will tell how this loss will compare to past heartbreaks. But while Oklahoma got the final word, Husker fans have some pretty nice consolation prizes from the series, including memories of breathtaking wins in 1959, 1971, 1978 and 2001.

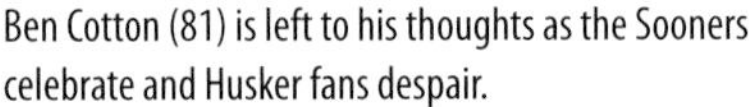

Ben Cotton (81) is left to his thoughts as the Sooners celebrate and Husker fans despair.

Oklahoma's James Winchester offers consolation to NU's Roy Helu (10) and Niles Paul (24) after the game, and the longtime rivals say goodbye.

Nebraska fans congratulate the Huskers in 2009 as they exit as victors in their last game at Colorado's Folsom Field.

ONE LAST GLANCE OUT THE BACK WINDOW

BY TOM SHATEL

Where we going today?

The bus is packed up and ready to move out. I'm headed to the back, next to the card game, where John Brooks, the wise guy Oklahoma play-by-play guy, is giving it to Vahe Gregorian, the young wordsmith from Missouri. I might try to sit next to the "Good Old Boy," Bob Hentzen, the venerable columnist from Topeka. I'm in the mood to hear some Pepper Rodgers stories.

Tom Shatel
has been following Big Eight and Big 12 football for more than 30 years.

Where we going today? The Big Eight Skywriters bus is packed and ready on the two-lane road in my memory. Every once in a while, when this game I love gets a little too corporate and a little too impersonal, I'll step back onboard in my time machine. That wonderful old bus.

Where we going today? As Nebraska prepares to jump off the cliff into the great Big Ten unknown, let's head back to a simpler time for college football. A better time, it says here.

The great thing about this book is that 10 years from now, 20 years, somebody will find it and learn the history. This is a story that needs to be told. A conference made up of eight schools that felt like a neighborhood? A league that was a mirror of a specific region of the United States? Nobody will ever believe it. It happened. I was there. A lot of us were.

The Big Eight was that way. It looked like it sprouted up from the very dirt – in some cases red dirt – in Missouri, Kansas, Nebraska, Iowa and Oklahoma. Pardon me if I don't acknowledge the Big 12 in this little farewell card. The Big 12 represented the awkward future of college athletics, the megaconference that made no sense. It was a predecessor of a lot of these superconferences people are talking about. They are corporate mergers made to increase TV portfolios. They tromp on simple things like tradition and history. The conference commissioner of the future should be Gordon Gekko.

Anyway, back to that bus. That Skywriters tour was a metaphor for the league. You looked out that window every day and it was hard to tell if you were in Concordia, Mo.; Atlantic, Iowa; Ashland, Neb.; or Paxico, Kan. That was the other thing about the Big Eight: every state, except for Colorado, even looked the same.

We were a little community, a fraternity, living on that bus for eight days. We were exactly like the Big Eight. The guy from Oklahoma may have had a twang, the Nebraska guy wore cowboy boots, the Missouri guy thought he could recite Shakespeare and the Colorado guy looked like Grizzly Adams. But we all spoke the same language.

In the Bill Callahan definition of things, we were all, ahem, hillbillies. That quote from Callahan back in 2004 crystallized what this league was about. When the former Nebraska coach walked off Owen Field at OU after a heated loss and called the OU fans "hillbillies," he did not score points with his own fan base. Nebraskans are Oklahomans are Kansans are Missourians are Iowans. Just plain

folks. Good folks. God-fearing folks who go to church on Saturday and Sunday. The church on Saturday just happened to be a football stadium.

That's not to say there weren't rivalries in the Big Eight. But it was like the rivalry you have with your neighbors. You wanted to have a nicer lawn than Tom Osborne or drive a cooler car than Barry Switzer. But in the end, everyone had pride in their neighborhood. And you wanted Big Eight football to stand up against the Big Ten or Pac-10 or SEC or Southwest Conference. Remember the SWC?

The Big Eight had iconic coaches and historic games and classic players. It was dirt kickin', hard hittin', helmet-splittin' football. But the thing I'll remember the most about the Big Eight was the community, the way the league was like a big small town. You won't see that again. The SEC still has that, but you wonder how future expansion might change that. Even though Nebraska looks like a good fit, the Big Ten will change. If the Pac-10 ever reaches into Texas or Oklahoma, that will be as weird as a dude surfing with a cowboy hat. You might see that, too.

These days I think about the old Big Eight schools. I worry about what might happen to them. If we have another expansion outbreak, you could see Kansas, Kansas State, Missouri and Iowa State break apart from OU and Oklahoma State. They could split apart like a group of college friends after graduation. Would they keep in touch? Probably not.

I wonder what those schools are thinking about Nebraska. Sure, if the Huskers had stayed in the Big 12, you could argue that the thing may have held together. For a while. But the Big 12 changed that, Texas changed it, and so did Oklahoma. You wonder how bitter the old Big Eight schools are at Nebraska. You wonder if they are saying, "How could you do this to us?"

It happened, and it happened for good reasons: for security, for legacy, for Nebraska's obligation to Nebraska. You can say this wouldn't have happened if it had been the Big Eight, and you'd be right. But that's the thing. The Big Eight was gone a long time ago.

The old neighborhood lives on, in books like this one, and on a bus full of happy sportswriters, somewhere in the Twilight Zone.

ALL-TIME BIG EIGHT/BIG 12 FOOTBALL TEAM

BY LEE BARFKNECHT | WORLD-HERALD STAFF WRITER

LET'S START WITH some of the players who didn't make The World-Herald's all-time Big Eight/Big 12 football team: Gale Sayers, Ndamukong Suh, Vince Young, Billy Sims, Thurman Thomas, Ricky Williams, Hart Lee Dykes, Tommie Harris, Steve Owens, Broderick Thomas.

In shock yet? Take a deep breath. There are plenty more: Mike Brown, Ralph Neely, Bobby Anderson, Dean Steinkuhler, Dexter Manley, Troy Davis, Darren Sproles, Derrick Johnson, Terence Newman. Such is the star power necessary to fill one of 11 spots on offense, 11 on defense and three on special teams.

This team is heavy on players from Nebraska and Oklahoma, because those schools dominated from the mid-1960s into the 1990s. Both earned seven spots. Colorado got four and Oklahoma State three. The Big 12 began in 1996, making it more difficult for the four schools from Texas to earn spots.

OFFENSE

QUARTERBACK

Tommie Frazier

Nebraska, 1992-95

He won two national titles, was the MVP of three consecutive national title games (Orange, Orange and Fiesta Bowls) and should have been the 1995 Heisman winner over Ohio State's Eddie George. Tom Osborne said the only other player in his NU football career who impacted a game like Frazier was Johnny Rodgers. Frazier won't ever win the most-popular player vote at Nebraska. But he had ultimate respect on the field, as his 33-3 record as a starter shows.

RUNNING BACK

Mike Rozier

Nebraska, 1981-83

After one season at Coffeyville (Kan.) Junior College, he arrived in Lincoln and found Roger Craig entrenched at I-back. But in the final full-scale scrimmage that fall, Rozier – working with the No. 3 offense against the No. 1 defense – rushed for 230 yards. When a reporter asked if Rozier would consider redshirting, he replied with the word "no," preceded by a word we need not repeat. He ran for 2,148 yards as a senior, earning the Heisman and a reputation for being one of the toughest guys to play at NU.

RUNNING BACK

Barry Sanders

Oklahoma State, 1986-88

In 1987, Nebraska drilled Oklahoma State 35-0 and held All-America tailback Thurman Thomas to 7 yards in nine carries. But another OSU back scampered for 60 yards in seven carries. Inside the locker room, I asked NU players Broderick Thomas and Neil Smith about the effort on Thurman Thomas. "We shut his (bleep) down," Broderick said. "Yeah," said Smith, who grudgingly added: "But we couldn't tackle that other little (blankety-blank)." The "other little blankety-blank" was Sanders, who the next season won the Heisman with 2,628 yards – a record that may stand forever.

WIDE RECEIVER

Michael Crabtree

Texas Tech, 2007-08

He was an option quarterback in high school. Looks like the position change worked out pretty well. Texas tried to recruit Crabtree to play defense, but he spurned the Longhorns, saying: "I want to score touchdowns." One of the biggest he scored at Tech was with one second left to beat No. 1 Texas 39-33 in 2008. The two-time All-American was the first two-time winner of the Biletnikoff Award.

WIDE RECEIVER

Johnny Rodgers

Nebraska, 1969-72

Tom Osborne said Rodgers was the first player he coached who was worth 10 to 14 points a game. That estimate might have been a bit low. Rodgers rightfully drew a lot of attention for his spectacular long gains. But the number of plays he made on third down to produce first downs was remarkable. Rodgers' punt return work also drove opponents nuts. Bob Devaney always said Rodgers' punt return for a touchdown in the 1971 Oklahoma game was the greatest play he had ever seen.

TIGHT END

Keith Jackson

Oklahoma, 1984-87

Missouri's Kellen Winslow and Nebraska's Junior Miller brought a new dimension to tight end. But Jackson truly transformed the position with his speed, power and size. The two-time All-American averaged 28.8 yards a catch as a junior and 27.5 yards as a senior. His ability to break long runs on reverses added to opponents' misery.

TACKLE

Russell Okung

Oklahoma State, 2006-09

The All-American started his final 47 games at OSU, which won three Big 12 rushing titles in that stretch. When he was a senior, pro scouts considered him the best offensive lineman in college. He was the overall No. 6 pick in the 2010 NFL draft.

GUARD

Joe Romig

Colorado, 1958-61

Three-time all-conference, two-time All-American and the nastiest astrophysicist you'll ever come across. Romig performed an experiment in college in which he and a teammate crashed into each other at full speed. The Rhodes Scholar filmed the collision so he could study the effects in slow motion. But that was the only time Romig, sixth in the 1961 Heisman voting, was in slow motion, according to teammates such as former NU assistant Charlie McBride.

CENTER

Dave Rimington

Nebraska, 1979-82

For all of Rimington's many awards, this is the most memorable: The United Press International's 1981 All-Big Eight team featured him as the offensive player of the year.

GUARD

Will Shields

Nebraska, 1988-92

This professorial-looking sort was a three-time All-Big Eight choice and a two-time All-American who won the Outland Trophy. Nebraska won national rushing titles in three of his four seasons, and he received Big Eight offensive player of the year votes. Then Shields became a 12-time Pro Bowl pick with the Kansas City Chiefs.

TACKLE

Jammal Brown

Oklahoma, 2001-04

A powerful résumé: three-time All-Big 12, two-time All-American, Outland Trophy winner. Brown didn't allow a sack in 2004, and just one in 2003.

ALL-TIME BIG EIGHT/BIG 12 FOOTBALL TEAM

DEFENSE

DEFENSIVE END

Alfred Williams

Colorado, 1987-90

A two-time All-American on the defenses that helped transform the Buffaloes from mediocre to national champions in 1990. Williams averaged almost a sack a game for his career despite playing against mostly run-oriented offenses.

MIDDLE GUARD/DEF. TACKLE

Rich Glover

Nebraska, 1969-72

How do you leave out Ndamukong Suh? True, Suh had arguably the greatest single defensive season ever. But he didn't make first-team All-Big 12 as a junior in the coaches' vote. Glover was a two-time All-American, finished third in the Heisman voting and had a 22-tackle game against an All-America center in the 1971 NU-OU Game of the Century.

DEFENSIVE TACKLE

Lee Roy Selmon

Oklahoma, 1972-75

Barry Switzer calls the two-time All-American and Lombardi and Outland winner the best player he ever coached. That's a good enough recommendation for me. Any of the three Selmon brothers from Eufaula, Okla. – Lee Roy, Dewey (a two-time All-American) or Lucious (an All-American, too) – would have been a great anchor to a defensive line.

DEFENSIVE END

Grant Wistrom

Nebraska, 1994-97

This two-time All-American was NU's fourth Lombardi Award winner. Wistrom, known for his relentless style, still holds the school record for tackles for loss (58.5). As much as anything, he brought a will to win and a contagious fire that spread through the entire program.

LINEBACKER

Brian Bosworth

Oklahoma, 1983-86

For all his showboating, the Boz could hit. He's the only player to have won the Butkus Award twice, and he led OU in tackles for three straight seasons while twice earning All-America honors.

SPECIAL TEAMS

KICKER

« Mason Crosby

Colorado, 2003-06

Crosby nailed field goals of 60, 58 (at sea level), 57, 56, 56, 55, 54 and 54 yards. And he was clutch – 10 for 10 in the final nine minutes of games. He was the Big 12's player of the week eight times.

PUNTER

« Daniel Sepulveda

Baylor, 2003-06

He joined the Bears as a walk-on linebacker. He left as the school's second three-time All-American (LB Mike Singletary is the other) and as the only two-time winner of the Ray Guy Award. Sepulveda's career average was 45.2 yards.

PUNT/KICK RETURNER

« Cliff Branch

Colorado, 1970-71

In just two seasons, this star track sprinter returned six punts and two kickoffs for touchdowns, a record that lasted 30 years. He went on to a 14-year NFL career as a receiver in which he was All-Pro four times.

LINEBACKER

George Cumby

Oklahoma, 1977-79

Barry Switzer said Cumby was the only defender he saw go one-on-one against Heisman winner Earl Campbell of Texas and knock Campbell backward. Cumby was a two-time All-American and two-time Big Eight defensive player of the year.

LINEBACKER

Rod Shoate

Oklahoma, 1972-74

The "Hit Man" of college football was a three-time All-American, one of only two Sooners with that distinction (guard Buddy Burris is the other). Shoate was one of the early players with running back speed (4.5-second 40) to play defense.

CORNERBACK

Rickey Dixon

Oklahoma, 1984-87

The Jim Thorpe Award winner had 16 career interceptions. Dixon was a star in the 1985 national championship win against Penn State. In the 1987 "Game of the Century II" at No. 1 Nebraska, his two interceptions were critical to OU's win.

CORNERBACK

Roger Wehrli

Missouri, 1965-68

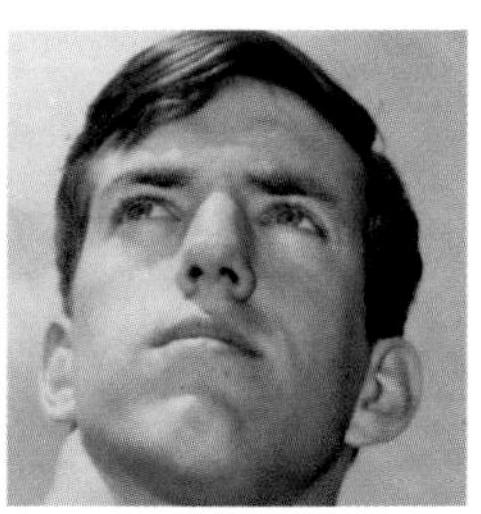

"Roger the Dodger" was an All-American who as a senior set school records for career and single-season interceptions (10 and 7), led the country in punt returns and was voted Big Eight defender of the year. He went on to a 14-year NFL career and is a member of the College and Pro Football Halls of Fame.

SAFETY

Michael Huff

Texas, 2002-05

An All-American and Thorpe winner with a big-play résumé. In Texas' 2005 title win over Southern Cal, Huff recovered a Reggie Bush fumble that got the Longhorns back in the game. Huff then made the key hit on LenDale White on fourth-and-2 to set up UT's winning drive.

SAFETY

Mark Moore

Oklahoma State, 1983-86

The two-time All-American was an anchor of the vaunted Jimmy Johnson-Pat Jones defenses that raised hell in the mid-1980s. Moore made 311 career tackles. Said Jones: "Pound for pound, he was maybe the most violent hitter we ever had."

COACH

« Tom Osborne

Nebraska

- Thirteen Big Eight/ Big 12 titles
- Career record of 255-49-3, winning percentage of .836
- Inducted into College Football Hall of Fame
- Three national championships
- Career victories total (255) ranks sixth among major college football coaches.

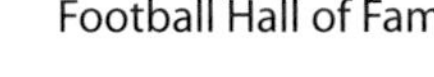

COACH

« Barry Switzer

Oklahoma

- Twelve Big Eight titles
- Career record of 157-29-4, winning percentage of .837
- Inducted into College Football Hall of Fame
- Three national championships
- Career winning percentage (.837) ranks fourth among major college football coaches.

HUSKERS
COTTON
81
49
BLUE
14
82

BIG RED RIVALS

LASTING IMPRESSIONS

IMAGES FROM THE RIVALRIES NEBRASKA IS LEAVING BEHIND

« Kansas State fans Travis Owens and Samantha Coleman don't share the joy of John Martinez after a Husker score in the 2010 game in Manhattan.

« Nebraska takes the field for pre-game warmups after most of the lights went out at Missouri's Faurot Field in 2009.

BIG RED RIVALS

THE SPIRIT

≈ NU cheerleaders and Herbie stand tall at the 1995 Kansas State game.

» A K-State Wildcat delivers a blow to a mock Husker fan before the 2002 game in Manhattan.

» The Huskers take the field against Iowa State at Memorial Stadium in 2001.

Red balloons rise after NU's first score against K-State in 2007.

Cheerleaders spell out their support before the Kansas State game in Lincoln in 2009.

The Cornhusker Marching Band steps out for a pregame performance against Iowa State at Memorial Stadium in 2009.

BIG RED RIVALS
THE FANS

⌃ Jarrod Hinrichs shows his support for Ndamukong Suh in 2009.

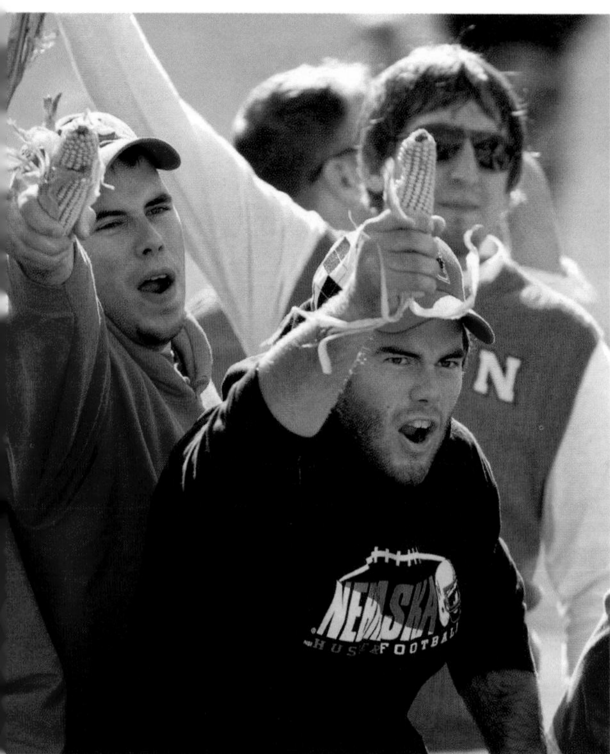

⌃ Brothers Josh and Jake Henn bring the real stuff to a Cornhusker game in 2008.

» A homemade flag salutes the defense in 1987.

« Newlyweds Jake and Mellisa Renter took a vow to always support the Huskers, no matter the score. The couple married the night before the Texas game in Lincoln in 2010 and exchanged a kiss after the loss.

« NU fans (far left) enjoyed the road trip to Stillwater in 2010.

« Jeff Krueger (left) roots on the Huskers against Kansas in Lawrence in 2009.

BIG RED RIVALS THE FOES

» Oklahoma State fan Tom Dougherty was having the time of his life in 2002 when the Cowboys beat NU for the first time since 1961.

≈ Colorado fans brought a message to Lincoln in 1967, and the Buffs backed it up on the field.

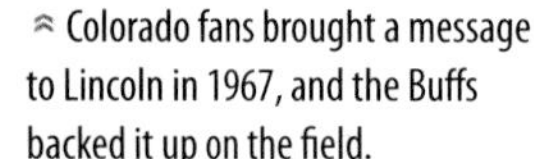

» Texas fan Chris Langer cheers on the Longhorns in 2010 amid the sea of red at Memorial Stadium.

» K-State student Courtney Sutherland turns thumbs down on NU in 2010.

⩓ Mizzou fans conduct a postmortem after beating NU in Columbia in 1973.

« Iowa State students pass out "Beat Nebraska" T-shirts in Ames in 2006.

BIG RED RIVALS
THE BRAINS

» Texas' Mack Brown and NU's Frank Solich before the 2002 game in Lincoln.

« Defensive coordinator Monte Kiffin and Bob Devaney at the 1970 Kansas game.

« Then-Iowa State assistant Barney Cotton and coach Dan McCarney celebrate a win over Nebraska in 2004.

» Oklahoma's Bud Wilkinson leaves the field after NU's 1959 victory in Lincoln.

» Bo Pelini (far right) with longtime friend Bob Stoops of Oklahoma in 2008.

^ Colorado's Bill McCartney in 1993.

« Tom Osborne with K-State's Bill Snyder in 1995 in Lincoln.

BIG RED RIVALS
THE BRAWN

Nebraska center Kurt Mann pushes back against K-State's Ian Campbell in Manahttan in 2006.

Nebraska's Zach Potter is double-teamed by Adrian Mayes and Ryan Cantrell of Kansas in 2008.

« NU's Kerry Weinmaster goes nose to nose with Kansas State's center in 1978.

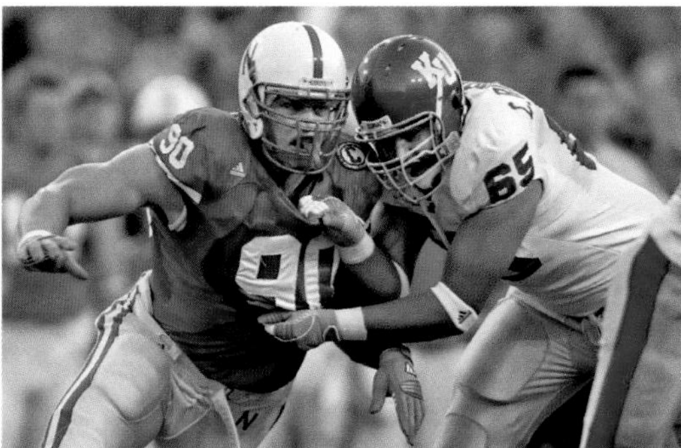

« NU's Cameron Meredith (far left) takes a Wildcat hit in 2010.

« Adam Carriker (center) battles KU's Cesar Rodriguez in 2006.

« Nate Kolterman (left) hooks up with Texas' Cory Redding in 2002.

^ Nebraska's Tom Alward struggles with Roger Stuckey of Kansas State at Memorial Stadium in Lincoln in 1972.

THE RUNS

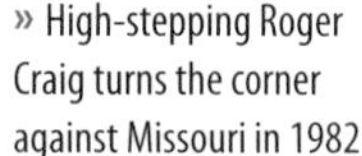

» High-stepping Roger Craig turns the corner against Missouri in 1982.

» Taylor Martinez breaks free against Kansas State in 2010.

︽ NU's Roy Helu Jr. secures the ball as he blows past K-State defenders in 2009.

« Colorado running back Bobby Purify (far left) leaves the Huskers in the dust in 2001 .

« Nebraska's Blake Tiedtke (left) is no match for Oklahoma's Adrian Peterson in 2005.

BIG RED RIVALS

THE THROWS

» Joe Ganz has plenty of protection as he releases the ball against Kansas State in 2007.

≈ Tommie Frazier spots a target against Oklahoma in 1993.

» Husker Frank Patrick (10) prepares to unload as Tom Penney (85) makes his move against Kansas in 1967.

« Colt McCoy of Texas finds a receiver in the snow against the Huskers in 2006.

≚ Texas Tech quarterback Steven Sheffield gets rid of the ball as Jared Crick arrives in 2009.

≈ Oklahoma's Sam Bradford prepares to deliver a strike in 2008.

» Iowa State's Seneca Wallace eyes a target in 2002.

BIG RED RIVALS
THE HITS

⌃ Stewart Bradley (34) and Steve Octavien (15) stop Oklahoma's Chris Brown in his tracks in the 2006 Big 12 title game.

⌃ Husker Phillip Dillard knocks down Kansas' Tim Biere after a reception in 2009.

⌃ Iowa State's Steve Karber punishes Nebraska end Jim McFarland on a pass play in 1969.

« Nebraska's Dick Davis butts heads with Kansas State's Paul Henney in 1967.

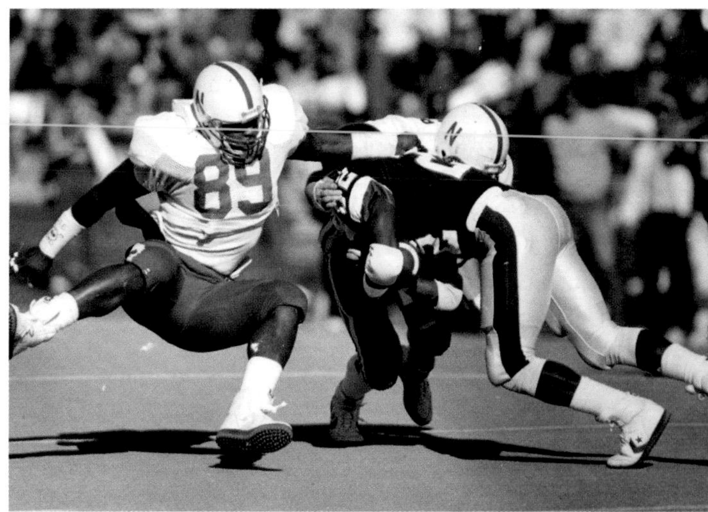

^ Husker Broderick Thomas (89) reaches out to help bring down Kansas' Arnold Snell in 1986.

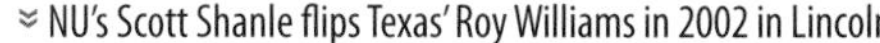

˅ NU's Scott Shanle flips Texas' Roy Williams in 2002 in Lincoln.

THE HURTS

« Kansas State's Derrick Evans loses his helmet in a collision with Scott Shanle in 2002.

» Steve Kriewald and Jake Andersen (71) check on teammate Cory Ross in 2004.

≈ Jamel Williams drops Colorado quarterback Koy Detmer in 1996.

« Kansas' Gary Coleman props up his injured ankle in 1980.

≈ Kansas' Johnny McCoy is left holding Jammal Lord's helmet in 2002.

BIG RED RIVALS
THE GRIEF

« A Jayhawk (top) finds a 56-6 whipping in 1984 is too much to bear.

« Missouri's Chris Hall (above) is brought low by a fumble against the Huskers in 1988.

« Oklahoma's Jay Jimerson and NU's Randy Theiss have opposing views of a Husker fumble in 1980.

« The face of Seppo Evwaraye (77) reflects the scoreboard, which showed a 70-10 drubbing by Texas Tech in 2004.

« Tom Osborne slaps the turf after Oklahoma's second successful "fumbleroosky" play set up a touchdown in the 1989 game.

» Kansas quarterback Todd Reesing, hounded by the Blackshirts in 2008, is dismayed over an intentional grounding call.

« Kansas State's Eric Mack cannot believe he dropped a pass in 1982. Huskers Mike Knox (44) and Allen Lyday (18) are unsympathetic.

THE JOY

» It's a quarterback thing, as Latravis Washington (15), Cody Green (17) and Zac Lee (5) enjoy a touchdown against K-State in 2009.

^ NU assistant coach Monte Kiffin jumps into the arms of Jimmy Burrow after a touchdown against Missouri in 1975.

« Nebraska fullback Jeff Makovicka after a fourth-quarter touchdown against K-State in 1994.

« Quarterback Joe Ganz after a touchdown against Kansas State in 2008.

« Husker Troy Dumas after a pass breakup on Oklahoma State's Robert Kirksey in 1991.

Nebraska halfback Dale Bradley goes in for a score against Iowa State in the Cornhuskers' 14-0 victory in Ames in 1941.

Staff Writers

Michael Kelly

Lee Barkfknecht

Tom Shatel

Retired Writers

Tom Ash

Larry Porter

Steve Sinclair

TO OUR READERS,

THE OMAHA WORLD-HERALD in 2010 celebrates its 125th year of publishing, and 120 of those years have been devoted to covering University of Nebraska football. We reported on the first game, a 10-0 Thanksgiving Day victory over the Omaha YMCA in 1890. "The Lincoln team had the better teamwork and the locals had the better individual players, who failed to play into each other's hands," the article said. "It was the first game of rugby football that had been seen in Omaha, and there were several hundred out to see the boys enjoy themselves and break each other's shins. It resembled an old-fashioned game of log-heap more than anything else."

The newspaper's archives provide a rich, detailed history of Nebraska football, from that 19th century shin-breaker against the Omaha YMCA, all the way to the 21st century helmet-bangers against Texas.

This book looks back on the Huskers' football series with their conference rivals, as the school leaves the Big 12 and heads off to the Big Ten. The story is told through the photos and words of the talented people who have worked for The World-World over the years.

Columnists Michael Kelly, Lee Barfknecht and Tom Shatel, along with members of our sports staff, took time out of their hectic schedules to assist with the writing. Our coverage of the 1970s and 1980s was enhanced with contributions from retired writers Tom Ash, Larry Porter and Steve Sinclair. We also are indebted to former staff writers James Denney, Howard Silber and the late Hollis Limprecht for their valuable work in "Go Big Red," a World-Herald book published in 1967.

But the story is incomplete without the photos that display the drama and action from the games. Soak in the atmosphere that jumps from the crisp digital images of recent years and from the decades-old photos that were brought back to life by our imaging wizard, Jolene McHugh.

Enjoy reliving the memories, and we hope that any suffering that is inflicted by the retelling of "Sooner Magic" is overcome by the "Miracle in Missouri."

Dan Sullivan

Dan Sullivan

Editor, Big Red Rivals

Designer
Christine Zueck

Photo Imager
Jolene McHugh

Assistant Editors
Frank Hassler
Rich Mills

Contributing Writers
Rich Kaipust
Steven Pivovar
Jon Nyatawa
Mitch Sherman
Dirk Chatelain
Dan Sullivan

Copy Editors
Jim Anderson
Kevin Cole
Bob Glissmann
Jolene McHugh
Chris Nigrin
Juan Perez Jr.
Mike Reilly
Duane Retzlaff
Jeffrey Robb
Aaron Sanderford
Kent Savery
Larry Sparks
Kathy Sullivan
Mary Kay Wayman
Christine Zueck

From Our Archives
Tom Allan
Harold W. Andersen
Howard Brantz
Kevin Cole
Gregg McBride
Elizabeth Merrill
Floyd Olds
Eric Olson
Wally Provost
Conde Sargent
Dave Sittler
Doug Thomas
Bob Tucker

Researchers
Rebecca S. Gratz
Michelle Gullett
Jeanne Hauser

Print and Production Coordinators
Pat "Murphy" Benoit
Wayne Harty

Sports Editor
Thad Livingston

Director of Photography
Jeff Bundy

Director of Marketing
Rich Warren

Nebraska captains Keith Williams, Mathew May, Roy Helu Jr. and Prince Amukamara leave the tunnel for the 2010 Missouri game.

HUSKERS PICTURED IN BIG RED RIVALS

Colorado's Ralphie takes aim at Tom Osborne before the start of the 1980 game in Boulder. "I think they ought to think about not doing that," Osborne said of the buffalo's charge onto the field. "Conceivably, someone might not see it coming."

OTHERS PICTURED IN BIG RED RIVALS

KANSAS

IOWA STATE

MISSOURI

KANSAS STATE

OKLAHOMA

COLORADO

OKLAHOMA STATE

TEXAS

TEXAS TECH

BAYLOR

TEXAS A&M

COACHES

ALSO

The sun sets on the final Big 12 Conference game played at Memorial Stadium – Nebraska vs. Colorado in 2010.

Photographers Index

Indexes do not include photos from the Big 12 championship game.

Reprints of all Omaha World-Herald photos are available from the OWHstore for a fee.

Call 402-444-1014 to place an order or go to owhstore.com.